He Ascended into Heaven

A Study in the History of Doctrine

J. G. Davies

James Clarke & Co.
Cambridge

Published by
James Clarke & Co.
P.O. Box 60
Cambridge
CB1 2NT
England

e-mail: **publishing@jamesclarke.co.uk**
website: **http://www.jamesclarke.co.uk**

ISBN 0 227 17231 0 paperback

British Library Cataloguing in Publication Data:
A catalogue record is available from the British Library.

First published 1958
reprinted 2004

Extract
FROM THE LAST WILL AND TESTAMENT
of the Late Rev.
JOHN BAMPTON
Canon of Salisbury

". . . I give and bequeath my Lands and Estates to the Chancellor, Masters, and Scholars of the University of Oxford for ever, to have and to hold all and singular the said Lands or Estates upon Trust, and to the intents and purposes hereinafter mentioned; that is to say, I will and appoint that the Vice-Chancellor of the University of Oxford for the time being shall take and receive all the rents, issues, and profits thereof, and (after all taxes, reparations, and necessary deductions made) that he pay all the remainder to the endowment of eight Divinity Lecture Sermons, to be established for ever in the said University, and to be performed in the manner following:

" 'I direct and appoint that, upon the first Tuesday in Easter Term, a Lecturer be yearly chosen by the Heads of Colleges only, and by no others, in the room adjoining to the Printing-House, between the hours of ten in the morning and two in the afternoon, to preach eight Divinity Lecture Sermons, the year following, at St. Mary's in Oxford, between the commencement of the last month in Lent Term and the end of the third week in Act Term.

" 'Also I direct and appoint, that the eight Divinity Lecture Sermons shall be preached upon either of the following Subjects—to confirm and establish the Christian Faith, and to confute all heretics and schismatics—upon the divine authority of the holy Scriptures—upon the authority and writings of the primitive Fathers, as to the faith and practice of the primitive Church—upon the Divinity of our Lord and Saviour Jesus Christ—upon the Divinity of the Holy Ghost—upon the Articles of the Christian Faith, as comprehended in the Apostles' and Nicene Creeds.

" 'Also I direct, that thirty copies of the eight Divinity

7

Lecture Sermons shall be always printed, within two months after they are preached; and one copy shall be given to the Chancellor of the University, and one copy to the Head of every College, and one copy to the Mayor of the City of Oxford, and one copy to be put into the Bodleian Library; and the expense of printing them shall be paid out of the revenue of the Land or Estates given for establishing the Divinity Lecture Sermons; and the Preacher shall not be paid, nor be entitled to the revenue, before they are printed.

" 'Also I direct and appoint, that no person shall be qualified to preach the Divinity Lecture Sermons, unless he hath taken the degree of Master of Arts at least, in one of the two Universities of Oxford or Cambridge; and that the same person shall never preach the Divinity Lecture Sermons twice.' "

PREFACE

OF ALL THE articles in the Creed there is none that has been so neglected in the present century as that which affirms our Lord's Ascension into heaven. Only one book has been published in English on the subject—in 1910[1]—and of this three-quarters of the contents are more properly to be described as concerned with the Session. No history of the doctrine exists, as far as I have been able to discover, and only a limited number of articles, of very differing worth, has been devoted to it.

From the days of Justin Martyr's Trypho, the Ascension has had its detractors, and from Reimarus onwards it has been subjected to a long-sustained attack,[2] but the chief reason for this contemporary neglect lies without question in the scientific temper which became so predominant in the last decades of the nineteenth century. The Lucan account of the Ascension appeared to be so naïvely pre-Copernican that few could take it seriously. It must have brought a sense of great relief, therefore, to those who adopted this attitude when the great German scholar, A. Harnack, declared that, quite apart from its outmoded cosmology, the Lucan record was suspect, since the Ascension was wanting to the first three Gospels and was not mentioned in the First Epistle to the Corinthians nor by any of the Apostolic Fathers. He went on to assert that it had no separate place in the primitive tradition, being undifferentiated from the Resurrection, and that to give it any prominence at all was to be guilty of a deviation from the original Gospel.

The pamphlet in which Harnack formulated these views, *Das apostolische Glaubensbekenntniss* (1892), was so popular that within a year of its being issued it had run through twenty-five editions. In 1893 a translation was made by Mrs. Humphry Ward and published in the *Nineteenth Century* (XXXIV, pp. 158-76), and from then onwards Harnack's opinions made a profound impression upon English scholarship. Even to-day his

[1] H. B. Swete, *The Ascended Christ*, 1910. In 1901 there was issued a third reprint of the second edition of W. Milligan, *The Ascension and Heavenly Priesthood of Our Lord*, first published in 1891.
[2] The literature is surveyed by V. Larrañaga, *L'Ascension de Notre-Seigneur dans le Nouveau Testament*, 1938, pp. 18-124.

9

interpretation of the New Testament evidence regarding the Ascension is frequently reproduced, without any fresh examination of the Biblical material and without any recognition of the fact that New Testament studies are no longer in the position that they were sixty years ago.

It is my purpose in this present work to undertake such an examination, and then to continue the history of the doctrine through the period of the ante-Nicene Church, through the age of the Conciliar Creeds to the first homilists and on to their remote descendants of the Carolingian Renaissance and of the reforming monastic movements in the eleventh and twelfth centuries.

The limits that I have set to this survey are necessarily artificial and a word of explanation is perhaps required. Two factors have prevented me carrying the subject further. First, the period corresponds to that covered by the volumes in Migne's two *Patrologiae*. Although new critical editions are constantly appearing, Migne will undoubtedly remain the standard work of general reference for many years to come, and since it provides a convenient, if not complete, corpus for ready consultation I have refrained from going beyond its chronological limits. In the second place, a rapid excursion through the later literature has led me to believe that neither the mediaeval divines nor the Reformation teachers—with the notable exception of Calvin—had much of significance to add to what had already been written on the subject by their predecessors in the faith. If my impression be correct, then there is little advantage to be gained by pursuing the history of the doctrine much beyond these limits, which, in any case, my own interests have predisposed me to observe.

We begin then with the Old Testament prefigurement and follow the doctrine through to the dawn of the scholastic era. On the basis of this historical review, I propose, in the final lecture, to call attention to those features which would appear to be of permanent value and which require re-emphasis if the Ascension is to be rescued from the oblivion to which so much neglect has temporarily consigned it.

J. G. D.

The University, Birmingham
July, 1957

CONTENTS

NOTE

IN THE CASE of well-known documents, e.g. the epistles of Ignatius or the treatises of Tertullian, chapter and/or section references have alone been given. The same practice has also been followed where the chapters or sections are sufficiently brief to enable a citation to be found without difficulty. Where less familiar texts are concerned or where the chapters and sections are of considerable length Migne's *Patrologiae* is usually cited, occasional reference being also made to the 'Berlin Corpus' (*C.G.S.*).

Of the hundred or so Ascension homilies which have survived from the period under review, less than half a dozen have ever been translated into English. Not all of them merit translation, but there are many which contain valuable insights into the meaning of the Ascension; I have therefore included numerous extracts in their appropriate contexts.

1

THE OLD TESTAMENT PREFIGUREMENT

Novum testamentum in vetere latet, vetus testamentum in novo patet.[1]
The basis upon which St. Augustine formulated this well-known dictum comprised a belief in the verbal inspiration of Holy Scripture, and the method which he employed to demonstrate its validity, while not excluding literal exegesis,[2] was chiefly that of allegorical interpretation.[3] To-day, due to the painstaking labours of Biblical critics, both lower and higher, neither the foundation of St. Augustine's principle nor the way in which he put it into operation can be accepted. There are indeed few informed modern scholars who would assert that the Old Testament was predictive either of the details of the Gospels or of the events of early Christian history.[4] But the recognition that Christianity divorced from its roots in the Old Testament would cease to be Christianity, that to penetrate the thought forms of the New Testament writings we must start from the Old, and that if not predictive the Old Testament may be legitimately read as prefigurative—these factors have each contributed to a renewed emphasis on the unity of Scripture. Thus the wheel has gone full turn, and the Christian theologian may accept St. Augustine's thesis and use it as a principle of exegesis, even though the method of his application will necessarily differ.

I trust that these brief prefatory remarks will serve as sufficient justification, if justification be necessary, for my procedure in beginning this survey of the doctrine of the Ascension with a consideration of the Old Testament prefigurement. Yet it must be frankly acknowledged that only those passages may be deemed relevant where the literal and historical sense, as far as it can be discovered, corresponds with and is not

---

[1] Augustine, *Quaest. in Hept.*, 2. 73.
[2] *De Doct. Christ.*, 3. 26-28.
[3] *Conf.*, 6. 4, 5.
[4] H. F. D. Sparks, *The Old Testament in the Christian Church*, 1944, p. 43.

contradictory of the typological.[1] These passages may be classified conveniently into two groups, the first consisting of those accounts that predicate an ascension of an individual, the second of those pronouncements that were applied in later Christian exegesis to the Ascension of Christ.

The Old Testament presents us with two individuals of whom an ascension is predicated, viz. Enoch and Elijah. At the period or periods from which these accounts date a shadowy existence in Sheol was all that awaited the normal person, and the authority of Yahweh would seem to have been limited to this side of the grave, the dead being beyond the exercise of His grace.[2] All the more remarkable, therefore, are the narratives of these translations, and in order to understand how they could have been conceived, before there was any developed view of an after-life, it is necessary to investigate their background.

Enoch, according to Gen. 5, was the seventh from Adam. Now the seventh of the antediluvian Babylonian kings was Edōranchus, who is most probably to be identified with Enmeduranki, a legendary king of Sippar, the city sacred to the sun god Shamash. From a ritual tablet, discovered in the library of Asshurbanipal, we learn that Enmeduranki was summoned by the god and initiated into the secrets of heaven and earth.[3] Here then is one source of the Enoch account, for Enoch is stated to have lived 365 years, i.e. his age corresponds to the number of days in the solar year—this being the sole surviving trait of his connexion with a devotee of the sun god. There is, however, no mention of a translation of Enmeduranki; for this we must turn to the Gilgamesh epic. In the eleventh canto, Gilgamesh is treated to the life story of his ancestor Utnapishtim, whose narration concludes with the following lines:

Then Enlil went up into the ship.
He took my hand and caused me to go aboard.
He caused my wife to go aboard (and) to kneel down at my side.

[1] E. Jacob, "A propos de l'Ancien Testament: Méthode christologique ou méthode historique," *Études Théologiques et Religieuses*, XX, Montpellier, 1945, pp. 76-82.
[2] R. H. Charles, *A Critical History of the Doctrine of a Future Life*, 1899, p. 56.
[3] S. R. Driver, *The Book of Genesis*, 1926, p. 78.

Standing between us, he touched our foreheads and blessed us:
"Hitherto Utnapishtim has been but a man;
But now Utnapishtim and his wife shall be like unto us gods.
In the distance, at the mouth of the rivers, Utnapishtim shall
dwell!"
So they took me and caused me to dwell in the distance, at the
mouth of the rivers.[1]

Here indeed is the immediate source of the Enoch legend, for
the Hebrew *lakah*, i.e. take, which is used of Enoch in Gen.
5: 24—"God took him"—corresponds philologically with the
Akkadian *leku* found in the final line of the above quotation.
We are now in a position to appreciate the meaning of the
Genesis story: just as the gods took Utnapishtim because he
had pleased them by his previous conduct and so deserved to
escape the common lot of humanity, so Yahweh took Enoch
because he had "walked with God", i.e. as the LXX expresses
it, "pleased God".[2] Hence Enoch, whose piety merited something better than Sheol, is represented as not descending there
at all but as ascending into the presence of God.

The same conception underlies the account of the ascension
of Elijah in 2 Kings 2, and indeed the identical verb *lakah*
is employed as in Gen. 5: 24. So the godly prophet goes up
in a chariot of fire[3] by a whirlwind into heaven, thus escaping
death and being raised to the society of God. Whether or not
the author of the passage in 2 Kings had the Enoch incident
in mind and chose his words deliberately one cannot determine, but in psalms 49 and 73 there is reason to suppose that
the Psalmist is choosing his words with reference to the translation of Enoch, the verb *lakah* being again used in each case.[4]

But God will redeem my soul from the power of Sheol:
For he shall take[5] me.[6]

Thou shalt guide me with thy counsel,
And afterward take[5] me to glory.[7]

[1] A. Heidel, *The Gilgamesh Epic and Old Testament Parallels*, 1949, p. 88.
[2] cp. Heb. 11: 5.
[3] This may indicate solar associations.
[4] C. F. Burney, *Israel's Hope of Immortality*, 1909, pp. 43, 47; *Outlines of Old Testament Theology*, 1930, p. 128.
[5] R.V. "receive".   [6] 49: 15.   [7] 73: 24.

B   17

Thus the belief is expressed that men may be delivered from Sheol and may enjoy a future which is to be compared with that of the patriarch. It is interesting, therefore, to note that even within the Old Testament the account of Enoch, and probably of Elijah also, is regarded as prefigurative of the lot of the truly righteous individual and may then be accepted as a legitimate type of Him who knew no sin.[1] But neither of these two psalms was used of the Ascension by Christian writers, although the second, with its reference to glory, could have been most appropriately applied to that event which was the glorifying of the Servant of Yahweh.[2] If, however, these two psalms were neglected, there are four others which were not: these form our second group of pericopes, viz. those pronouncements which were applied by later Christian exegetes to the Ascension of Christ. They are psalms 24, 47, 68 and 110. To define their background is a far more complex task than was the case with Gen. 5 and 2 Kings 2.

The present century has witnessed a considerable change in the method of studying the Psalter.[3] The old atomistic approach, i.e. the labelling of psalms according to their subject matter coupled with the dating of each in an entirely individualistic manner, has given way to their classification according to type, with an examination of the *Sitz im Leben* of each psalm against the general cultural background of early civilization in the Middle East. The pioneer in this field was Hermann Gunkel,[4] who distinguished five main categories of psalms. His third class comprised what he termed "Royal Psalms" (*Königspsalmen*), in which he included one of those which concerns us, viz. 110. Sigmund Mowinckel carried this work further and, stressing above all the formative influence of the cultus, argued for the existence in pre-exilic Israel of an autumnal New Year Festival which celebrated the enthronement of Yahweh as universal King.[5] Among the psalms which he associated with this feast were 24 and 47.

[1] 2 Cor. 5: 21.   [2] Acts 3: 13.
[3] For an excellent survey of the main trends in the modern study of the Psalter see A. R. Johnson, "The Psalms", in *The Old Testament and Modern Study*, ed. H. H. Rowley, 1951, pp. 162-209.
[4] *Ausgewählte Psalmen*, 1904; "Psalmen" in *Die Religion in Geschichte und Gegenwart*, IV, 1913, cols. 1927-49; *Die Psalmen*, 1926.
[5] *Psalmenstudien II. Das Thronbetsseigungsfest Jahwäs und der Ursprung der Eschatologie*, 1922.

If few scholars have accepted Mowinckel's theory exactly as it stands, many have followed the lead which he offered, and in particular the so-called Myth-and-Ritual school in England of which S. H. Hooke may be styled the leader.[1] Amongst the more recent contributions to be noted is an article by J. R. Porter,[2] in which, on the basis of 2 Sam. 6, he not only supports the case for the existence of an Israelite New Year Festival but argues, with some cogency, that it was David himself who was responsible for its introduction and that the occasion was that of his accession in Jerusalem: included in the evidence are psalms 24 and 68. Thus it is to be noted that each of the four psalms which were applied by Christian writers to the Ascension has been referred by one scholar or another to this festival, and indeed both Dr. W. O. E. Oesterley[3] and Dr. A. R. Johnson[4] have linked all four together with this celebration. At the same time it must be stressed that this has so far no more than the character of a provisional thesis, and that there is a tendency, notable in certain authors, to go beyond the evidence and to assume too readily the unity of ancient near-eastern culture without recognizing that whatever Israel borrowed from her neighbours she transformed in the process. Nevertheless, as a consequence of this new approach, although voices are still raised in protest,[5] there is a growing agreement on the cultic background of the Psalter. In what then did this New Year Festival consist and how are the psalms that particularly concern us said to fit into that context?

In the Israelite New Year Festival there were, it is contended, four principal elements. First, a procession which ascended the hill of Zion and escorted both the ark of Yahweh and the Davidic king into the Temple precincts. Second, a ritual combat which re-enacted the triumph of Yahweh and of his anointed representative over the forces of death and chaos. Next, the re-enthronement of Yahweh as King and of

---

[1] But see his guarded statements in *C.Q.R.*, CLVII, 1956, pp. 386-92.
[2] "The Interpretation of 2 Samuel vi and Psalm cxxxii", *J.T.S.*, V, 1954, pp. 161-73.
[3] *Myth and Ritual*, ed. S. H. Hooke, 1933, pp. 126, 130, 132f.
[4] *The Labyrinth*, ed. S. H. Hooke, 1935, pp. 87, 89, 96, 109f.; *Sacral Kingship in Ancient Israel*, 1955, pp. 63-76, 121f.
[5] e.g. N. H. Snaith, *The Jewish New Year Festival*, 1947.

the contemporary ruler and, finally, the sacred marriage.[1] There is a certain incongruity in the presence in this ritual of both Yahweh, of whom the ark was the focal manifestation, and of the king, who was His adopted son,[2] there being thus two principal *dramatis personae*; but consistency and logic are not to be expected in early religious conceptions and practice.

We have now to fit into this cultic pattern the four psalms that are our especial concern.

In psalm 47 we have what would appear to be a graphic description of the procession:

> O clap your hands, all ye peoples;
> Shout unto God with the voice of triumph.
> For the Lord Most High is terrible;
> He is a great King over all the earth . . .
> God is gone up with a shout,
> The Lord with the sound of a trumpet.
> Sing praises to God, sing praises:
> Sing praises unto our King, sing praises.
> For God is the King of all the earth:
> Sing ye praises with understanding.
> God reigneth over the nations:
> God sitteth upon his holy throne . . .
> He is greatly exalted.[3]

Particularly to be noted here are the references to the blast on the Shophar or ram's horn[4] and to the enthronement and Kingship of Yahweh.[5] A second vivid account of this procession seems to be provided by psalm 68:

> They have seen thy goings, O God,
> Even the goings of my God, my King, into the sanctuary.
> The singers went before, the minstrels followed after,
> In the midst of the damsels playing with timbrels.
> Bless ye God in the congregations,
> Even the Lord, ye that are of the fountain of Israel.[6]

We notice also a possible reference to the triumph after a ritual combat:

---

[1] S. H. Hooke, *The Origins of Early Semitic Ritual*, 1938, pp. 51-56.
[2] A. R. Johnson, "The Role of the King in the Jerusalem Cultus", in *The Labyrinth*, pp. 73-111.
[3] vv. 1, 2, 5-9. [4] v. 5. [5] v. 8. [6] vv. 24-26.

Thou hast ascended on high, thou hast led thy captivity captive;
Thou hast received gifts among men,
Yea, among the rebellious also, that the Lord God might dwell
with them.[1]

Psalm 24 may add further details to our picture. As the worshippers ascend the hill of Zion, they sing:

> Who shall ascend into the hill of the Lord?
> And who shall stand in his holy place?
> He that hath clean hands, and a pure heart;
> Who hath not lifted up his soul unto vanity,
> And hath not sworn deceitfully.

Then they halt at the Temple gates and cry:

> Lift up your heads, O ye gates;
> And be ye lift up, ye everlasting doors:
> And the King of glory shall come in.

The Levites reply:

> Who is the King of glory?

And the people respond:

> The Lord strong and mighty,
> The Lord mighty in battle.
> Lift up your heads, O ye gates;
> Yea, lift them up, ye everlasting doors:
> And the King of glory shall come in.

Again the Levites demand:

> Who is this King of glory?

And again the answer is given:

> The Lord of hosts,
> He is the King of glory.

So bearing Yahweh in His chariot,[2] the triumphal procession
enters the Temple precincts.

---

[1] v. 18.
[2] Ps. 68: 17, as emended by W. O. E. Oesterley, *The Psalms*, II, 1939, pp. 322ff.

In psalm 110 the actual enthronement of the king as the divine representative may be in the writer's mind. A cultic prophet[1] conveys a message from Yahweh to the king:[2]

The Lord saith unto my lord, Sit thou at my right hand,
Until I make thine enemies thy footstool.
The Lord shall send forth the rod of thy strength out of Zion:
Rule thou in the midst of thine enemies.[3]

We are then told by the same minister of the cult what the nature of this kingship is:

The Lord hath sworn, and will not repent,
Thou art a priest for ever
After the order of Melchizedek.[4]

Thus the king by his enthronement has succeeded not only to the throne of David, but also to the traditional priesthood of Melchizedek,[5] for David himself upon his accession in the former Jebusite stronghold[6] had thereby entered the royal priestly order of Melchizedek, a previous priest-king of Jerusalem.[7]

The disentanglement of this ritual pattern is more difficult than its application to the Ascension of Christ—assuming that this cultic background is indeed a reality. The first feature of the New Year Festival, according to this interpretation, was the ascent of Mount Zion and the entrance into the Temple; so Christ has ascended on high and entered heaven itself of which the holy of holies was but a shadow. The second feature was the triumph over the forces of evil; so the ascended Christ can say: "He that overcometh, I will give to him to sit down with me in my throne, as I also overcame, and sat down with my Father in his throne."[8] This verse also points to the third

---

[1] S. Mowinckel, *Psalmenstudien III. Die Kultprophetie und prophetische Psalmen*, 1923, p. 3.
[2] According to G. Widengren, *Psalm 110 och det sakrala kungsdömet i Israel*, 1941, pp. 9ff., and I. Engnell, *Studies in Divine Kingship in the Ancient Near East*, 1943, pp. 11, 12, this psalm also has reference to the sacred marriage. I remain unconvinced.
[3] vv. 1, 2. [4] v. 4.
[5] Johnson, *op. cit.*, pp. 109f.
[6] *Ibid.*, pp. 81-84. [7] Gen. 14: 18ff. [8] Rev. 3: 21.

feature of the cult,[1] viz. the enthronement, and the consequent entrance of the Lord's Anointed upon the royal priestly order of Melchizedek; so of Christ it is said: "We have such a high priest, who sat down on the right hand of the throne of the Majesty in the heavens",[2] being "named of God a high priest after the order of Melchizedek",[3] even He who is "Lord of lords, and King of kings."[4] To press these points further would be to trespass upon New Testament exegesis which must await the next lecture, but before we leave these psalms[5] whose literal meaning, if this interpretation be correct, provides a justification for their use of the Ascension by Christian writers, we may notice that three of them, in the LXX translation, contain the verb ἀναβαίνω, which came to be employed of Christ's Ascension. It may well be therefore that an investigation of the LXX usage of this word will help to shed further light on our subject.

The primary meaning of ἀναβαίνω is movement from a lower to a higher level. Thus it is used of the seven kine in Pharaoh's dream who came up out of the river on to the bank.[6] It is used of going up on to a roof,[7] of getting up on to a bed,[8] of mounting into a chariot,[9] of ascending stairs[10] and of climbing out of a well.[11] It is used also of going up to a high place,[12] and very frequently of going up to the house of the Lord.[13] We find it employed of mounting the steps of an altar,[14]

---

[1] A. R. Johnson (*Sacral Kingship, op. cit.*, pp. 64, 81, 116) also finds a place in the ritual for an ascension of Yahweh in glory, returning in triumph from a victory over His foes and in particular over death. The correspondence with Christ's Ascension in glory, after His conquest of evil and His Resurrection from the dead, is close.

[2] Heb. 8: 1.

[3] Heb. 5: 10.

[4] Rev. 17: 14.

[5] The theme of the sacred marriage is not connected with the Ascension, but Christ was represented as the bridegroom (Matt. 25: 1-13; Mark 2: 20; cp. Luke 14: 8-11) and the Church, His Body, as His Bride (Eph. 5: 22-32).

[6] Gen. 41: 2.

[7] Josh. 2: 8.

[8] 2 Kings 1: 4.

[9] 2 Chron. 10: 18.

[10] Neh. 12: 37.

[11] 2 Sam. 17: 21.

[12] 2 Sam. 15: 30.

[13] e.g. 2 Kings 20: 8; 23: 2; 2 Chron. 29: 20; Isa. 38: 22; Mic. 4: 2

[14] Exod. 20: 26.

and also, quite commonly, of offering a sacrifice or making an oblation.[1] The cry of the oppressed Israelites in Egypt,[2] the laments of the men of Ekron,[3] the arrogancy of Sennacherib[4] and the wickedness of the Ninevites[5] all come up to God in heaven. It is used further of the cloud of the divine presence being taken up from the tabernacle[6] and of the divine glory departing from the holy of holies.[7] It describes the return of God from earth to heaven,[8] e.g. after His promise to Abraham[9] and after His visitation of Jacob at Bethel.[10] Finally, ἀναβαίνω is used of the angels of God ascending to heaven after the completion of their tasks upon earth.[11] It is remarkable how this LXX usage of the word anticipates many of the features of the later doctrine of the Ascension. There is the going up to the Temple and the offering of sacrifice which is the central theme of the teaching of the Epistle to the Hebrews, even though its author does not actually use ἀναβαίνω itself. There is the connexion with the cloud and the divine glory, both of which features are stressed in the Lucan writings, and there is also the return after the successful execution of a mission, quite apart from its use in the psalms in reference to the triumphal procession and enthronement of the priest-king, the Lord's Anointed. But perhaps the most interesting passage is one which provides an example of the last usage listed above, viz. of an angel ascending to heaven.

The passage in question is to be found in Tobit 12. It recounts how Raphael, after complimenting Tobit on his care for the dead, discloses to him and to his son Tobias his real nature which he has hitherto concealed. The immediate effect of this news upon his hearers is that "they were both troubled, and fell upon their faces; for they were afraid" (ἐταράχθησαν

---

[1] 1 Kings 12: 32, 33; 18: 29; 2 Kings 3: 20; 16: 12; 23: 9; 2 Chron. 29: 21; Ezra 3: 3; Jer. 48: 35.
[2] Exod. 2: 23.
[3] 1 Sam. 5: 12.
[4] 2 Kings 19: 28.
[5] Jonah 1: 2.
[6] Exod. 40: 36, 37; Num. 9: 17, 21.
[7] Ezek. 9: 3; 11: 23.
[8] Since it means movement from a lower to a higher level, it can also be used of the dead coming up from Sheol to the earth (1 Sam. 28: 13, 14).
[9] Gen. 17: 22.
[10] Gen. 35: 13.
[11] Gen. 28: 12; Judges 13: 20; Tobit 12: 20.

THE OLD TESTAMENT PREFIGUREMENT

οἱ δύο καὶ ἔπεσον ἐπὶ πρόσωπον, ὅτι ἐφοβήθησαν).¹ The angel
reassures them, saying: "Be not afraid, ye shall have peace;
but bless God for ever" (Μὴ φοβεῖσθε, εἰρήνη ὑμῖν ἔσται· τὸν
δὲ θεὸν εὐλογεῖτε εἰς τὸν αἰῶνα).² He then explains how "all
these days did I appear unto you; and I did neither eat nor
drink, but ye saw a vision. And now give God thanks: because
I ascend to him that sent me . . . and they rose up, and
saw him no more" (πάσας τὰς ἡμέρας ὠπτανόμην ὑμῖν, καὶ
οὐκ ἔφαγον οὐδὲ ἔπιον, ἀλλὰ ὅρασιν ὑμεῖς ἐθεωρεῖτε. καὶ νῦν
ἐξομολογεῖσθε τῷ θεῷ, διότι ἀναβαίνω πρὸς τὸν ἀποστείλαντά
με³ . . . καὶ ἀνέστησαν, καὶ οὐκ εἶδον αὐτόν).⁴
The most remarkable feature of this account is that all its
principal ingredients, albeit not in exactly the same order,⁵
appear in the final chapter of the third Gospel. St. Luke's
24th chapter opens with a reference to the women who are
going to take care of the dead; we hear how when they beheld
the angels "they were affrighted, and bowed down their faces
to the earth" (ἐμφόβων δὲ γενομένων αὐτῶν καὶ κλινουσῶν τὰ
πρόσωπα εἰς τὴν γῆν).⁶ Later, the disciples, too, when they
saw Jesus, were "affrighted" (ἔμφοβοι)⁷ and "troubled"
(τεταραγμένοι),⁸ but He said to them: "Peace be unto you"
(Εἰρήνη ὑμῖν),⁹ and they blessed God (εὐλογοῦντες τὸν Θεόν).¹⁰
Initially the disciples "supposed that they beheld a spirit"
(ἐδόκουν πνεῦμα θεωρεῖν),¹¹ but Jesus demonstrated that, unlike the "vision of angels" (ὀπτασίαν ἀγγέλων)¹² seen by the
women, it was indeed He by eating before them (ἐνώπιον αὐτῶν
ἔφαγεν).¹³ Finally, the risen Lord "parted from them, and was
carried up into heaven" (διέστη ἀπ' αὐτῶν καὶ ἀνεφέρετο εἰς
τὸν οὐρανόν),¹⁴ and like certain of the faithful who had gone
previously to the empty tomb "him they saw not" (αὐτὸν
δὲ οὐκ εἶδον).¹⁵ From this coincidence of detail in Tobit 12 and
Luke 24 it is reasonable to conclude that St. Luke saw in the
story of Raphael a type of the Resurrection appearances and
Ascension of Christ, and so we may add to our total of Old

¹ Tobit 12: 16.   ² v. 17.   ³ cp. John 7: 33; 16: 5.   ⁴ Tobit 12: 19-21.
⁵ To facilitate comparison the material from Luke 24 is presented in the order
of Tobit 12. The parallels are also set out in Table A on p. 185.
⁶ Luke 24: 5.   ⁷ v. 37.   ⁸ v. 38.   ⁹ v. 36.   ¹⁰ v. 53.
¹¹ v. 37.   ¹² v. 23.   ¹³ v. 43.   ¹⁴ v. 51.
¹⁵ v. 24; note πάσας τὰς ἡμέρας ὠπτανόμην ὑμῖν Tobit 12: 19‖δι' ἡμερῶν τεσσεράκοντα ὀπτανόμενος αὐτοῖς Acts 1: 3.

25

Testament prefigurations this further passage. One other section also requires attention, and the telling will then be complete.

In Dan. 7 the seer describes his first vision, as he who had formerly interpreted the dreams of kings now dreams on his own account.[1] He beholds four monsters coming up out of the deep, signifying the four empires which have afflicted Israel from the days of the Exile, viz. Babylonia, Media, Persia and Greece. One succeeds to the other and the last divides into rival kingdoms. Then God's judgment upon the affairs of earth takes place: "I beheld till thrones were placed, and one that was ancient of days did sit: his raiment was white as snow, and the hair of his head like pure wool; his throne was fiery flames, and the wheels thereof burning fire. A fiery stream issued and came forth from before him: thousand thousands ministered unto him, and ten thousand times ten thousand stood before him: the judgment was set, and the books were opened."[2] The sentence is passed: "and as for the rest of the beasts, their dominion was taken away",[3] and to the kingdoms of earth succeeds the Kingdom of the Most High. "I saw in the night visions, and, behold, there came with the clouds of heaven one like unto a son of man, and he came even to the ancient of days, and they brought him near before him. And there was given him dominion, and glory, and a kingdom, that all the peoples, nations, and languages should serve him: his dominion is an everlasting dominion, which shall not pass away, and his kingdom that which shall not be destroyed."[4] Whether we conceive of the "one like unto a son of man" in a collective sense or in an individualistic, and both shades of meaning tend to merge into one, we are presented with a triumphal "coming" to the Ancient of days which became for many later exegetes a prefiguration of the Ascension of the Son of man to His Father's throne. *Novum testamentum in vetere velebatur: vetus testamentum in novo revelatur.*[5]

---

[1] For a brief but brilliant examination of Daniel, see A. Farrer, *A Study in St. Mark*, 1951, pp. 251-64.

[2] Dan. 7: 9, 10.   [3] v. 12.   [4] vv. 13, 14.   [5] Augustine, *Sermo*, 160. 6.

2

THE NEW TESTAMENT RECORD—I

FROM the Old Testament prefigurement we must now pass to the New Testament record of the event which was its fulfilment. But before we do so, there is one preliminary observation to be made. For centuries it has been the invariable practice to understand the Ascension in the light of the Lucan account in Acts. It would be a mistake, however, to approach the New Testament evidence with any such fixed preconception. *A priori* it is conceivable, in view of the acknowledged differences between the Apostolic writers, that allusions to the Ascension may take a great variety of forms. But if St. Luke is accepted as providing the norm, we may possibly fail to discern any other references to an Ascension that do not strictly conform to it. For this reason it is necessary at the outset to enter a caveat against the domination of the Lucan point of view. It may be that we shall reach the conclusion that the Lucan description is accurate and comprehensive— it may be not—but we can only determine this satisfactorily after, and not before, examining the New Testament witness as a whole. In this lecture, therefore, one aspect alone of that record will be considered: namely, the evidence of belief in an Ascension. It is only when this has been assessed that one can undertake an examination of the meaning of the event.

For St. Paul, to whose letters we turn as the earliest written documents in the New Testament, there would seem to be no adequate grounds for doubting that an Ascension has taken place.[1] In his Epistle to the Romans, he quotes from the Book of Deuteronomy, farcing his citation with his own exegetical comments: "Who shall ascend into heaven? (that is, to bring Christ down:) Or, Who shall descend into the abyss? (that is, to bring Christ up from the dead)."[2] By substituting ἄβυσσος,

[1] Albeit St. Paul did not share St. Luke's conception of the event; see below, pp. 49, 59.
[2] Rom. 10: 6, 7; Deut. 30: 12, 13.

27

with its direct reference to Sheol, for the LXX θάλασσα, St. Paul focuses attention upon two reciprocal features of Christ's redemptive work,[1] viz. the *descensus ad inferos* and the Ascension.[2] These complementary events, which serve to affirm the universality of Christ's saving act, are again brought together though less explicitly in the Epistle to the Philippians: Christ became "obedient even unto death, yea, the death of the cross. Wherefore also God highly exalted him, and gave unto him the name which is above every name; that in the name of Jesus every knee should bow, of things in heaven and things on earth and things under the earth, and that every tongue should confess that Jesus Christ is Lord."[3]

It may, however, be argued that the word translated "highly exalted" in this last quotation does not involve a direct reference to the Ascension. We must therefore examine both ὑπερυψόω and ὑψόω to determine the exact meaning of this passage. 'Υπερυψόω is not used elsewhere in the New Testament and is employed very sparingly in the LXX; in one instance it means to increase one's power or wealth,[4] in another to give praise,[5] and in a third to lift up, viz.:

> For thou, Lord, art most high (ὕψιστος) above all the earth:
> Thou art exalted (ὑπερυψώθης) far above all gods.[6]

It is this last rendering which would seem to fit best the context of Phil. 2: 9. 'Υψόω is used frequently in the LXX. Its primary meaning is movement from a lower to a higher level. Thus it is used of the ark being borne up of the flood above the earth;[7] of picking something up from the ground;[8] of erecting a high wall;[9] of an eagle soaring into the sky;[10] of a tree

[1] cp. Tertullian, *De anima*, 55.

[2] It is the use of ἄβυσσος which makes it more likely that the reference is to the *descensus* and Ascension than to the Incarnation and Resurrection. The Peshitta introduces an explicit mention of Sheol.

[3] Phil. 2: 8-11; cp. Acts 2: 36.

[4] Ps. 37: 35.

[5] Dan. 4: 34.

[6] Ps. 97: 9.

[7] Gen. 7: 17.

[8] 2 Kings 2: 13; 6: 7.

[9] 2 Chron. 33: 14.

[10] Job 39: 27. This verse was used as a text for an Ascension sermon by Peter of Celles; see below, p. 163.

growing up to the clouds;[1] of the mountain of the Lord's house being elevated above all other hills[2] and of a throne set in a high and prominent position.[3] It is also used of lifting up one's voice[4] and so of praising,[5] and of the cry of the men of Sodom waxing great before the Lord.[6] A comparison of these usages with those of ἀναβαίνω listed in the previous lecture reveals a remarkable similarity; the two words in fact in many instances are all but synonyms, except that the one is intransitive and the other transitive. This may be further illustrated from the third Gospel, where Christ is represented as loosely quoting from Isa. 14: 13, 15, with the substitution of ὑψόω for the ἀναβαίνω of the original.[7] Moreover, ὑψόω is never used in the New Testament of the Resurrection, although it is employed in reference to the Crucifixion.[8] It does, however, appear in Acts 2: 33[9] with direct reference to the Ascension, where St. Luke affirms that Christ has been "by the right hand of God exalted" (ὑψωθεὶς), and to Him the words of Ps. 110: 1 may now be applied, for David, its reputed author, unlike Christ, "ascended (ἀνέβη) not into the heavens".

This linguistic study points to one conclusion, viz. that ὑψόω and its intensive form ὑπερυψόω may be taken as the equivalents of ἀναβαίνω and may, therefore, if the context warrants it, be understood to refer to the Ascension. In Phil. 2: 8-11, St. Paul speaks of the three levels of the universe above which Christ has been "highly exalted"; his immediate reference is then to the Ascension.[10]

Other statements of St. Paul to be noted are those concerning the Session and the Parousia, both of which involve his

---

1 Ecclus. 50: 10.
2 Isa. 2: 2.
3 Jer. 17: 12.
4 Gen. 39: 15, 18.
5 Tobit 13: 4.
6 Gen. 19: 13.
7 Luke 10: 15‖Matt. 11: 23; they read ἕως οὐρανοῦ ὑψωθήσῃ; ἕως τοῦ ῞Αδου καταβήσῃ,where Isa. 14: 13, 15 has εἰς τὸν οὐρανὸν ἀναβήσομαι . . . εἰς ᾅδην καταβήσῃ.
8 John 3: 14; 8: 28; 12: 32, 34. Even here, however, there is probably an implied reference to the Ascension (O. Cullmann, Early Christian Worship, E.T., 1953, pp. 51-52).
9 cp. 5: 31.
10 Also to be noted is the association of ὑψόω and δοξάζω in the LXX. Isa. 4: 2; 33: 10; 52: 13; Ecclus. 43: 30. cp. L. H. Brockington, "The Septuagintal Background to the New Testament Use of ΔΟΞΑ", Studies in the Gospels, ed. D. Nineham, 1955, p. 2n.

belief in an Ascension as an accomplished fact. So the Colossians are to "seek the things that are above, where Christ is, seated on the right hand of God";[1] while the Thessalonians are bidden to serve the living and true God "and to wait for his Son from heaven",[2] for "the revelation of the Lord Jesus from heaven with the angels of his power".[3]

It must be acknowledged, however, that certain modern critics would contend that although St. Paul speaks of Christ being in heaven this does not of itself necessarily involve an Ascension as distinct from the Resurrection. "The Resurrection of Jesus", according to R. Bultmann, "means simultaneously his exaltation."[4] Thus they would deny the force of the argument I have just used, i.e. that the Session and Parousia involve belief in an Ascension as an accomplished fact, and they would cite as part of the evidence Rom. 8: 34 to the effect that this plainly states that the Resurrection is the *only* necessary immediate antecedent to the Session. The verse reads: "It is Christ Jesus that died, yea rather, that was raised from the dead, who is at the right hand of God, who also maketh intercession for us."

Two factors, however, militate against this position. First there is the Philippian passage that we have already considered and seen to be a direct reference to the Ascension. Second, there is the use of the verbs ἐγείρω and ἀνίστημι which examination shows never refer to any exaltation beyond the recall from death.

The root meaning of ἐγείρω, both in the LXX and in the New Testament, is "to set upright". Thus it is used of lifting up the statue of Dagon that had fallen down;[5] of rebuilding a house,[6] or restoring the walls of Jerusalem.[7] Hence it can mean to set someone on their feet; so the elders raised up David from the ground where he lay in sorrow for Bathsheba's son;[8] Judith, prostrate before Holofernes, was taken up by the king's servants;[9] Jesus took Peter's mother-in-law by the hand and raised her up.[10] Hence it can be employed of waking up or getting out of bed; so Pharaoh, after dreaming of the kine and the ears of corn, awoke;[11] Samson, his hair woven together

[1] Col. 3: 1.　　[2] 1 Thess. 1: 10; cp. Phil. 3: 20.　　[3] 2 Thess. 1: 7.
[4] *Theology of the New Testament*, E.T., I, 1952, p. 45.　　[5] 1 Sam. 5: 3.
[6] 1 Esdras 5: 44; cp. John 2: 20.　　[7] Ecclus. 49: 13.　　[8] 2 Sam. 12: 17.
[9] Judith 10: 23.　　[10] Mark 1: 31; cp. Acts 3: 7.　　[11] Gen. 41: 4, 7.

by Delilah, "awaked out of his sleep, and plucked away the pin of the beam";[1] the disciples, terrified by the storm, awoke Jesus, who was asleep on a cushion in the stern of the boat;[2] and Jesus said to the sick of the palsy, "Arise, and take up thy bed, and walk";[3] and to Jairus' daughter: "Damsel, I say unto thee, Arise."[4] This last quotation indicates how ἐγείρω can also be used of those who have entered upon the sleep of death. So when the king of Babylon descended to Sheol the "chief ones of the earth" were stirred up to taunt him.[5] So too Gehazi tried to restore the Shunammite's child to life and, being unable, reported to his master: "The child is not awaked";[6] and Elijah is described as the one "who didst raise up a dead one from death, and from the place of the dead, by the word of the most High".[7] The reference here is to the widow's son at Zarephath whose raising up was no more than a recall to life,[8] as is also the case with the eschatological fragment incorporated in Isa. 26: "Thy dead shall live; my dead bodies shall arise" when "the earth shall cast forth the dead".[9] The LXX rendering of this verse—"the dead shall arise (ἀναστήσονται) and those in the tombs shall be raised (οἱ ἐν τοῖς μνημείοις ἐγερθήσονται)"—may well be the source of the statement in Matthew: "And the tombs (τὰ μνημεῖα) were opened; and many bodies of the saints that had fallen asleep were raised (ἠγέρθησαν); and coming forth out of the tombs (ἐκ τῶν μνημείων) after his resurrection (ἔγερσιν) they entered into the holy city and appeared unto many."[10] In this verse the raising up certainly involves no immediate entry into heaven, and this is also the case in other New Testament passages. Herod supposes that Jesus is "John the Baptist risen from the dead";[11] the result of Jesus' healing ministry is that "the dead are raised up",[12] and so Lazarus, alive again and restored to his family, is the one "whom Jesus raised from the dead",[13] and Jesus, after He Himself is raised up, will go before the disciples into Galilee.[14] There is certainly no implication in these statements that Resurrection implies any Ascension into

---

[1] Judges 16: 14; cp. 1 Esdras 3: 9; Ps. 108: 2; Prov. 6: 9; Isa. 5: 11; Rom. 13: 11.
[2] Mark 4: 38. [3] Mark 2: 9. [4] Mark 5: 41. [5] Isa. 14: 9.
[6] 2 Kings 4: 31. [7] Ecclus. 48: 5. [8] 1 Kings 17: 17-24. [9] Isa. 26: 19.
[10] Matt. 27: 52, 53. [11] Mark 6: 14. [12] Luke 7: 22; cp. Matt. 10: 8.
[13] John 12: 1. [14] Mark 14: 28.

heaven—quite the contrary, and the same is also true of those passages where ἀνίστημι is used.[1]

The root meaning of ἀνίστημι is "to rise from a recumbent or sitting position to an upright one". So Abraham "rose up early in the morning" to send Hagar and her child into the wilderness;[2] Rachel, sitting upon the teraphim, excused herself from standing;[3] Ruth, after lying at Boaz's feet all night, "rose up before one could discern another";[4] Samuel, asleep in the temple at Shiloh, rose at the Lord's summons;[5] Saul, overcome by calamity, fell full length upon the earth, but was induced by his servants to rise and sit on the bed;[6] Solomon, after his prayer at the dedication of the Temple, "arose from before the altar of the Lord, from kneeling on his knees"[7] and Tobit and his son, after falling on their faces before Raphael, rose up and saw him no more because the angel had ascended to Him that sent him.[8] Jesus rose up early in the morning and departed to a desert place to pray;[9] blind Bartimaeus, at the Lord's summons, cast away his garments and sprang up to meet Him.[10] So ἀνίστημι came to mean "to stand"; Jehoshaphat "stood in the congregation of Judah and Jerusalem, in the house of the Lord",[11] just as Caiaphas stood up in the midst of the Sanhedrin to interrogate Jesus;[12] while Jesus Himself stood up in the synagogue at Nazareth to read.[13] As applied to the dead, ἀνίστημι, like ἐγείρω, has no further reference than a recall to life.

> Wilt thou shew wonders to the dead?
> Shall they that are deceased arise and praise thee?[14]

"After two days will he revive us: on the third day he will raise us up, and we shall live before him."[15] So the dead man, hurriedly thrown into Elisha's tomb, as soon as he touched the prophet's bones, "revived and stood up (ἀνέστη) on his feet".[16] Tyre is to descend into Sheol and not arise in the land of the living,[17] for "they that are dead, they shall not live; they

---

[1] There are certain figurative uses of ἐγείρω in the LXX, not listed above as they have no direct bearing on the Resurrection, e.g. to stir up strife (Prov. 29: 22) and to raise up judges (Judges 2: 16; 3: 9; cp. 1 Kings 11: 14).
[2] Gen. 21: 14.   [3] Gen. 31: 35.   [4] Ruth 3: 14.   [5] 1 Sam. 3: 6.
[6] 1 Sam. 28: 23.   [7] 1 Kings 8: 54.   [8] Tobit 12: 21.   [9] Mark 1: 35.
[10] Mark 10: 50.   [11] 2 Chron. 20: 5.   [12] Mark 14: 60.   [13] Luke 4: 16.
[14] Ps. 88: 10.   [15] Hos. 6: 2.   [16] 2 Kings 13: 21.   [17] Ezek. 26: 20 LXX.

are deceased, they shall not rise".[1] The third of the seven brethren, martyred by Antiochus, was confident that "the King of the world shall raise us up . . . unto an eternal renewal of life", and that this is to be upon the earth is evident from his avowal that he will then have restored his tongue and his hands.[2]

Similarly in the New Testament there are some who think that Jesus is one of the old prophets risen again,[3] while in His parable of Dives and Lazarus He represents the former as pleading for one to go to his brethren from the dead, only to be told that they would not be persuaded even "if one rise from the dead".[4] In exact accord with this is St. Paul's description of the End. "The Lord himself shall descend from heaven, with a shout, with the voice of the archangel, and with the trump of God: and the dead in Christ shall rise first: then we that are alive, that are left, shall together with them be caught up in the clouds, to meet the Lord in the air."[5] The order of events could not have been more clearly expressed. First, the Lord descends. Second, the dead rise, unquestionably to life on this earth since the third stage is that those who have risen and those that are still alive are together "caught up in the clouds, to meet the Lord in the air". Resurrection is certainly not Ascension.

Two further considerations will complete this brief study in lexicography. First, in the LXX ἀνίστημι and ἀναβαίνω are not infrequently associated in a manner that indicates that they are distinct. God says to Jacob, "Arise, go up to Bethel (ἀναστὰς ἀνάβηθι)",[6] and to Joshua He commands, "Arise, go up to Ai".[7] The watchers of Ephraim shall cry: "Arise ye, and let us go up to Zion unto the Lord our God",[8] and Judas, encamped at Elasa, bids his troops: "Let us arise and go up against our adversaries."[9] Hence *anastasis* precedes *anabasis*. Second, ἀνίστημι and ἐγείρω are obviously very close in meaning, and indeed on occasion they may be regarded as synonymous.[10] Thus where the LXX of Dan. 12: 2 uses ἀναστήσονται Theodotion reads ἐξεγερθήσονται, and where St. Luke,

[1] Isa. 26: 14. [2] 2 Macc. 7: 9, 11; cp. 12: 44. [3] Luke 9: 8.
[4] Luke 16: 30, 31. [5] 1 Thess. 4: 16, 17. [6] Gen. 35: 1. [7] Joshua 8: 1.
[8] Jer. 31: 6; cp. 6: 5; 8: 4; 49: 28, 31. [9] 1 Macc. 9: 8.
[10] cp. also the LXX application of ἀνίστημι to the setting up of the Tabernacle (Exod. 26: 30; Num. 1: 51) and to the rearing up of an idol (Lev. 26: 1).

describing the healing of Peter's mother-in-law, has ἀναστᾶσα
διηκόνει αὐτοῖς,[1] St. Matthew has καὶ ἠγέρθη, καὶ διηκόνει αὐτῷ.[2]
We are bound to conclude on the basis of this evidence that
when St. Paul speaks of Jesus being in heaven an antecedent
Ascension, distinct from though possibly to be closely connected with the Resurrection, is undoubtedly implied. When
therefore he tells the Philippians "our citizenship is in heaven;
from whence also we wait for a Saviour, the Lord Jesus Christ",[3]
we may be confident that this and similar statements provide
evidence of an Ascension.

In the Epistle to the Ephesians, the Session of Christ at the
right hand of God and the consequent co-session of believers
in the heavenlies is affirmed,[4] and Ps. 68: 18 is quoted with
the comment: "Now this, He ascended, what is it but that
he also descended into the lower parts of the earth? He that
descended is the same also that ascended far above all the
heavens, that he might fill all things."[5] Here again, according to one interpretation of the passage,[6] the Pauline reci-
procals, *descensus* and Ascension, are brought together,[7] as they
are also in 1 Peter 3: 18-22 where, after recording Christ's
mission to the departed,[8] the writer informs us that He "is
on the right hand of God, having gone into heaven; angels
and authorities and powers being made subject unto him".

With this background of Apostolic testimony we may reasonably expect, when we turn to the first Gospel to have been
written, to find further witness to the fact of the Ascension;
but initially this expectation would seem to be unrealized,
since, except in the spurious Longer Ending, few critics have
found in Mark any reference to it. This in itself need occasion

[1] Luke 4: 39.
[2] Matt. 8: 15.
[3] Phil. 3: 20.
[4] Eph. 1: 20; 2: 6; cp. 1: 3.
[5] Eph. 4: 9, 10.
[6] Bultmann, *op. cit.*, p. 175, disputes the reference to the *descensus* and refers the passage to the pre-existent Son's journey to earth (cp. T. K. Abbott, *The Epistles to the Ephesians and to the Colossians, I.C.C.*, 1897, pp. 144f.).
[7] E. G. Selwyn, *The First Epistle of St. Peter*, 1947, p. 321.
[8] Bultmann, *op. cit.*, p. 176, who considers 1 Peter 3: 18-22 to be part of a Christ-hymn used and misunderstood by the author, asserts that the original reference was not to the descent into Hades, but to a Gnostic myth "according to which the prison of the dead is not in the interior of the earth but in the region of the air, where the spirits of the stars, or of the firmament, keep them confined"; the Ascension is therefore simultaneously the mission to the departed and the act of subjugating the demonic world-rulers.

34

no surprise, since equally there is scant direct reference to the Resurrection appearances; we should, however, scarcely use the *argumentum e silentio* to the effect that St. Mark was ignorant of them, even though they may never have been included in the Gospel itself. Nevertheless, there are two passages[1] which should not be passed over, in the first and fourteenth chapters respectively. In the former, which records the Baptism of Jesus in the River Jordan, the evangelist describes how when He was coming up (ἀναβαίνων) out of the water, the heavens were rent asunder and the Spirit descended as a dove.[2] On the basis of this use of ἀναβαίνω, coupled with the reference to the Spirit, it has been suggested that this account points to the Ascension as the precondition of Pentecost.[3] These two factors by themselves, however, are scarcely sufficient to allow one to affirm with confidence that St. Mark did in fact have the Ascension in mind when he wrote this section of his Gospel, since, as we have seen, in our examination of the LXX usage, ἀναβαίνω would be the normal word to employ in this context, and is indeed so used in Gen. 41: 2 of coming up out of a river, and since also the word may be a reminiscence of a detail in the ritual of Jewish proselyte baptism, i.e. the "coming up" of the candidate from the water to signify his entrance upon a new life.[4]

There is, however, a third feature which serves to lift this interpretation out of the realm of conjecture, viz. the typology which may be said to underlie the Marcan presentation of the opening stages of Jesus' ministry. To St. Mark, John is Elijah come again;[5] and Jesus, who is a second John in so far as like His forerunner He preaches repentance,[6] is also a second Elijah. Thus like Elijah Jesus spent forty days in the wilderness and was succoured by angels:[7] like Elijah,

---

[1] D. Daube, *The New Testament and Rabbinic Judaism*, 1956, pp. 23-24, calls attention to another passage, Mark 15: 38. He argues that there may have been a connexion "at some stage of the tradition" between the Ascension and the rending of the Temple veil because both may be associated with Elijah, so 2 Kings 2: 12||Mark 15: 38, and 2 Kings 2: 11||Luke 24: 51. If this ever were the case, and I remain unconvinced, it is demonstrably so no longer in the Gospels as we have them, since Mark has no Ascension account and Luke places the rending of the Temple veil before Jesus' death (23: 45).
[2] Mark 1: 10.
[3] G. W. H. Lampe, *The Seal of the Spirit*, 1951, p. 43.
[4] Daube, *op. cit.*, pp. 111f. If this were correct, the reason why St. Mark has preserved the detail could still be because it suggested the Ascension.
[5] Mark 9: 13. [6] 1: 15. [7] 1: 13||1 Kings 19: 8.

He called His disciples from their daily work,[1] but as Elijah's disciple did not receive the Spirit until after his master's ascension,[2] so too the disciples of Jesus must persevere in hope. When Christ ascended out of the water He was baptized with Spirit, so the disciples' baptism waits upon His Ascension into heaven.[3] With the conclusion then that St. Mark had the Ascension in mind when he wrote this passage in his first chapter, we turn to the account of Jesus' trial before the Sanhedrin in the fourteenth chapter.

In answer to the high priest's question: "Art thou the Christ?" Jesus says: "I am: and ye shall see the Son of man sitting at the right hand of power, and coming with the clouds of heaven."[4] This reply combines two Old Testament passages, viz. Ps. 110: 1 and Dan. 7: 13. We have already seen, in our consideration of the Old Testament prefigurement, that this latter pericope describes a coming *unto* the Ancient of days, and it has therefore been suggested that these words should be taken to refer to the exaltation of the Son of man to the right hand of God, having been brought there on the clouds of heaven.[5] If this were correct, we should then have a second reference by St. Mark to the Ascension.

Before accepting this interpretation, we must recognize that this logion cannot be considered in isolation from two others in Mark, clearly reminiscent of the same verse in Daniel, which are usually taken to foretell the Parousia.[6] These two statements are: "For whosoever shall be ashamed of me and of my words in this adulterous and sinful generation, the Son of man also shall be ashamed of him, when he cometh in the glory of his Father with the holy angels";[7] and "then shall they see the Son of man coming in clouds with great power and glory".[8] According to these verses, the Son of man has been glorified, since He comes in glory; but in Daniel it is not until *after* the Son of man has come to the Ancient of days

---

[1] 1: 16, 17‖1 Kings 19: 19.
[2] 2 Kings 2: 9.
[3] A. Farrer, *A Study in St. Mark*, 1951, pp. 62-63.
[4] Mark 14: 62.
[5] W. K. Lowther Clarke, "The Clouds of Heaven: An Eschatological Study", *Theology*, XXXI, 1935, p. 130.
[6] Dr. Lowther Clarke appreciates this and argues, incorrectly it seems to me in view of the reasons given below, that these two also refer to the Ascension (*op. cit.*, p. 129).
[7] 8: 38. [8] 13: 26.

that "there was given him dominion, and glory,[1] and a kingdom".[2] Hence these pronouncements in Mark presuppose that the Ascension has taken place; they do not, however, refer to it explicitly, but instead predict the Second Advent. The question then arises, is Jesus' answer to the high priest to be understood in the same sense? Superficially the order of events —sitting, coming—might suggest that this should be so, since to speak of the Ascension after the Session would seem to reverse the natural sequence of events. But there is significantly no reference to "glory" and moreover the two predictions "are to be seen as parallel expressions, static and dynamic, of the same assertion",[3] and that assertion is concerned with Jesus' vindication.

By combining Ps. 110 and Dan. 7, both "enthronement" passages, Jesus intimates that though He is to suffer a shameful death, He is also in fact about to enter upon His reign, i.e. the Cross for Him does not involve defeat, instead it is to be the means of His entrance into glory.[4] Just as the destiny of the Servant was "to pour out his soul unto death"[5] and then to be "exalted and lifted up",[6] so Jesus' death is to issue in His glorification, and the priests will become aware of this fact, not by means of a visible portent—they will not "see" the Ascension—but by the effects in the lives of men that will reveal the fulfilment in the person of Jesus of these Old Testament prophecies.[7]

That both St. Matthew and St. Luke understood the saying in this way is evident from their additions: ἀπ' ἄρτι in Matthew[8] and ἀπὸ τοῦ νῦν in Luke.[9] Since by the time they came to compose their accounts history had falsified any claim to an immediate return,[10] these insertions make it very plain

---

[1] LXX τιμή, not δόξα; a difference obscured in the English versions, but doubtless this includes "glory".
[2] Dan. 7: 14.
[3] J. A. T. Robinson, "The Second Coming—Mark xiv. 62", *Expository Times*, LXVII, 1956, p. 337.
[4] T. F. Glasson, *The Second Advent*, 1945, pp. 64-65.
[5] Isa. 53: 12.
[6] Isa. 52: 13.
[7] V. Taylor, *The Gospel According to St. Mark*, 1952, pp. 568-69.
[8] 26: 64.
[9] 22: 69.
[10] It is evident that St. Matthew at least anticipated a long period of waiting before the Parousia, cp. his phrase μετὰ πολὺν χρόνον (25: 19) in his version of the Parable of the Talents.

that they regarded the logion as referring to an imminent vindication—"from now". Indeed, it is possible that some such
expression originally stood in Mark,[1] and in the Sinaitic Syriac
and in one of the manuscripts of the Sahidic version there are
equivalents of ἀπ' ἄρτι. But whether in Mark or not, the meaning in all three Synoptic Gospels is the same, i.e. the seeming
defeat of Jesus is the beginning of His triumph; His exaltation through death, Resurrection and Ascension is shortly to
take place. So the trial logion contains a direct reference to
the Ascension, and moreover the title "Son of man" itself
implies such a reference.

In Mark 8: 38, quoted above, Jesus speaks of the Son of
man as a person other than Himself: "whosoever shall be
ashamed of me . . . the Son of man also shall be ashamed of
him, when he cometh." Hence Jesus in His earthly ministry
is to be distinguished from the Son of man to come. In so
far as on occasion He applied the latter title to Himself during His ministry,[2] it may be said that He did so because He
was proleptically exercising the functions of the coming Son
of man. And in so far as the title is also found in the predictions of the Passion,[3] it could be so employed because suffering was one of the essential elements in that process whereby
He was to come to the Ancient of days and be glorified as the
Son of man.[4] The Son of man is indeed primarily a triumphant
figure, and it was not until Jesus had triumphed over sin and
death *and* ascended that He received the dominion and glory
inseparable from that status. Thus the presence of the title
"Son of man" in Mark must be regarded as evidence of a
belief in the Ascension.

Closely parallel in meaning and implication to the title
"Son of man" is also the designation "Messiah" or "Christ".
It was central to the Jewish eschatological expectation that
the day would come when God would establish His Kingdom;
then His rule would be exercised either directly or through
His Anointed, i.e. the Messiah. The Messiah himself would

[1] Glasson, *op. cit.*, pp. 66-68.
[2] e.g. Mark 2: 10.
[3] e.g. Mark 8: 31.
[4] The evidence for this thesis is more fully set out by R. H. Fuller, *The Mission and Achievement of Jesus*, 1954, pp. 95-108. It is also upheld by S. Mowinckel, *He That Cometh*, 1956, pp. 445-50. (I am grateful to the translator, the Rev. G. W. Anderson, for allowing me to consult the latter work in galley proof.)

only be known and acknowledged as such when he had revealed his identity through his work of salvation. "According to Jewish thought", states Mowinckel, "it is only then that He will become Messiah in the full sense of the term. Before that time we may say that He is but *Messias designatus*, a claimant to Messianic status"[1]—thus it is the Messianic work that makes him the Messiah and manifests him as such. Hence Jesus during His earthly ministry was the Messiah designate; only when He had accomplished His mission through death, Resurrection and Ascension was He enthroned as Messiah and His kingly rule began. So in Mark, Jesus' answer to Peter's confession is to direct attention to His imminent Passion,[2] and His acknowledgment before the high priest that He was the Christ[3] was only possible because He was then standing within the context of His Passion through which He was destined to become the triumphant Son of man. Again, when Jesus raised the question: "How say the scribes that the Christ is the son of David?"[4] His answer, quoting Ps. 110: 1, indicates that He thought of Christ as a title to be applied not to an earthly figure but to one who has been exalted to God's right hand.[5] Hence St. Mark by his use of the title "Messiah" witnesses to an implicit belief in the Ascension.

St. Luke, handling his material with his customary freedom, omits ἀναβαίνω from his account of the Baptism, but his reason for so doing may well be that he considered it superfluous in view of his use of the Transfiguration story as a prefigurement of the Ascension. I have elsewhere[6] sought to show in detail how exactly St. Luke has done this, and to save needless repetition I will limit my observations to summarizing the main points of that analysis.

In the first place, a comparison of the complex of ideas to be found in Luke 9: 1-34 with that in Acts 1: 1-12 reveals an identity of which the most reasonable explanation is that the one was regarded by its author as the prefigurement of the

---

[1] *op. cit.*, p. 303.
[2] 8: 29-31.
[3] 14: 61, 62.
[4] 12: 35-37.
[5] Fuller, *op. cit.*, pp. 108-11.
[6] "The Prefigurement of the Ascension in the Third Gospel", *J.T.S.*, VI, 1955, pp. 229-33.

other.[1] In the second place, it is to be noted that at Luke 9: 51 there is an explicit reference to the ἀνάλημψις of Christ. It is of course often stated that this is not to be referred to the Ascension as a single incident but also to the death and Resurrection of Christ,[2] but such an interpretation fails to take note of the context in which St. Luke uses the term. It is found in the opening verse of the pericope which records the refusal of the Samaritans to receive Jesus and the consequent request of James and John to call down fire from heaven upon them. The underlying Elijah typology is here unmistakable, and indeed a great number of Western manuscripts make it patent by adding the words ὡς καὶ 'Ηλίας ἐποίησεν. But that incident was the final one in Elijah's career, immediately prior to his ascension,[3] which from Acts 1 we know was also used typologically by St. Luke. Hence ἀνάλημψις in conjunction with the saying about fire from heaven should be taken as a direct reference to the Ascension of Christ.

The third reason for regarding the Transfiguration story as a prefigurement of the Ascension is given by St. Luke's additions to and alterations of his Marcan source, which are provided thereby with a ready explanation: thus we note that (a) ἀναβαίνω[4] is employed instead of ἀναφέρω,[5] (b) καὶ ἰδοὺ ἄνδρες δύο[6] is inserted, a phrase which is repeated in Acts 1: 10,[7] (c) ἔξοδος is added,[8] a word which in view of St. Luke's use of εἴσοδος[9] of Christ's coming into the world must mean not only His death but also His Resurrection and Ascension,[10] (d) δόξα[11] is explicitly mentioned, and whereas this word does

[1] The parallels are set out in Table B on p. 186.
[2] So E. Klostermann, Das Lukasevangelium, 1919, p. 473, followed by A. Loisy, L'Evangile selon Saint Luc, 1924, p. 284, and J. M. Creed, The Gospel According to St. Luke, 1942, p. 141.
[3] 2 Kings 1: 10ff.
[4] Luke 9: 28.
[5] Mark 9: 2.
[6] Luke 9: 30.
[7] J. Mánek ("The New Exodus in the Books of Luke", Novum Testamentum, II, 1957, p. 19) argues that these two men were also Moses and Elijah.
[8] Luke 9: 31.
[9] Acts 13: 24.
[10] H. J. Cadbury suggests that as both Elijah, according to the Old Testament, and Moses, in later thought, ascended, the discussion of Jesus' exodus, a feature peculiar to Luke, involved reference to their own assumption experiences. ("Acts and Eschatology", The Background of the New Testament and Its Eschatology, ed. W. D. Davies and D. Daube, 1956, pp. 308-09.)
[11] Luke 9: 31f.

not appear in the Acts' account of the Ascension, it is evident that St. Luke considered that to be the occasion of Christ's entry into δόξα.[1] Finally, both Dr. Boobyer[2] and Dr. Ramsey[3] have shown that the Transfiguration was understood by the first three evangelists to be a foreshadowing of the Parousia; but St. Luke also affirms that the latter is foreshadowed by the Ascension;[4] if therefore the Transfiguration was a pre-figurement of the Parousia, it must logically be a prefigurement of the Ascension too, and as such it is presented in the third Gospel.

St. Luke provides us not only with a prefigurement but also, in his final chapter, with a brief account of the event itself.[5] "And he led them out until they were over against Bethany: and he lifted up his hands, and blessed them. And it came to pass, while he blessed them, he parted from them, and was carried up into heaven."[6] The words "and was carried up into heaven" are omitted in certain manuscripts and are therefore suspect as a Western non-interpolation. Yet it is more easy to explain an excision than an insertion, on the grounds either that the former was to remove an apparent chronological contradiction between the Gospel and Acts[7]—a contradiction that will occupy us later—or that it was prompted by a desire to

---

[1] Acts 3: 13; 7: 55; 22: 11.
[2] G. H. Boobyer, *St. Mark and the Transfiguration Story*, 1942.
[3] A. M. Ramsey, *The Glory of God and the Transfiguration of Christ*, 1949.
[4] Acts 1: 11.
[5] It was suggested by Kirsopp Lake (*The Beginnings of Christianity*, V, 1933, p. 3), following a conjecture by F. C. Burkitt (*J.T.S.*, XXVIII, 1926, pp. 180, 198) that Luke 24: 50-53, summarizing Acts 1: 6ff., was added to the Gospel when it was separated from Acts. This thesis has been revived recently in a slightly different form by P. Menoud ("Remarques sur les textes de l'ascension dans Luc-Actes", *Neutestamentliche Studien für R. Bultmann*, 1954, pp. 148ff.); he argues that Acts 1: 1-5 was also added when the hypothetical division took place. There is little or no evidence to support this thesis, and Menoud's detailed arguments are not convincing. So, e.g., he asserts that in Acts 1: 1-5 there are several linguistic phenomena which distinguish this passage from the rest of Luke-Acts, but, as Professor C. F. D. Moule points out, in a private communication, "whereas οὐ μετὰ in v. 5 is correctly contrasted by Menoud with μετ' οὐ in Luke 15: 13 and Acts 27: 14, 'do and teach' (Acts 1: 1) is paralleled in Luke 24: 19 as a description of the ministry. The ἅπαξ λεγόμενα in Acts 1: 3f. are not surprising considering the subject matter, while the transition from *oratio obliqua* to *oratio recta*, v. 4, so far from being un-Lucan, can be paralleled from Luke 5: 14; Acts 17: 3; 23: 22." Again, Menoud maintains that there is a contradiction between Luke 24: 49 and 50, since in the former Jesus bids His disciples stay in the city and in the latter is stated to have led them out, but "the alleged conflict between the command to stay in Jerusalem and the leading out of the disciples is nugatory: 'stay' might simply mean that they were not to return to Galilee, not that they were not to go beyond the city wall." See further E. Haenchen, *Die Apostelgeschichte*, 1956, pp. 155ff.
[6] 24: 50, 51.   [7] B. H. Streeter, *The Four Gospels*, 1930, pp. 142f.

avoid an explicit statement as to how and in what form Jesus was taken up on the part of an editor who objected to the idea of a bodily Ascension.[1] However, whether the ultimate verdict of the textual critics is for the retention[2] or omission of this phrase,[3] there can be little doubt that when St. Luke states that "he parted from them", it is the Ascension that he has in mind.[4] Not only is the solemn blessing which he records consonant with a final parting, but this interpretation is confirmed by the Raphael typology which we have suggested may underlie this section, by the close parallelism of Luke 24 and Acts 1, and also by the Longer Ending of Mark.

The parallelism between Luke 24: 46-53 and Acts 1: 4-14 is most striking;[5] exactly the same main features are found in each. In both accounts (1) the Apostles are told not to leave Jerusalem until the coming of the Spirit; (2) they are thus to await the fulfilment of the Father's promise; (3) they are to preach to all nations, bearing witness to Christ from Jerusalem to the ends of the earth; (4) after the parting the eleven return to the city; (5) they continue steadfastly in prayer. There is thus too close an identity of ideas and expressions to allow of any other explanation than that the two passages are concerned with the same event, i.e. the Ascension.

A comparison of Mark 16: 9-20 with Luke 24: 13-52[6] also indicates that the former is in the main a summary of the latter.[7] So in both there are references to the appearance on

[1] This is the thesis cogently presented by D. Plooij, *The Ascension in the "Western" Textual Tradition*, 1929. He maintains that this would explain not only the omission of καὶ ἀνεφέρετο εἰς τὸν οὐρανόν from 24: 51 but also of ἀνελήμφθη in Acts 1: 2 and the change of ἐπήρθη to ἀπήρθη in Acts 1: 9.
[2] The phrase is probably original according to C. S. C. Williams, *Alterations to the Text of the Synoptic Gospels and Acts*, 1951, pp. 51-53, and it is accepted by J. Jeremias, *The Eucharistic Words of Jesus*, E.T., 1955, p. 99. For a very thorough defence of the inclusion of the phrase see V. Larrañaga, *L'Ascension de Notre-Seigneur dans le Nouveau Testament*, 1938, pp. 145-67.
[3] It is frequently argued that Luke 24: 51 must refer to the Ascension in view of Acts 1: 2, which speaks of the "day in which he was received up" (e.g. Creed, *op. cit.*, p. 302), but these very words in Acts are also regarded by some critics as a Western non-interpolation (J. H. Ropes, *The Beginnings of Christianity*, III, 1926, pp. 256-61). Larrañaga, *op. cit.*, pp. 174-207, again provides a full discussion.
[4] W. J. Sparrow Simpson, *Our Lord's Resurrection*, 1905, p. 113.
[5] The parallels are set out in Table C on p. 187.
[6] The parallels are set out in Table D on p. 188.
[7] There is little reason to suppose that the Longer Ending was indebted to John (Streeter, *op. cit.*, pp. 348-50); the two possible points of contact with Matthew (Mark 16: 9, 15; Matt. 28: 9, 19) could be derived from oral tradition, but equally they could be developed from hints in Luke (Luke 24: 10, 47; cp. 8: 2).

the Emmaus road,[1] to the appearance to the eleven as they sat at meat,[2] and to the command to preach.[3] Furthermore, corresponding to the Lucan description of the parting[4] we have in Mark: "so then the Lord Jesus, after he had spoken unto them, was received up into heaven, and sat down at the right hand of God."[5] Thus the spurious Longer Ending of Mark provides us with both an additional witness—one cannot say an independent witness—to belief in the Ascension in the first century and with a means of understanding St. Luke's own witness in the concluding chapter of his Gospel; i.e. the event he is recording is indeed an Ascension.

In the first chapter of his second volume a full description of that event is provided by St. Luke. An examination of the details of this narrative may be postponed until we come to consider the circumstances of the Ascension; all that is necessary here is to note it as an additional item of evidence. Reference is also made to it in three of St. Peter's speeches, on the day of Pentecost,[6] in Solomon's porch[7] and before the Sanhedrin;[8] it is moreover implied in St. Stephen's vision of the Son of man standing at the right hand of God[9] and in St. Paul's heavenly vision on the road to Damascus.[10] Finally, the use of the titles "Son of man" and "Christ", in both Gospel and Acts, rests upon a belief in the Ascension,[11] and this connexion is made very evident by St. Luke's statement that at Jesus' exaltation God "*made* him both Lord and Christ".[12]

In St. Matthew's Gospel there are four passages that are relevant to our investigation. The first of these is his account of the Baptism, which preserves the Marcan use of ἀναβαίνω and the reference to the Spirit, but also contains a significant difference. Where Mark has "he saw the heavens rent asunder" (σχιζομένους),[13] Matthew reads "the heavens were opened" (ἠνεῴχθησαν),[14] and some manuscripts add "unto him". The appropriateness of this alteration when the incident is understood as a prefigurement of the Ascension scarcely needs emphasis. The second passage is the Matthean version of the

---

[1] Mark 16: 12, 13‖Luke 24: 13-35.   [2] Mark 16: 14‖Luke 24: 36, 41ff.
[3] Mark 16: 15‖Luke 24: 47.   [4] Luke 24: 51.   [5] Mark 16: 19.
[6] Acts 2: 33, 34.   [7] 3: 21.   [8] 5: 31.   [9] 7: 56.   [10] 9: 5.
[11] See Luke 12: 8, which draws a distinction between Jesus and the exalted Son of man parallel to that in Mark 8: 38. In Matt. 10: 32 the distinction is obscured by the use of the first person throughout.
[12] Acts 2: 36.   [13] 1: 10.   [14] 3: 16.

Parable of the Talents,[1] in which the merchant has become
an allegory of Christ; his journey is the Ascension and his
return μετὰ πολὺν χρόνον is the Parousia.[2] The third passage
is the trial logion with its quotation of Daniel,[3] and there is
no reason to suppose that St. Matthew was unaware of its
implications. Our final section is to be found in the concluding verses of the Gospel, where the risen Christ tells His disciples: "All authority hath been given unto me in heaven and
on earth" (ἐδόθη μοι πᾶσα ἐξουσία ἐν οὐρανῷ καὶ ἐπὶ τῆς
γῆς),[4] which is an almost verbatim quotation of Dan. 7: 14:
"authority was given unto him" (ἐδόθη αὐτῷ ἐξουσία). In
Daniel this investment with authority is consequent upon the
coming to the Ancient of days of the Son of man whom all
the nations (πάντα τὰ ἔθνη) are to serve; in Matthew this
investment has evidently taken place through the Ascension
of Him whose command is to make disciples of all the nations
(πάντα τὰ ἔθνη).[5]

The fourth Gospel contains several unequivocal references
to the Ascension, although its author, like St. Matthew, does
not provide any description of it. So we read: "No man hath
ascended into heaven, but he that descended out of heaven,
even the Son of man, which is in heaven."[6] When certain of
the disciples murmur against Jesus because of the difficulty of
His teaching, He replies: "Doth this cause you to stumble?
What then if ye should behold the Son of man ascending
where he was before?"[7] Finally,[8] when the risen Christ appears
to Mary Magdalene in the garden, He bids her: "Touch me
not; for I am not yet ascended unto the Father: but go unto
my brethren, and say to them, I ascend unto my Father and
your Father, and my God and your God."[9]

The author of the Epistle to the Hebrews is less concerned

1 Matt. 25: 14-30.
2 J. Jeremias, The Parables of Jesus, E.T., 1954, p. 51. He states that in Luke
(19: 12-27) the process of allegorization has been carried still further and points
out that the merchant becomes a king.
3 Matt. 26: 64.
4 28: 18.
5 28: 19.
6 John 3: 13.
7 6: 61, 62.
8 W. Bauer, Das Johannesevangelium, 3rd Edit., 1933, p. 108, would also include
7: 8, where he takes ἀναβαίνω to have a double sense: "go up to the feast" and
"ascend into heaven".
9 20: 17.

44

with testifying to the fact of the Ascension than with expounding its theological significance; yet, needless to say, the latter rests upon the former. Thus he informs his readers that they have "a great high priest, who hath passed through the heavens",[1] who has indeed been "made higher than the heavens"[2] and has "entered . . . into heaven itself".[3] As a consequence He has "sat down on the right hand of the throne of the Majesty in the heavens",[4] having been "named of God a high priest after the order of Melchizedek"[5]—and we note the threefold citation of Ps. 110.[6]

To the seer of the Apocalypse, Christ is essentially the ascended and glorified Lord who has overcome and sat down with His Father in His throne.[7] Through His *descensus* He possesses the keys of death and of Hades,[8] through His Ascension He has become the ruler of the kings of the earth.[9] His unity with the Father is revealed by His description as one like unto a son of man and "his head and his hair were white as white wool"[10] even as the hair of the Ancient of days in Daniel's vision was like pure wool.[11] It is to Him that the two witnesses ascend in the cloud ($\dot{a}\nu\dot{\epsilon}\beta\eta\sigma\alpha\nu$ $\epsilon\dot{\iota}s$ $\tau\dot{o}\nu$ $o\dot{\upsilon}\rho\alpha\nu\dot{o}\nu$ $\dot{\epsilon}\nu$ $\tau\hat{\eta}$ $\nu\epsilon\phi\dot{\epsilon}\lambda\eta$).[12] He is the man-child of whom the woman was delivered and who was "caught up unto God, and unto his throne"[13]—direct references to the two terms of Christ's mission, His Incarnation and His Ascension.[14] This is He of whom the author of the Pastoral Epistles, documents which in their present form are among the latest of those included in the New Testament, testifies, saying: "He who was manifested in the flesh, justified in the spirit, seen of angels,[15] preached among the nations, believed on in the world, received up in glory."[16]

The witness of the New Testament writings to the Ascension of Christ is remarkable in its universality. We have

[1] Heb. 4: 14.　　[2] 7: 26.　　[3] 9: 24.　　[4] 8: 1; cp. 10: 12; 12: 2.
[5] 5: 10.　　[6] 5: 6; 7: 17, 21.　　[7] Rev. 3: 21.　　[8] 1: 18.
[9] 1: 5.　　[10] 1: 14.　　[11] Dan. 7: 9.　　[12] Rev. 11: 12.　　[13] 12: 5.
[14] cp. R. H. Charles, *The Revelation of St. John*, I, 1920, p. 321; A. Farrer, *A Rebirth of Images*, 1949, p. 144.
[15] This phrase, "seen of angels", is probably to be understood as referring to the beholding of the ascending Christ by the angelic powers, a theme which was elaborated by the interpolator of the *Ascension of Isaiah* and used by Irenaeus (see below, pp. 75, 79).
[16] 1 Tim. 3: 16.

45

observed references to it in all four Gospels, in the Acts of the
Apostles, in the Pauline Epistles, in the Epistles to the Ephesians
and to the Hebrews, in the Pastorals, in 1 Peter and in the
Book of Revelation.[1] We may confidently assert therefore that
the inclusion of the words "he ascended into heaven" in the
Apostles' Creed is amply justified by the evidence.

[1] 1 John should possibly be added in view of 2: 1.

3

THE NEW TESTAMENT RECORD—II

OUR survey of the New Testament record, in the previous lecture, has enabled us to affirm that this provides ample evidence of belief in an Ascension of Christ. This conclusion forms the essential basis for a further examination of the Apostolic writings in order to determine (1) the occasion of the Ascension; (2) its attendant circumstances, and (3) its meaning as understood by the first generation of Christians.

1. *The Occasion of the Ascension*

For many centuries it has been the custom of the Church to celebrate the Ascension on the fortieth day after Easter. The authority for so doing is provided by the Acts of the Apostles where it is stated that Christ appeared unto the disciples "by the space of forty days".[1] In partial agreement with this would seem to be the further statement, in the same book, to the effect that Christ "was seen for many days of them that came up with him from Galilee to Jerusalem".[2] Biblical critics at the present day, however, have not been slow to point out that this evidence as to the occasion of the Ascension is in apparent conflict with what St. Luke had already written in the final chapter of his first book, where the Ascension would seem to be represented as taking place on the evening of the day of the Resurrection. Against such a reading of the Lucan narrative it has been argued (1) that this would allow insufficient time for all the recorded events to take place, and (2) that it is unthinkable that the Ascension happened late at night.[3] Neither of these contentions can be said to carry conviction.

[1] 1: 3. The thesis of B. W. Bacon ("The Ascension in Luke and Acts", *Expositor*, VII, 1909, pp. 254-61), that Acts 1 implies not an Ascension after forty days but an Ascension on Easter Day followed by forty days of appearances, is not convincing.
[2] 13: 31. [3] Larrañaga, *op. cit.*, pp. 457-61.

The two disciples arrived at Emmaus "towards evening (πρὸς ἑσπέραν)" when "the day is now far spent",[1] i.e. shortly before 6 p.m. when one Jewish day ended and the next began. The couple immediately returned to Jerusalem (three score furlongs) and we are left with a meal, a discourse, and a walk to the Mount of Olives, which involves no more than the Last Supper with its accompanying discourse and the walk to Gethsemane—the one could as easily culminate in the Ascension as the other had done in the arrest. As for the statement that the Ascension could not possibly have been at night, this completely lacks critical support, and such tenuous indications as there are might indeed be taken to suggest the exact opposite. The Lucan handling of the Transfiguration story provides a possible hint. We have already had occasion to remark that St. Luke altered the Marcan account in several particulars in order to represent the Transfiguration as the prefiguration of the Ascension. Besides those details previously listed, he made two additions which indicate the time of day of the occurrence. Thus he inserted: "Peter and they that were with him were heavy with sleep"[2]—this suggests a late hour—and also, unlike St. Matthew and St. Mark, he affirms that the party did not descend the mountain until the following day.[3] So according to St. Luke the Transfiguration took place at night. It may be that his reason for emphasizing this was to provide another pointer to the Ascension which took place at night. This is anything but proof, but at least it has some basis in the text, even if fanciful, whereas the contention it is designed to refute has none.

There can indeed be no gainsaying that the final chapter of Luke does read like a continuous narrative, and this would seem to be guaranteed by the introduction of its final section with a phrase, εἶπεν δὲ,[4] so characteristic of St. Luke that it is found fifty-nine times in the Gospels, fifteen in Acts and only once elsewhere in the New Testament. This phrase nearly always indicates the continuation of a narrative and never necessarily the contrary.[5] Just as εἶπεν δὲ πρὸς αὐτούς at Luke 24: 17 implies no break in the narrative, so the identical words at 24: 44 may be understood in the same way.

[1] 24: 29.   [2] 9: 32.   [3] 9: 37.   [4] 24: 44.
[5] K. Lake, *The Resurrection of Jesus Christ*, 1907, p. 108.

THE NEW TESTAMENT RECORD—II

Nevertheless, it must be frankly admitted that St. Luke was not a writer who was much concerned to indicate precise intervals of time[1] or to give details of exact location,[2] but there is one item of evidence that would endorse our understanding of Luke 24 as affirming that the Ascension occurred on Easter Day, and that is the Longer Ending of Mark. As we have seen, this addition is mainly a summary of the final chapter of Luke. At Mark 16: 14 Christ appears to the disciples and bids them go forth and preach the Gospel: the passage continues: "So then the Lord Jesus, after he had spoken unto them, was received up into heaven."[3] The undoubted continuity of this passage substantiates the conclusion that the Lucan narrative, upon which it is most probably based, equally implies no break in the action. What then are we to make of this apparent contradiction in the Lucan records?

It is not infrequently argued that in the interval that may be supposed to have elapsed between the writing of the Gospel and Acts, St. Luke came across further evidence which he deemed to be more reliable and therefore he included it in his second volume, thereby correcting, by implication, what he had written in his first. But the close relationship between chapter 9 of the Gospel and chapter 1 of Acts would seem to render this a doubtful supposition, and, moreover, it is just as reasonable to suppose either that St. Luke was familiar with two distinct traditions and, following the method so common in the Old Testament, recorded the two as of equal value, without presuming to adjudicate between them, or that he inserted the forty days on his own initiative for reasons yet to be discovered. In order to decide between these alternatives, it will be necessary first to consider what evidence there is for the existence of two separate traditions.[4]

In 1 Cor. 15: 5-8 St. Paul lists the witnesses of the Resurrection, of whom the last is himself. Now whether we say that

[1] F. H. Chase, *The Meaning of the Creed*, ed. G. K. A. Bell, 1918, p. 122.
[2] cp. 17: 11.
[3] Mark 16: 19.
[4] The varying Gnostic traditions need not concern us—18 months according to the Valentinians (Irenaeus, *Adv. Haer.*, 1. 3. 2.), to the Ophites (1. 30. 14), and to the Ethiopic *Ascension of Isaiah* (9.16. 545 days = 18 months); 12 years according to *Pistis Sophia* (1.1). A. Harnack (*S.B.A.*, 1912, pp. 677f.) suggested that the 18 months might represent a correct tradition as to the date of St. Paul's conversion and the appearance on the Damascus road was the last of the risen Lord.

the Ascension took place on Easter Day or forty days later, it is quite clear that the appearance to St. Paul was after the Ascension; yet he sees no distinction between his experience and those of Peter and the twelve. The implication therefore is that for St. Paul all the appearances were not only post-Resurrection but also post-Ascension. It is probable that St. Matthew shared this same conception. As we have seen, the charge which Christ is represented as delivering in the concluding verses of this Gospel implies that the Ascension has already taken place. But if this final appearance is compared with the first appearance to the women, it is noticeable that the circumstances of the two events are not presented as being in any way strikingly different; on the contrary, on both occasions προσεκύνησαν αὐτῷ.[1] It would not be unreasonable to see in this evidence that St. Matthew, like St. Paul, considered all the appearances to have taken place after the Ascension.

According to John, the gift of the Spirit was consequent upon the Ascension: "the Spirit was not yet given; because Jesus was not yet glorified."[2] Jesus was about to leave the world and "go unto the Father";[3] He would then send to them the Comforter from the Father.[4] On Easter Day, Jesus' first action, after saluting the disciples, is to breathe on them saying: "Receive ye the Holy Ghost."[5] The implication is clear that the Ascension has taken place.[6] That this is indeed so is confirmed by Jesus' statement to Mary at the tomb: "Touch me not; for I am not yet ascended unto the Father: but go unto my brethren, and say to them, I ascend unto my Father and your Father."[7] When He appears to the disciples He shows them His hands and later bids Thomas handle

---

[1] 28: 9‖28: 17.

[2] John 7: 39.

[3] 16: 28. This "going to the Father" is represented as a single act comprising three distinct events, viz. death, Resurrection and Ascension.

[4] 15: 26; cp. 16: 7.

[5] 20: 22.

[6] This is a commonplace of contemporary New Testament scholarship. One of its clearest expositions is by Archimandrite Cassien, *La Pentecôte Johannique*, 1939, pp. 9-91.

[7] 20: 17; cp. the comment of Marius Victorinus (*c. Arianos*, 3. 15), who states that Christ, before He could allow Himself to be touched, had to go to the Father with the human life which He had recovered from Hades (as distinct from His divine life as Logos) in order to have it sanctified.

Him;[1] again the implication is that the Ascension is an accomplished fact. We conclude therefore that, for St. John, the occasion of the Ascension was Easter Day.

Evidence for the persistence of this tradition is to be found in the *Epistle of Barnabas* (*c.* A.D. 130): "We also celebrate with gladness the eighth day in which Jesus also rose from the dead, and was made manifest, and ascended into heaven."[2] Again, according to the *Apology of Aristides* (*c.* 140): "after three days he rose again and went up into the heavens."[3] According to the *Epistle of the Apostles* (*c.* 150): "He said unto us again: Behold, on the third day and at the third hour shall he come which hath sent me, that I may depart with him. And as he so spake, there was thunder and lightning and an earthquake and the heavens parted asunder, and there appeared a light cloud which bore him up."[4] According to the *Gospel of Peter* (*c.* 150), when the women come to the tomb on Easter Day, an angel informs them: "He is risen and is departed thither whence he was sent."[5] In the Pseudo-Tertullian treatise *Against the Jews*[6] there is the statement: "Why, accordingly, after His Resurrection from the dead, which was effected on the third day, did the heavens receive him back? It was in accordance with the prophecy of Hosea uttered on this wise: 'Before daybreak they shall arise unto me, saying, Let us go and return unto the Lord our God, because he himself will draw us and free us. After two days, on the third day',[7] which is His glorious Resurrection, He received Him back from earth into the heavens (whence the Spirit Himself had come to the Virgin) even Him whose Nativity and Passion alike the Jews had failed to recognize." Finally there is to be noted the interesting reading of the *Codex Bobiensis*, which at Mark 16: 2 inserts the words: "*subito autem ad horam tertiam tenebrae diei factae sunt per totum orbem terrae et descenderunt de caelis angeli et surgent in claritate vivi dei simul ascenderunt cum eo et continuo lux facta est.*"[8]

[1] John 20: 20, 27.   [2] 15: 8, 9.   [3] 15.
[4] M. R. James, *The Apocryphal New Testament*, 1926, p. 503.
[5] 56 (James, *op. cit.*, p. 93). According to this same docetic work (19, p. 91), the divine power ascended at the death on the Cross.
[6] 13. (*P.L.* 2. 636-37.)
[7] cp. Hos. 6: 1, 2.
[8] To these examples may be added (*a*) The Syriac Diatessaron (Aphraates, *Dem.*, 20. 11). (*b*) The Old Syriac Calendar which observes the Ascension on a Sunday (Lake, *op. cit.*, p. 114).

The persistence and extent of this tradition, to which even St. Luke himself is probably a witness, tells strongly against accepting the chronology of Acts, which is after all the sole certain evidence opposed to the view that the Ascension took place on Easter Day.[1] Whence then did St. Luke derive his forty-day period? It is remarkable that in two separate documents we find evidence for such a period prior to an ascension. Thus in the *Apocalypse of Baruch* we read that the scribe had to wait forty days on a mountain before his assumption;[2] while in 2 Esdras it is stated that Ezra spent forty days transcribing the Law before his exaltation into heaven.[3] In neither of these cases, however, can we posit any direct influence upon St. Luke, as the first was probably written between A.D. 70 and 100 and the second between A.D. 100 and 120; but they serve to emphasize the fact that the number forty was a traditional one in sacred history. So, at the time of the flood it rained upon the earth for forty days and forty nights; Moses was forty days on Mount Sinai; the Israelites wandered forty years in the wilderness, and Jesus was forty days in the desert tempted of the devil. There was ample precedent therefore for the use of the number forty, and we may be confident that its typological possibilities were not lost upon St. Luke.

The typological basis of Acts 1 is not difficult to discern; St. Luke is quite evidently using the Elijah story as a prefigurement of the Ascension.[4] So in 2 Kings 2: 11 Elijah is received up into heaven (ἀνελήμφθη Ἠλειού . . . ὡς εἰς τὸν οὐρανόν), while his disciple watches the incident and then receives the gift of the Spirit, and in Acts 1: 11 Jesus is received up into heaven (Ἰησοῦς ὁ ἀναλημφθεὶς . . . εἰς τὸν οὐρανόν),

[1] In a recent article ("The Ascension—Acts i. 9", *Expository Times*, LXVIII, 1957, pp. 205-9), C. F. D. Moule accepts the forty days and suggests that the Jerusalemite and Galilean traditions of the Resurrection appearances fit into this chronology. The disciples would naturally return home to Galilee after the Week of Unleavened Bread, and would there see Jesus; they would then return for the next festival shortly before Pentecost, to which period the Ascension may be reasonably assigned. This is a cogent argument, once the forty days is accepted, but in my view Professor Moule has not given sufficient attention to the evidence against it as listed above.

[2] 76: 4.
[3] 14: 9, 23, 44.
[4] It may be that St. Luke had Enoch also in mind, as his translation immediately precedes Babel (Gen. 5: 24; 6: 1-8) as the Ascension precedes Pentecost which reverses Babel (J. G. Davies, "Pentecost and Glossolalia", *J.T.S.*, III, 1952, pp. 228-31).

while His disciples watch the incident and later receive the gift of the Spirit at Pentecost.

In 1 Kings 19: 8 there is a further passage, also referring to Elijah, which is most striking and particularly relevant to our present investigation; it reads, in the original Greek, as follows: καὶ ἀνέστη καὶ ἔφαγεν καὶ ἔπιεν· καὶ ἐπορεύθη ἐν τῇ ἰσχύι τῆς βρώσεως ἐκείνης τεσσεράκοντα ἡμέρας καὶ τεσσεράκοντα νύκτας ἕως ὄρους Χωρήβ. If we read this statement not from the standpoint of modern criticism but in the way that St. Luke would have done, i.e. as a prefiguration of Christ, we notice three features:

(i) καὶ ἀνέστη, and he rose: so St. Luke uses ἀνίστημι of the Resurrection of Christ.[1]

(ii) καὶ ἔφαγεν καὶ ἔπιεν, and he ate and drank: so St. Luke says that Christ was manifested to certain witnesses who ate and drank with Him after He rose from the dead (συνεφάγομεν καὶ συνεπίομεν αὐτῷ μετὰ τὸ ἀναστῆναι αὐτὸν ἐκ νεκρῶν).[2]

(iii) ἐπορεύθη . . . τεσσεράκοντα ἡμέρας καὶ τεσσεράκοντα νύκτας ἕως ὄρους, he went forty days and forty nights unto the mount: so, according to St. Luke, Jesus, after forty days (δι' ἡμερῶν τεσσεράκοντα), went unto the mount of Olives (ὄρους)[3] and thence went (πορευομένου) into heaven.[4]

In the account of the Ascension in his Gospel St. Luke, as we have seen, most probably took the story of Raphael as his type; in Acts he would appear to be using the Elijah saga and he points the connexion by referring to a forty-day period.[5] There is no reason to suppose that in so doing he expected his readers to press the details literally or that he thought that this involved any serious contradiction of what he had previously written.[6]

We cannot, however, rest satisfied with this conclusion without examining another passage which may seem to weigh

[1] Luke 24: 46; Acts 2: 24, 30-32; 3: 26.
[2] Acts 10: 41; cp. Luke 24: 43.
[3] Acts 1: 12.
[4] Also to be noted are the references to πνεῦμα, συσσεισμός, πῦρ, φωνή, 1 Kings 19: 11, 12; the first, third and fourth appear in Acts 2: 1-6 and the second in its doublet Acts 4: 31. See further Table E, p. 189.
[5] It is interesting to note that Maximus of Turin associated Elijah's forty days in the desert with his translation, viz. "Elijah, after forty days' fast, was translated from this world." *Sermo* 18 *de Temp.* (*P.L.* 57. 568).
[6] The close parallelism between Luke 24: 46-53 and Acts 1: 1-14, previously noted, would also suggest that he saw no conflict in the two accounts.

against it. In Acts 13: 31 St. Paul is represented as saying, during the course of a sermon at Antioch of Pisidia, that Jesus "was seen for many days of them that came up with him from Galilee to Jerusalem".[1] The "many days" of this statement might well be taken to be a less precise expression of the forty-day period of Acts 1: 3, in which case the latter could hardly be, as I have suggested, no more than a typological detail with no direct bearing on chronology. If we could assume that St. Luke was a consistent and at the same time a lucid writer there would be much force in this argument; in fact, however, he was anything but perspicuous.[2] One example must suffice to demonstrate the correctness of this description. To St. Luke the Ascension was the occasion of the glorification of Jesus; He then assumed a radiant, shining form which had been revealed beforehand to the three disciples on the mount of Transfiguration and later dazzled St. Paul on the Damascus road.[3] If St. Luke had been a consistent writer then he must have described any other post-Ascension appearance of Christ in the same manner; in fact, he did not do so. When the Lord comes to St. Paul in the house of Titus Justus at Corinth[4] and when He stands by him in the castle at Jerusalem,[5] there is not the slightest hint of a heavenly luminosity. It would therefore be a mistake to assume too readily on the grounds of St. Luke's alleged consistency that the "many days" of Acts 13: 31 must refer to the forty days of Acts 1: 3. It could equally be that the "many days" was taken unaltered by him from a source which envisaged a series of appearances after Jesus had both risen and ascended on Easter Day.[6] When therefore there is inescapable uncertainty, it would be a mistake to press Acts 13: 31 against the interpretation of the forty days as a deliberate reminiscence of Elijah for typological ends.

---

[1] The inclusion of ἡμέρας τεσσαράκοντα in 10: 41 in certain manuscripts is undoubtedly a late explanatory gloss.

[2] If C. F. Evans ("The Central Section of St. Luke's Gospel", *Studies in the Gospels*, ed. D. Nineham, 1955, pp. 37-53) be correct in his suggestion that the sequence of Luke 10: 1-18: 14 is determined by the Book of Deuteronomy, we have a striking example of St. Luke's disregard of modern canons of historical writing. To attempt to understand him by these canons, of which he knew nothing, is unlikely to produce accurate results.

[3] So Boobyer, *op. cit.*, p. 67. This is a view I would endorse against the thesis of P. Benoit, "L'Ascension", *Revue Biblique*, LVI, 1949, pp. 198-203, which has been accepted by J. A. T. Robinson, *Jesus and His Coming*, 1957, pp. 135f. See further below p. 110 n.1.

[4] 18: 9.   [5] 23: 11.   [6] e.g. John 20: 21.

Assessment of the validity of this suggestion will obviously be in part determined by preconceptions; that is to say, to one who rejects typology the above argument will seem fanciful, while to one who considers that the thought of the New Testament writers, and of St. Luke in particular, was cast in a typological mould, the thesis will deserve to be examined on its merits. This is obviously not the place to embark upon a discussion of typology as a whole,[1] but certain observations are pertinent to my theme. It is evident that typology can run riot; there is no need to adduce examples from the Fathers to prove this, but *abusus non tollit usum*, and the primary question then becomes, once it is acknowledged that typology is an element in New Testament thought and expression, how to differentiate between passages which are *by the writer's intention* typological and those which are not. Two factors seem to me above all essential: first, a point by point parallelism between a New Testament and an Old Testament episode (a parallelism, however, which need not involve an identical order), and second, a direct quotation or distinct reminiscence of the Old Testament passage. I am not suggesting that where these features are absent typology is not present, but it obviously becomes very difficult to detect—one might even say that one man's guess is as good as another's. However, in this case under discussion—the Lucan reference to the forty days —both canons seem to me to be observed, and for this reason I put it forward as a possible explanation of St. Luke's source and intention.[2] Thus there seems no adequate reason for questioning our acceptance of the tradition that Easter Day was the occasion of the Ascension and that the apparent contradiction of this by St. Luke in Acts is a formal one only.

This conclusion, however, brings us back to the statement with which this section opened, viz. that for centuries it has been the custom of the Church to celebrate the Ascension on the fortieth day after Easter. How is this to be reconciled with the outcome of our investigation? If we regard the calendar

---

[1] See the illuminating discussion by G. W. H. Lampe and K. J. Woollcombe, *Essays on Typology*, 1957.
[2] J. Mánek ("The New Exodus in the Books of Luke", *Novum Testamentum* II, 1957, p. 19) suggests that the typological basis is to be found in the events of the Exodus, the crossing of the Red Sea corresponding to the Crucifixion and Resurrection, the forty years in the wilderness to the forty days of the Appearances, and the entry into the Promised Land to the Ascension.

primarily as a series of historical commemorations, then it is doubtful if any reconciliation is possible, for it is one thing, e.g., to observe the Nativity of Christ on a fictitious date when we have no possible means of discovering the correct one, and quite another to persist in observing the Ascension on a day known to be incorrect. If, however, we can recover something of the significance of the primitive liturgical cycle, which was essentially eschatological, its festivals proclaiming and manifesting the fact of Redemption and representing the inauguration of the world to come[1] rather than a series of historical facts, we shall have less difficulty in approving the Church's practice which does provide an opportunity for teaching, which a unitive observance on Easter Day would preclude.[2]

2. The Circumstances of the Ascension

Although, as we have seen, there is scarcely a New Testament writer who does not testify to the Ascension, St. Luke is the only one who has preserved a description of the circumstances of the event. Consequently the sole criterion at our disposal for assessing the reliability of his account would seem to be its intrinsic probability.

If we take the description in the first chapter of Acts literally and regard the cloud as a conveyance which carries Christ up to a localized heaven in much the same way that an elevator may carry a man to the top of the highest skyscraper in New York, we are bound to conclude that such an occurrence is not only improbable but impossible. Although we may perhaps consider that as the Resurrection appearances can be understood to be accommodations to the sense perceptions of the disciples, so this event may be regarded as an accommodation to their pre-Copernican cosmology. But the moot point is precisely whether St. Luke did or did not intend his account to be interpreted literally.

The description comprises two main details: first, He was taken up; second, a cloud received Him out of their sight. The latter feature need occasion no difficulty to anyone familiar with Biblical imagery, for the cloud is not primarily a cloud

---

[1] G. Dix, *The Shape of the Liturgy*, 1945, p. 336.
[2] C. S. Mann, "The New Testament and the Lord's Ascension", *C.Q.R.*, CLVIII, 1957, p. 464.

of our atmosphere at all, but the cloud of the divine presence —that cloud which rested on the Mount of Transfiguration and was the sign of the divine presence in the Tent of Meeting in the wilderness. St. Luke in fact is affirming by the use of this imagery that the Ascension was no more and no less than the entrance of Christ into the divine glory. It is when we turn to the first feature, viz. the taking up, that difficulties arise, for it has to be admitted that the Hebrew regarded the universe as a three-storeyed construction, of which heaven was the first and earth the ground floor with Sheol as the basement. Yet it would be a mistake to regard this as in any sense a systematized conception. Heaven itself had been created by God,[1] but the Hebrew never asked where God was before this act of creation took place. Again, it was recognized that "the heaven of heavens cannot contain" Him,[2] and so God could not be said to be confined in space, although one might also affirm that heaven was His throne.[3] The clue to these statements and indeed to the whole Hebrew cosmology, which was a theological and not a scientific one, lies in the Hebrew manner of thinking.

The Hebrew, unlike the Greek, knew of no natural sciences or physics. He never objectified the world as a natural order whose laws are to be discerned nor did he regard it as a closed system susceptible of mathematical measurement.[4] The world, to him, was the scene of God's encounter with man, the sphere in which God's over-all purpose was being carried out. When he spoke of God's act of creation he was not concerned to make an objective statement of observed fact nor to formulate a scientific theory of origins, but to praise God for His mighty acts of which creation was but one among many. Consequently to treat the three-storeyed concept as if it were the defined result of the Greek way of thinking and observing is to misconceive its nature. Moreover, the Hebrew invariably thought in terms of the concrete. There are indeed few abstract nouns in the language, and the Hebrew thinker inevitably pictorialized his theological ideas. When St. Luke came to describe

---

[1] Gen. 1; Exod. 20: 11; 2 Kings 19: 15; Ps. 121: 2, etc.
[2] 1 Kings 8: 27.
[3] Isa. 66: 1.
[4] R. Bultmann, *Primitive Christianity in Its Contemporary Setting*, E.T., 1956, pp. 12, 23.

the Ascension, which to him, as to his fellow New Testament writers, was the occasion of Christ's entrance into the divine presence, he did so pictorially—Christ was taken up. It would seem impossible, however, to determine whether St. Luke intended this to be understood as involving a movement in space or not. Here indeed fact and interpretation are so closely welded as to be inseparable.

We may say, if we choose, that we do not like this picture, but that is only another way of saying that we do not like the Hebrew way of thinking, for if pictorial language is to be used of the Ascension it is difficult to see how otherwise it could have been expressed than in the way that St. Luke has adopted. Moreover, the extent to which this way was natural to contemporary writers with a Hebraic cast of mind may be seen from a comparison with two other passages in the New Testament.[1] In St. Paul's account to the Thessalonians of the Parousia, as we have already had occasion to notice, Christ is represented as being in the air, and both those still alive and those resurrected are to be "caught up in the clouds, to meet the Lord";[2] while in the Apocalypse, the two witnesses, after the breath of God has entered into them and they stand upon their feet, ascended "into heaven in the cloud".[3]

The translation of this Hebraic imagery into abstract terms does not *ipso facto* make the result any more accurate. If, therefore, with these considerations in mind, we seek to determine the intrinsic probability of Acts 1: 9, it must be admitted that St. Luke has adopted a by no means inadequate method to convey what he wished to express, even if we may feel bound to maintain a reverent agnosticism as to the exact historical circumstances of the event that he is interpreting for us.

There is, however, one other aspect of this whole problem which should not be neglected. According to St. Luke, both in his Gospel and in Acts, there were witnesses of the Ascension;[4] but according to St. John, since the Ascension took

---

[1] cp. Josephus who, in rehearsing the story of Moses' death, introduces quite naturally a reference to a cloud (*Ant. Jud.*, 4. 8. 48).

[2] 1 Thess. 4: 17.

[3] Rev. 11: 12.

[4] Did St. Luke stress the presence of witnesses, who "looked steadfastly" after their ascending Master, to emphasize the typological basis according to which Elisha had to see his master's ascent in order to obtain the gift of the Spirit?

place after the appearance to Mary Magdalene and before the first appearance to the disciples, there were, as far as we can tell, no witnesses of the Ascension.[1] St. Matthew might be taken to imply the same circumstances. St. Paul's testimony is less easy to disentangle, and in order to appreciate it we have to recognize that his view of the Ascension differed in one important particular from that of his companion, St. Luke. It was the latter's belief that the Ascension was the final event in the series of Resurrection appearances; then Christ received what may be termed a body of glory, i.e. a heavenly body of shining, ethereal substance,[2] which was revealed in the post-Ascension appearance to St. Paul on the Damascus road. But St. Paul, as we have seen, did not consider that there was any distinction between the appearances to Peter and the Twelve and his own visitation; i.e. for him there was no finality about the Ascension. Moreover, in 1 Cor. 15: 35-44, where he discusses the nature of the resurrection body in terms which suggest that he thinks of Christ's resurrection body and that of the Christian as similar, he describes it as "raised in glory"; hence Christ's resurrection body is a body of glory and so resurrection and ascension, i.e. glorification, are represented in this passage as two aspects of one occurrence; or, perhaps, since elsewhere he distinguishes the two events, it would be more accurate to say that they are so closely linked that on occasion they may be regarded as two parts of a single process. In which case we must affirm that St. Paul's evidence precludes the presence of witnesses. Thus at the one point where we can check St. Luke's account of the Ascension we find that his description is not supported by what is the most primitive and probably, in view of St. John, the most accurate conception of the event. We have to conclude therefore that any certain knowledge of the circumstances of the Ascension, as indeed of the Resurrection also, is impossible since St. Luke's is the sole account of it, and we have found grounds

---

[1] The newly discovered *Epistle of James* represents the Ascension as taking place, after 550 days (i.e. 18 months), in the presence of Peter and James only. Christ ascends in a chariot of *pneuma*—a feature probably borrowed from Elijah's ascension. G. Quispel (*The Jung Codex*, ed. F. L. Cross, 1955, pp. 45-47) is not prepared to assert that it is a Gnostic work. W. C. van Unnik ("The Origin of the recently discovered 'Apocryphon Jacobi' ", *Vig. Christ.*, X, 1956, pp. 149-56) argues that it is not of Gnostic but Egyptian provenance, c. A.D. 125-50.

[2] Boobyer, *op. cit.*, p. 23.

for considering this to be not so much intrinsically improbable as unreliable.

3. *The Meaning of the Ascension according to the New Testament*

Because of the unity of event and interpretation in the New Testament writings, it has not been possible to avoid hitherto some trespassing upon the subject of this third and final section. But a broad survey of the meaning of the Ascension in all its variety is still required as a necessary preliminary to assessing the contributions of later writers, although, in view of the final lecture, which will be devoted to a more systematic exposition of the doctrine, the treatment here of the New Testament teaching may be less than exhaustive.

To St. Paul the Ascension is primarily the occasion when Jesus was elevated to the status of Lord. "Wherefore also God highly exalted him, and gave unto him the name which is above every name . . . that every tongue should confess Jesus Christ is Lord."[1] "No man can say, Jesus is Lord, but in the Holy Spirit";[2] but the mission of the Spirit, so St. Paul taught, is consequent upon and subsequent to the mission of the Son,[3] therefore it is not until after the Ascension that men are enabled by the Spirit to confess Christ to be the Lord. "For to this end Christ died, and lived again, that he might be Lord of both the dead and the living."[4] The centrality of this belief in St. Paul's thought is demonstrated not only by his explicit statement that "we preach not ourselves, but Christ Jesus as Lord",[5] but also by his constant use of the title κύριος and his not infrequent description of himself as δοῦλος Χριστοῦ.[6] St. Paul's relation to Christ is indeed not that of discipleship but of religious dependence upon a glorified Messiah, and his devotion is not primarily directed to Jesus as a figure of the past but towards Jesus as the exalted Lord of present and future.[7] Hence the Christianity which St. Paul both embraced[8] and expounded was one "of which the essential and distinguishing

---

[1] Phil. 2: 9, 11.   [2] 1 Cor. 12:3.   [3] Gal. 4: 4-6.   [4] Rom. 14: 9.   [5] 2 Cor. 4: 5.
[6] e.g. Rom. 1: 1; Gal. 1: 10; Phil. 1: 1. "Son of man" does not appear in the Pauline writings; its meaning is included in the titles "Lord" and "Christ".
[7] A. E. J. Rawlinson, *The New Testament Doctrine of the Christ*, 3rd impress., 1949, p. 118.
[8] The cult of Jesus as Lord derives, *pace* Bousset and Bultmann, from the primitive Palestinian Church (cp. Rawlinson, *op. cit.*, p. 106).

characteristic was the *cultus* of Jesus as 'Lord' ".[1] Thus Christians are those who at their Baptism, which involved the solemn liturgical invocation of Jesus as Lord, confessed Him in the same formula;[2] they are too those who call upon Him under that title in their worship[3] when they assemble to celebrate the Lord's Supper.[4] To St. Paul, then, Christ is Lord, and He is so in virtue of His Resurrection and Ascension.

So closely allied with this conception of the Ascension that it is all but indistinguishable from it is the further belief that the Ascension issues in the enthronement of Christ in Messianic majesty as King at the right hand of God; "for he must reign, till he hath put all his enemies under his feet".[5] Thus through the Ascension Christ has become God's vicegerent over the universe, yet His reign is not one of peace but of glorious warfare as He continues "to subject all things unto himself".[6] St. Paul has here in mind psalm 8, and indeed he directly quotes from the sixth verse,[7] but the preceding verse equally expressed another aspect of the Apostle's understanding of the Ascension,[8] viz.:

For thou hast made him but little lower than God,
And crownest him with glory and honour.

The Ascension is indeed the glorification,[9] "for our citizenship is in heaven; from whence also we wait for a Saviour, the Lord Jesus Christ: who shall fashion anew the body of our humiliation, that it may be conformed to the body of his glory".[10]

Finally, St. Paul sees in the Ascension one of the four closely-knit elements in Christ's atoning act, which comprises not only His death, but also His descent into Sheol, His Resurrection and His exaltation viewed as one single process effecting deliverance from the power of darkness and translation into the kingdom of the Son.[11] This is the *Christus Victor* theme which presents the atonement as a great triumph over Satan and his minions; they have been deprived of their dominion over man, which dominion has passed to Christ.[12] Thus by the Cross He has triumphed over the principalities and powers;[13] by His

---

[1] Rawlinson, *op. cit.*, pp. 93-94. [2] Rom. 10: 9; 1 Cor. 6: 11. [3] 1 Cor. 1: 3.
[4] 1 Cor. 11: 20. [5] 1 Cor. 15: 25. [6] Phil. 3: 21. [7] 1 Cor. 15: 27.
[8] C. H. Dodd, *According to the Scriptures*, 1952, pp. 32-34.
[9] 1 Cor. 15: 43; Col. 3: 1-4. [10] Phil. 3: 20, 21; cp. 2 Thess. 2: 14. [11] Col. 1: 13.
[12] Rom. 14: 9. [13] Col. 2: 15; cp. 1 Cor. 2: 8.

descensus He has entered the abyss[1] which is the very abode of Satan, and by His exaltation, through Resurrection and Ascension, He has become the "head of all principality and power",[2] the One to whom all created things, in heaven, on earth, and under the earth,[3] are subject.

According to the Epistle to the Ephesians,[4] Christ Jesus is the "Lord",[5] and in so far as it is through His Ascension that He has become "head over all things to the church"[6] His present sovereignty may be said to rest upon that event. Thus He rules in exalted majesty, since God has "put all things in subjection under his feet".[7] It is, however, in connexion with Christ's Ascension as part of His atoning act that this Epistle has its most important contribution to make. The Christians' foe is no material adversary but a spiritual one: "for our wrestling is not against flesh and blood, but against the principalities, against the powers, against the world-rulers of this darkness, against the spiritual hosts of wickedness in the heavenly places."[8] It is against "the prince of the power of the air"[9] that believers must struggle. But their eventual victory is assured, because when God raised Christ from the dead He "made him to sit at his right hand in the heavenly places, far above all rule, and authority, and power, and dominion".[10] Hence all spiritual forces have been subordinated to Christ who at His Ascension led them captive in His triumphal train,[11] and in this victory the faithful may share, since God "raised us up with him, and made us to sit with him in the heavenly places, in Christ Jesus".[12] Finally, it is to be noted that the exaltation of Christ is also connected with the power that is at work in the members of His Church, and this is emphasized by the alteration made in the quotation from Ps. 68: 18 when "he received gifts" becomes "he gave gifts".[13] These are the

---

[1] Rom. 10: 7.   [2] Col. 2: 10.   [3] Phil. 2: 10.
[4] If it be held that Ephesians is Pauline, then these observations should be read as complementary to those that precede.
[5] Eph. 1: 2, 3, 15, 17; 2: 21; 4: 1, 17; 5: 8; 6: 23, 24.   [6] Eph. 1: 22.
[7] *Ibid.*   [8] 6: 12.   [9] 2: 2.   [10] 1: 20, 21.   [11] 4: 8.   [12] 2: 6.
[13] Thus agreeing both with the Targum and the Peshitta. G. Kretschmar ("Himmelfahrt und Pfingsten", *Zeitschrift für Kirchengeschichte*, LXVI, 1954-55, pp. 216f.) makes the interesting suggestion that a Moses typology underlies this form of the quotation, for the rabbis referred this verse to Moses and associated it with Exod. 19: 3, interpreting the "gifts" as the "Law". It is also to be noted, as H. Schrade has emphasized ("Zur Ikonographie der Himmelfahrt Christi", *Vorträge der Bibliothek Warburg. Vorträge 1928-1929. Über die Vorstellungen von der Himmelsreise der Seele*, 1930, pp. 89f.), that the early Christian iconography of the

fruits of His triumph, the largess which He distributes from the spoils of war, and they comprise a diversity of functions given by the Ascended Lord for the varied and harmonious development of His Church.

St. Peter's interpretation of the Ascension is relatively simple to summarize. It is the occasion both of the glorification of Christ[1] and of His enthronement, "angels and authorities and powers being made subject unto him".[2] St. Mark equally regards the Ascension as the glorification[3] and enthronement[4] when Jesus is invested with the status of "Son of man" and His hidden Messiahship is disclosed.[5] It is further the necessary preliminary to the descent of the Spirit.[6]

St. Luke, on the other hand, gives a fuller exposition. To him the Ascension marks the reversal of man's verdict upon Jesus of Nazareth by the verdict of God.[7] So St. Peter can say of Jesus "he is Lord of all".[8] This investiture with supreme Lordship involves His enthronement as King: "Him did God exalt with his right hand to be a Prince and a Saviour."[9] It is therefore the occasion when "the God of Abraham, and of Isaac, and of Jacob, the God of our fathers, hath glorified his Servant Jesus".[10] It is further the necessary prelude to the descent of the Spirit: "being therefore by the right hand of God exalted, and having received of the Father the promise of the Holy Ghost, he hath poured forth this, which ye see and hear."[11]

St. Luke's use of the Transfiguration story as a prefigurement of the Ascension, which we have observed above, also provides a clue to another aspect of his interpretation of the latter. At the Transfiguration Jesus entered into the cloud of the divine presence, but He did not remain there; at the

Ascension is very similar to the representation of the giving of the Law to Moses; hence there is an antithetical parallelism between Moses ascending Sinai prior to giving the Law to Israel, and Christ ascending into heaven prior to giving the Spirit to the Church. A similar connexion may also underlie the Epistle to the Hebrews, since the holy of holies represented cultically Mount Sinai, which Moses ascended to intercede for Israel when they worshipped the golden calf (T. F. Torrance, *Royal Priesthood*, 1955, p. 4).

[1] 1 Peter 1: 21.   [2] 3: 22.   [3] Mark 8: 38; 13: 26.   [4] 14: 62.
[5] The so-called Messianic Secret may in fact be interpreted in terms of the *Messias designatus*.
[6] Mark 1: 10.   [7] Acts 2: 34-36.   [8] Acts 10: 36.
[9] Acts 5: 31; cp. Luke 19: 12: "a certain nobleman went into a far country, to receive for himself a kingdom, and to return."
[10] Acts 3: 13.   [11] Acts 2: 33.

Ascension Jesus again entered the cloud and abides for ever-more with the Father. The Ascension thus both marks the passing of Jesus into the presence of God and the completion of His mission. So, to employ the typology which we have suggested underlies Luke 24, as Raphael when he had brought his errand of mercy to a successful conclusion returned to heaven, so Christ when His work of redemption was done returned to His heavenly abode. Consequently to St. Luke, although, as we have seen, this view was not shared by the other New Testament writers, the Ascension is a final parting which brings to an end the Resurrection appearances. This fact makes it all the more appropriate as a revelation of the mode of the Parousia[1] when Christ will come in His glory on a cloud.[2]

In comparison with St. Luke, St. Matthew's doctrine of the Ascension is more limited. To him it is the prelude to the gift of the Spirit;[3] it is the glorification of Christ,[4] and it is the means of His investment with universal authority.[5] In express-ing this last aspect St. Matthew makes use of an allusion to Dan. 7: 14, and since the scripture which a writer has in mind is not necessarily limited to the amount which he actually cites,[6] it is perhaps apposite to note that according to Daniel the Son of man is given not only authority but also a king-dom. It is reasonable, therefore, to assume that St. Matthew also considered the Ascension as culminating in the enthrone-ment of the Messiah as King of kings.

The author of the fourth Gospel associates the Ascension primarily with the glorification of Christ, but, unlike the Synoptists, he regards it as one of three elements in a process of glorification of which the other two are the Crucifixion and the Resurrection.[7] The Ascension is equally a "going to the

---

[1] Acts 1: 11.

[2] St. Luke is so concerned to emphasize the connexion of both the Transfigura-tion and the Ascension with the Parousia that in the prediction of the Parousia, taken from Mark, he alters the Marcan "clouds" to the single "cloud" of the Transfiguration and the Ascension (Mark 13: 26‖Luke 21: 27).

[3] Matt. 3: 16.

[4] 24: 30.

[5] 28: 18.

[6] C. H. Dodd, *According to the Scriptures*, p. 47, n. 1.

[7] 12: 23; 13: 31; 17: 1, 5. It is to be noted that acceptance of the Johannine chronology forbids any identification of Resurrection and Ascension.

Father",[1] and the purpose of this departure is twofold: first, to send the Spirit;[2] second, to prepare a place for His followers that "where I am, there ye may be also".[3]

The author of the Epistle to the Hebrews shares with his fellow New Testament writers several of their interpretations of the Ascension. Thus the Ascension marks the completion of Christ's mission on earth: "when he had made purification of sins, he sat down on the right hand of the Majesty on high."[4] It is the glorification and the Christ who was temporarily reduced to a status inferior to the angels has been exalted to sovereignty over all beings: "But we behold him who hath been made a little lower than the angels, even Jesus, because of the suffering of death crowned with glory and honour."[5] Consequently it leads to the enthronement:

> But of the Son he saith,
> Thy throne, O God, is for ever and ever;
> And the sceptre of uprightness is the sceptre of thy kingdom.[6]

> But of which of the angels hath he said at any time,
> Sit thou on my right hand,
> Till I make thine enemies the footstool of thy feet?[7]

So the Christ has been installed through the Ascension on "the throne of grace"[8] "from henceforth expecting till his enemies be made the footstool of his feet".[9] In thus citing Ps. 110: 1 the author was making use of one of the fundamental primitive proof-texts,[10] but in his application of verse 4 he plays the role of innovator and ascribes to the Ascended Christ not only kingship but also high priesthood, so

> Thou art a priest for ever,
> After the order of Melchizedek.[11]

The question immediately arises, when did this priesthood begin? Was the Ascension the occasion of His entering upon

[1] John 14: 12, 28; 16: 28.   [2] 7: 39; 14: 16; 15: 26.   [3] 14: 2, 3.
[4] Heb. 1: 3.   [5] Heb. 2: 9 after citing Ps. 8: 4-6.   [6] 1: 8, quoting Ps. 45: 6.
[7] 1: 13, quoting Ps. 110: 1.   [8] 4: 16.   [9] 10: 13; cp. 2: 8.
[10] Cited independently Mark 12: 36; Acts 2: 34-35; allusions in Mark 14: 62; Acts 7: 55; Rom. 8: 34; Eph. 1: 20; Col. 3: 1; 1 Pet. 3: 22; see Dodd, op. cit., pp. 34-35.
[11] 5: 6; 7: 17, 21.

it? There are not a few passages in the Epistle which suggest that the latter was indeed the view of its author. So it is stated that Christ was "addressed" or "designated" (προσαγορευθεὶς) as high priest subsequent to His having been made perfect,[1] and that He became a high priest after having "entered the veil".[2] On the other hand, there are some passages which would lead one to suppose that Christ performed priestly acts prior to His Ascension, and was both Priest and Victim when He was sacrificed upon the Cross.[3] The reconciliation of these two views may possibly lie in the recognition that as in the fourth Gospel the glorification of Christ is a single process consisting of three component parts, viz. Crucifixion, Resurrection and Ascension, so in the Epistle to the Hebrews the entrance of Christ upon His Priesthood is a single process consisting of these same three elements.[4] Alternatively, an explanation may be sought along the lines of the *Messias designatus*; i.e. as Jesus during His earthly ministry was Messiah designate and only after His Ascension was enthroned as Messiah, so He may be regarded as high priest designate during His earthly activity and only after His Ascension, through which He accomplished His offering, was He invested with the full status.[5]

By accomplishing this offering Christ made atonement,[6] and this act is a process: the dying, by which His blood is outpoured;[7] the rising, by which "God brings again from the dead the great shepherd of the sheep with the blood of the eternal covenant",[8] and the ascending, by which He enters into heaven itself with the blood[9] "now to appear before the face of God for us".[10]

There remain three other interconnected aspects of the Ascension to be considered. The Ascension is the means of

---

[1] 5: 9, 10.   [2] 6: 19, 20.   [3] 2: 17; 9: 11, 12.

[4] cp. W. Milligan, *The Ascension and Heavenly Priesthood of Our Lord*, 1901, pp. 72-83.

[5] It is apposite to note that, according to the Old Testament, sacrifice was a necessary part of the rite whereby a person was installed as high priest; it was only when the victim had been slain and offered that the candidate entered upon his office (Lev. 8: 22-32).

[6] In one passage only is there a hint of the Classic theory, viz. 2: 14.

[7] 2: 14; 9: 15.

[8] 13: 20.

[9] 9: 12, 14, 25; 10: 19.

[10] 9: 24; cp. J. G. Davies, *The Spirit, The Church and The Sacraments*, 1954, pp. 112-13.

opening to believers an entrance (εἴσοδος) into heaven, an entrance which Christ has renewed[1] (ἐνεκαίνισεν) in so far as He has made available for others the road by which He Himself travelled.[2] He is therefore, in virtue of His Ascension, the forerunner of those who are to follow after.[3] He is also the Mediator of the New Covenant[4] which has been dedicated by His blood outpoured on the Cross[5] and offered to God through the Ascension.[6] Christ is then the one who stands between the contracting parties and brings them into fellowship, so that Christians are in a heavenly presence and may enter even now upon the possession of those privileges which Christ through death, Resurrection and Ascension has obtained for them.[7]

To the seer of the Apocalypse the Ascension marks the triumph and enthronement of Christ: "I also overcame, and sat down with my Father in his throne."[8] Henceforth He is "Lord of lords, and King of kings"[9] and "ruler of the kings of the earth".[10] It is moreover by His Ascension that Christ has displaced Satan before God's throne,[11] so that the Church can sing: "Now is come the salvation, and the power, and the kingdom of our God, and the authority of his Christ: for the accuser of our brethren is cast down, which accuseth them before our God day and night."[12] Accusation thus gives way to intercession as the result of the Ascension.[13] But it is in his fifth chapter that the author describes most fully the consequences of Christ's exaltation in a vision which is concerned not with the remote eschatological future but with what had already taken place when the Lion that is over the tribe of Judah achieved His victory. He sees "a Lamb standing, as though it had been slain" whom the host of heaven hymns in these words:

Worthy is the Lamb that hath been slain to receive the power, and riches, and wisdom, and might, and honour, and glory, and

[1] There may be an implied reference to the Fall here.
[2] 10: 19, 20.
[3] 6: 20. J. Pearson, *An Exposition of the Creed*, 1869, p. 418, n. 7, notes that πρόδρομος has a second meaning, viz. the earliest fruit (Num. 13: 20; Isa. 28: 4): "now, as this early fruit doth forerun the latter fruit of the same tree, and comes to ripeness and perfection in its kind before the rest; so our Saviour goes before those men of the same nature with him, and they follow in their time to the maturity of the same perfection."
[4] 9: 15.   [5] 9: 18.   [6] 12: 24.   [7] 12: 22-24.   [8] Rev. 3: 21.
[9] 17: 14.   [10] 1: 5.   [11] 12: 1ff.   [12] 12: 10.
[13] E. Stauffer, *New Testament Theology*, E.T., 1955, p. 139.

67

blessing. And every created thing which is in the heaven, and on the earth, and under the earth, and on the sea, and all things that are in them, heard I saying, Unto him that sitteth on the throne, and unto the Lamb, be the blessing, and the honour, and the glory, and the dominion, for ever and ever. And the four living creatures said, Amen.[1]

[1] 5: 12-14. After this magnificent imagery, it would be an anticlimax to quote 1 Tim. 3: 16, although it is most probably to be dated later than Revelation; it adds nothing to the New Testament interpretation of the Ascension, merely equating it with glorification.

4

THE TEACHING OF THE ANTE-NICENE CHURCH

BETWEEN the writings of the New Testament and those of the Apostolic Fathers there is no chronological break, and indeed one at least of the latter antedates certain of the former. It is not surprising then to find a discernible echo of the Apostolic preaching in these documents, although they have the character, not of systematic expositions of the Christian faith, but of occasional utterances, pastoral in intent. References to the Ascension are present, but few in number: it is a doctrine more often implied than formulated. Thus there is frequent mention of the imminence of Christ's return[1] and of His high priesthood[2]—conceptions which necessarily involve the previous entrance of Christ into the heavenlies. It is in three passages only that we find explicit statement of the fact, and even then there is no attempt to interpret it.

The first of these in point of time is in the letter which Ignatius of Antioch wrote to the Magnesians, c. A.D. 110. He exhorts his readers to assemble together "even to one Jesus Christ, who came forth from one Father and is with One and departed unto One",[3] i.e. as at the commencement of His earthly ministry He came forth from One, as He is eternally with One, so also at the close of His mission He returned to One. The second reference is provided by the *Epistle of Barnabas* (c. 130), already quoted in our examination of the day of the Ascension, to the effect that the eighth day, i.e. Sunday, is observed by Christians because on it Jesus rose "and when He had manifested Himself He ascended into heaven".[4] Finally, Polycarp, in his letter to the Philippians (c. 135), cites 1 Peter and describes Christians as those who

---

[1] *I Clem.*, 23; Ignatius, *Ad Poly.*, 3; Barnabas, 21; Polycarp, *Ad Phil.*, 2; *II Clem.*, 17; *Didache*, 16.
[2] *I Clem.*, 36, 61; Ignatius, *Ad Philad.*, 9; Polycarp, *Ad Phil.*, 12.
[3] 7.   [4] 15.

have believed " 'in Him who raised up our Lord Jesus Christ from the dead, and gave Him glory' and a throne at His right hand".[1]

The second-century Apologists, with one notable exception, are as reticent as the Apostolic Fathers, but their silence is readily explicable as due to the nature of their writings. The task they set themselves was threefold: first, to lay the many unsavoury rumours which were current as to Christian behaviour and practice; second, to demonstrate the falsity of polytheism and the truth of theism, and, third, to commend the Christian faith.

Nearly all the extant apologies are in the form of legal documents, petitioning the state authorities for careful investigation of what Christianity really was,[2] and consequently they are chiefly concerned with the first two of these points and are by way of being prolegomena to the third, and so any detailed account of Christian beliefs is not to be expected. Moreover, since the audience in view was almost exclusively pagan, their authors largely rested their case, neither on the Old Testament nor on the Apostolic writings, but upon rational argument, and much as Paul had not disdained the use of rabbinic exegesis to confute his Judaic opponents, the Apologists were not adverse to the employment of philosophical categories to commend their position to the Hellenic world. So, e.g., Athenagoras, in his *Supplication for the Christians* (A.D. 177), defends a belief in the resurrection on rational grounds alone, with references to Pythagoras and to Plato,[3] and does not once allude to the Resurrection of Christ:[4] his failure to mention the Ascension is thus not difficult to understand. Similarly Tatian, in his vituperous attack on Greek culture in his *Discourse to the Greeks* (A.D. 177), does not see fit to speak of the Ascension, but that it was part of the tradition which he accepted is shown by his *Diatesseron*, a harmony of the four Gospels, the final page of which contains a skilful combination of the concluding verses

---

[1] 2.

[2] A. Ehrhardt, "Justin Martyr's Two Apologies", *Journ. Eccl. Hist.*, IV, 1952, pp. 1-12; R. M. Grant, "The Chronology of the Greek Apologists", *Vig. Christ.*, IX, 1955, pp. 25-33.

[3] 36.

[4] The *De Resurrectione* equally contains no reference to Christ, but this work is possibly to be dated in the early fourth century (R. M. Grant, "Athenagoras or Pseudo-Athenagoras", *H.T.R.*, XLVII, 1954, pp. 121-29).

of Luke with the Longer Ending of Mark. A further contributory factor to this reticence, at least on the part of the later Apologists, may well have been the *disciplina arcani*, which appears to have become operative in the latter part of the second century;[1] hence, earlier, Aristides, whose *Apology* (*c.* A.D. 143) is the first that has been preserved, is able to say of Christ that "after three days He rose again and went up into the heavens".[2]

Nevertheless, there is sufficient evidence to make it plain that both Jewish and pagan assailants of Christianity were not unaware of its teaching concerning the Ascension, and for this reason Justin Martyr and, later, Tertullian and Origen, sought to defend it against attack. The arguments they propounded are scarcely self-consistent when taken together, but as separate *argumenta ad hominem* they doubtless had their weight. Thus on the one hand it was contended that in affirming the Ascension Christians were proposing nothing different from what pagans believed regarding such persons as Aesculapius, Bacchus, the Dioscuri, Bellerophon[3] and Romulus;[4] and on the other hand that these pagan ascensions were either fictitious[5] or imitations of the Old Testament prophecies of Christ's true Ascension.[6]

The fullest witness to the Ascension is provided by Justin Martyr. That it was an integral part of his belief is evident from his frequent summaries of what was apparently a

---

[1] The arguments of J. Jeremias (*The Eucharistic Words of Jesus*, 1955, pp. 73-87), that the *disciplina* was operative even in the first century, are not convincing, for St. Paul saw no objection to the presence of unbelievers at the Christian assembly (1 Cor. 14: 23), and Justin was prepared to describe Sunday worship in some detail (*Apol.*, I. 65-67).

[2] 15.

[3] Justin, *Apol.*, I. 21.

[4] Tertullian, *Apol.*, 21; Min. Felix, *Octav.*, 23; Augustine, *De Civ. Dei*, 3. 15.

[5] Justin, *Apol.*, I. 54.

[6] Justin, *Dial.*, 69. The early attack on the Ascension, on the grounds that it is no more than an imitation of pagan ascensions, has been renewed at the present day through the study of comparative religion, and the assertion is made that it is no more than a legend developed from Babylonian, Mithraic, Iranian and even Parsee myths (cp. P. Jensen, *Das Gilgamesh-Epos in der Weltliteratur*, I, 1906, pp. 928-31; A. D. Martin, "The Ascension of Christ", *Expositor*, XVI, 1918, pp. 321-46; H. Diels, "Himmels- und Höllenfahrten von Homer bis Dante", *Neue Jahrb. f. das klass. Altertum*, 1922, pp. 239-44). But this influence, even if it exists, and that is highly questionable, is no more than indirect, i.e. through the Old Testament, which itself provides an all-sufficient background to the New Testament record (cp. E. Stauffer, *New Testament Theology*, E.T., 1955, Appendix VI, pp. 344-47).

developed Christological kerygma, already enjoying a measure of fixity. So he affirms:

> We say that the Word, who is the first offspring of God,
> was begotten without carnal intercourse,
> Jesus Christ our teacher,
> and that He was crucified,
> and died,
> and rose again,
> and ascended to heaven.[1]

This same formula, in almost identical words, is to be found repeated in no fewer than seven other passages in his works,[2] and there is no reason to doubt that this represents a faithful reproduction of the primitive kerygma in which the Ascension had a necessary place.

But Justin's principal contribution lies not in his witness to the contents of the embryonic Creed, but in his use of his favourite argument from prophecy which led him to associate certain scriptural passages with the Ascension. From the Apostolic writings he was already familiar with the application of psalms 68 and 110 to this subject, and this he repeats. So he asserts:

> that God the Father of all would bring Christ to heaven after He had raised Him from the dead, and would keep Him there until He has subdued His enemies the devils, and until the number of those who are foreknown by Him as good and virtuous is complete, on whose account He has still delayed the consummation—hear what was said by the prophet David . . .

and he then quotes Ps. 110: 1-3.[3] Elsewhere, in his *Dialogue with Trypho*, he acknowledges that the Jews expound this psalm as if it referred to King Hezekiah, but he argues that they are mistaken; on the contrary, it is to be understood of the Ascension of Christ and of His investiture with the high priesthood after the order of Melchizedek.[4] Similarly of Ps. 68, he says to his opponent:

> it was prophesied that after the Ascension of Christ to heaven He would deliver us from error and give us gifts. The words

---

[1] *Apol.*, I. 21.   [2] *Apol.*, I. 31; 42; 46; *Dial.*, 63; 85; 126; 132.
[3] *Apol.*, I. 45.   [4] 32, 33.

THE TEACHING OF THE ANTE-NICENE CHURCH

are these: "He ascended up on high: He led captivity captive; He gave gifts to men."[1]

These gifts, he further informs us, are the gifts of the Spirit, the pentecostal outpouring, foretold by Joel, being the consequence of the Ascension.[2]

To these two psalms, 68 and 110, Justin adds three others, viz. 19, 24 and 47. Quoting 19: 6 in the form "from the highest heaven is His going forth; and He returns to the highest heaven", Justin declares that this refers to the Incarnation and to the Ascension.[3] Quoting 24 in its entirety, a psalm which according to Jewish exegesis referred to Solomon, he comments:

> Solomon is not the Lord of hosts; but when our Christ rose from the dead and ascended to heaven, the rulers in heaven, under appointment of God, are commanded to open the gates of heaven, that He who is the King of glory may enter in, and, having ascended, may sit on the right hand of the Father until He make the enemies His footstool, as has been made manifest by another psalm. For when the rulers of heaven saw Him of uncomely and dishonoured appearance, and inglorious, not recognizing Him, they inquired, "Who is this King of glory?" And the Holy Spirit, either from the Person of His Father, or from His own Person, answers them, "The Lord of hosts, He is this King of glory."[4]

Finally he cites, without extended comment, Ps. 47: "God is gone up with a shout, the Lord with the sound of a trumpet ... God sits upon His holy throne."[5] By connecting these psalms with the Ascension, Justin added little to the New Testament interpretation of the doctrine, but he did lay the basis of all future exegesis.

Justin's practice of quoting quasi-credal formulae, referred to above, is to be noted in another Apologist, viz. Melito, Bishop of Sardis in Lydia († c. A.D. 190). Of his *Apology* only fragments have been preserved by Eusebius and in the *Chronicon Paschale*, but his *Homily on the Passion* has recently been discovered in an almost complete form. Melito brings this sermon to its conclusion with the following words:

[1] *Dial.*, 39. [2] 87. [3] 64.
[4] *Dial.*, 36. Ps. 24 is also used of the Ascension in *Dial.*, 85 and *Apol.*, I. 51.
[5] *Dial.*, 37.

This is He who first made heaven and earth, who in the beginning created man, who was proclaimed by Law and Prophets,
who was made flesh in a Virgin, who was hanged upon a tree,
who was buried in the earth, who rose from the dead and went
up (ἀνελθὼν) to the heights of heaven.[1]

To Melito the Ascension was the inevitable corollary of the
pre-existence of the divine Word: He descended, and then,
having completed His mission, He returned whither He had
come and "brought man safely home to the heights of heaven".[2]

These same two features are also found in the teaching of
Melito's contemporary and fellow bishop, Irenaeus of Lyons,
who both asserts that Christ is "He who descended and ascended
for the salvation of men",[3] and that the Son of God, made
the Son of man, did "ascend to the height above, offering and
commending to His Father that human nature which had been
found".[4]

It is, however, with Justin Martyr that Irenaeus has the
most affinities, as is to be expected in view of the latter's undoubted familiarity with and use of the writings of the former.[5]
Thus, like Justin, Irenaeus has preserved certain quasi-credal
statements in a more or less stereotyped form, containing distinct references to the Ascension. The Church believes:

in one God, the Father Almighty, maker of heaven and earth
and the sea and all things that are in them; and in one Christ
Jesus, the Son of God, who became incarnate for our salvation;
and in the Holy Spirit, who proclaimed through the prophets
the saving dispensations, and the advents, and the birth from
a Virgin, and the Passion, and the Resurrection from the dead,
and the Ascension into heaven in the flesh of the beloved Christ
Jesus, our Lord, and His manifestation from the heavens in the
glory of the Father to sum up all things and to raise up anew
all flesh of the whole human race.[6]

Elsewhere, Irenaeus appeals against the heretics to that deposit
of apostolic doctrine which has been preserved even by bar-
barians who believe in

[1] 17. Campbell Bonner, *Studies and Documents*, XII, 1940, p. 180.
[2] *Ibid.*
[3] *Adv. Haer.*, iii. 6. 2.
[4] iii. 19. 3.
[5] J. A. Robinson, *The Demonstration of the Apostolic Preaching*, 1920, pp. 6-23.
[6] *Adv. Haer.*, i. 10. 1.

74

one God, the maker of heaven and earth and all things therein, by means of Christ Jesus, the Son of God; who, because of His surpassing love towards His creation, condescended to be born of the Virgin, uniting in Himself man to God, and having suffered under Pontius Pilate, and rising again, and having been received up in splendour, shall come in glory, the Saviour of those who are saved, and the Judge of those who are judged.[1]

Irenaeus also follows Justin in applying to the Ascension not only psalms 68[2] and 110,[3] for which there was precedent in the Gospels and the Epistles, but also psalms 19 and 24. So he calls attention to the prophets

who spoke of His having slumbered and taken sleep, and of His having risen again because the Lord sustained Him, and who enjoined the principalities of heaven to set open the everlasting doors, that the King of glory might go in, proclaimed beforehand His Resurrection from the dead through the Father's power, and His reception into heaven. And when they expressed themselves thus: "His going forth is from the height of heaven, and His returning even to the highest heaven; and there is no one who can hide himself from His heat", they announced that very truth of His being taken up again to the place from which He came down, and that there is no one who can escape His righteous judgment.[4]

But although Irenaeus may start from Justin, he always goes beyond him. Thus, where Justin interprets Ps. 24 to the effect that it is the uncomely appearance of Christ which is the cause of the failure of the celestial powers to recognize Him at His Ascension, Irenaeus, possibly developing a hint in 1 Tim. 3: 16 and drawing most probably on the *Ascension of Isaiah*, a document which will be considered below, provides a different exegesis:

David says: "Lift up your gates, ye rulers; and be ye lift up, ye everlasting gates, and the King of glory shall come in." For the everlasting gates are the heavens. But because the Word descended invisible to created things, He was not made known in His descent to them. Because the Word was made flesh, He was visible in His Ascension;[5] and when the powers saw Him,

[1] iii. 4. 2. [2] ii. 20. 3. [3] iii. 6. 1; 10. 6. [4] iv. 33. 13.
[5] It may well be that Irenaeus had an anti-docetic, and therefore an anti-Gnostic, purpose in framing this exegesis, since according to Basilides Christ was invisible both in His descent and in His Ascension (*Adv. Haer.*, i. 24. 4).

the angels below cried out to those who were on the firmament: "Lift up your gates; and be ye lift up, ye everlasting gates, that the King of glory may come in." And when they marvelled and said: "Who is this?" those who had already seen Him testified a second time: "The Lord strong and mighty, He is the King of glory."[1]

At its simplest, however, Irenaeus's advance on Justin is to be seen in his additional quotations from the apostolic writings.

Towards the conclusion of his Gospel, Mark says: "So then, after the Lord Jesus had spoken to them, He was received up into heaven, and sitteth on the right hand of God", confirming what had been spoken by the prophet: "The Lord said to my Lord, Sit on my right hand, until I make Thy foes Thy footstool."[2]

The Lord rose from the dead on the third day, and manifested Himself to His disciples, and was in their sight received up into heaven.[3]

Irenaeus also cites Rom. 8: 34—"It is Christ Jesus that died, yea rather, that was raised from the dead, who is at the right hand of God"—with the comment:

He declares in the plainest manner that the same Being who was laid hold of, and underwent suffering, and shed His blood for us, was both Christ and the Son of God, who did also rise again and was taken up into heaven.[4]

But it is in connexion with his key doctrine of Recapitulation that Irenaeus makes his most notable contribution.

The term ἀνακεφαλαίωσις, as it is used by Irenaeus, has two principal meanings, viz. repetition and summing up. In the former sense Christ is the second Adam who traversed the same ground and faced the same temptations as the first Adam but with the opposite result; where the one was disobedient, the other was obedient. The outcome of the disobedience of the first Adam was his enslavement to the devil: the outcome

---

[1] *Demon.*, 84. [2] *Adv. Haer.*, iii. 10. 6.
[3] ii. 32. 3. This reads like a summary of either the Longer Ending of Mark or the final verses of Luke, and may possibly be taken as further evidence for the tradition that the Ascension took place on Easter Day.
[4] iii. 16. 9.

of the obedience of the second Adam was His enslavement of the devil.

He has therefore, in His work of recapitulation, summed up all things, both waging war against our enemy, and crushing him who had at the beginning led us away captive in Adam. . . . And justly indeed is he led captive, who had led man unjustly into bondage; while man, who had been led captive in time past, was rescued from the grasp of his possessor, according to the tender mercy of God the Father, who had compassion on His own handiwork, and gave to it salvation, restoring it by means of the Word—that is, by Christ—in order that man might learn by actual proof that he receives incorruptibility not of himself, but by the free gift of God.[1]

Wherefore he who had led man captive was justly captured in his turn by God; but man, who had been led captive, was loosed from the bonds of condemnation.[2]

This binding of Satan is achieved in part through the Passion of Christ:

for the Lord, by means of suffering, "ascending into the lofty place, led captivity captive, gave gifts to men" and conferred on those that believe in Him the power "to tread upon serpents and scorpions, and on all the power of the enemy"[3] that is, of the leader of apostasy.[4]

The Recapitulation is finally completed by the Ascension when Christ "ascended up on high, He led captivity captive . . ." and "by 'captivity' ", comments Irenaeus, "he means the destruction of the rule of the apostate angels."[5]

Where "summing up" is the primary meaning of Recapitulation, Christ is represented as the Head both of the old and the new creation, and

therefore does the Lord profess Himself to be the Son of man, comprising in Himself that original man out of which the woman was fashioned, in order that, as our species went down to death through a vanquished man, so we may ascend to life again through a victorious one[6] . . . in Himself raising up that which was fallen, lifting him up far above the heavens to the right hand of the glory of the Father.[7]

[1] v. 21. 1, 3.   [2] iii. 23. 1.   [3] Luke 10: 19.   [4] ii. 20. 3.
[5] Demon., 83.   [6] v. 21. 1.   [7] Demon., 38.

The process of Resurrection and Ascension is one which the individual believer will himself eventually undergo:

> For as the Lord "went away in the midst of the shadow of death",[1] where the souls of the dead were, yet afterwards arose in the body, and after the Resurrection was taken up, it is manifest that the souls of His disciples also, upon whose account the Lord underwent these things, shall go away into the invisible place allotted them by God, and there remain until the Resurrection, awaiting that event; then, receiving their bodies, and rising in their entirety, that is bodily, just as the Lord arose, they shall come thus into the presence of God. "For no disciple is above the Master, but every one that is perfect shall be as his Master."[2] As our Master, therefore, did not depart, taking flight, but awaited the time of His Resurrection prescribed by the Father, which had also been shown forth through Jonas, and, rising again after three days, was taken up; so ought we also to await the time of our resurrection prescribed by God, and foretold by the prophets, and so, rising, be taken up, as many as the Lord shall account worthy of this.[3]

The writers that we have been considering hitherto have at least one virtue in common: they do not seek to embroider the circumstances of the Ascension, but rest content with the simple fact as recorded in the Apostolic corpus. The authors of the apocryphal Gospels and Apocalypses,[4] however, which begin to appear in the second century, display no such praiseworthy reticence, and eager to supply the lacunae in those narratives which were undergoing the slow process of canonization, they resorted to imaginative reconstruction. Most remarkable of these productions is the very detailed description contained in the *Ascension of Isaiah*, a Jewish document, possibly of the later first century A.D., which has been extensively interpolated by a Christian editor, probably in the first half of the second century. After narrating how the Beloved of the Father descended through the seven heavens, assuming in each one the form of its occupants in order not to be recognized by them, the writer records His Virgin Birth, Crucifixion, descent into Sheol and Resurrection, and then continues:

[1] Ps. 23: 4.   [2] Luke 6: 40.   [3] v. 31. 2.

[4] In the developed Gnostic systems, as portrayed by Irenaeus, the Ascension is the essential counterpart of the descent of the supernatural Redeemer from the unknown Supreme Being. There is little to be gained from an examination of these statements (*Adv. Haer.*, i. 24. 4; 25. 1; 30. 14).

and I saw when He sent out the twelve Apostles and ascended. And I saw Him and He was in the firmament, but He had not changed Himself into their form, and all the angels of the firmament and the Satans saw Him and they worshipped. And there was much sorrow there, while they said: "How did our Lord descend in our midst, and we perceived not the glory, which we see hath been upon Him from the sixth heaven?" And He ascended into the second heaven, and He did not transform Himself, but all the angels who were on the right and on the left and the throne in the midst both worshipped Him and praised Him and said: "How did our Lord escape us whilst descending, and we perceived not?" And in like manner He ascended into the third heaven, and they praised Him and said in like manner. And in the fourth heaven and in the fifth also they said precisely after the same manner. But there was one glory and from it He did not change Himself. And I saw when He ascended into the sixth heaven, and they worshipped and glorified Him. But in all the heavens the praise increased. And I saw how He ascended into the seventh heaven, and all the righteous and all the angels praised Him. And then I saw Him sit down at the right hand of that Great Glory whose glory I told you that I could not behold.[1]

This quaint use of Jewish cosmology[2] is not without interest, but the main importance of this document lies both in its influence on Irenaeus, to which reference has already been made, and in its implied interpretation of psalm 24 which became normative among later Christian exegetes.

The second apocryphal work that requires notice is the *Apocalypse of Peter*, composed between A.D. 125 and 150. This records how Jesus led the disciples to the Mount of Olives where they were joined by two men, upon whose faces they were unable to look because of the light of glory that emanated from them. Upon learning that they were Moses and Elijah, Peter proposed to build three tabernacles, but was rebuked by Christ for his lack of understanding.

And behold, suddenly there came a voice from heaven saying: "This is my beloved Son in whom I am well pleased: He hath kept my commandments." And then came a great and exceeding white cloud over our heads and bare away our Lord and Moses and Elias. And I trembled and was afraid: and we looked

---

[1] 11. 21-32.   [2] Employed also by Irenaeus, *Demon.*, 9.

up; and the heaven opened, and we beheld men in the flesh, and they came and greeted our Lord and Moses and Elias and went into another heaven. And the word of the scripture was fulfilled: "This is the generation that seeketh Him and seeketh the face of the God of Jacob." And great fear and commotion was there in heaven, and the angels pressed one upon another that the word of the scripture might be fulfilled which saith: "Open the gates, ye princes." Thereafter was the heaven shut, that had been open.[1]

Here it is not Jewish cosmology upon which the writer has drawn to expand his account of the Ascension, but the Transfiguration story, and his combination of the two provides interesting corroboration of the thesis, outlined in the previous lecture, that the latter was regarded as a prefigurement of the former, by St. Luke in particular. Further, we may note that Ps. 24 is again being pressed into service.

The *Epistle of the Apostles* (c. A.D. 150) consists in the main of revelations which Christ made to His disciples after His Resurrection. It concludes with a description of the Ascension which, as already noted, takes place on Easter Day.

And when He had said this, and had finished His discourse with us, He said unto us again: "Behold, on the third day and at the third hour shall He come which hath sent me, that I may depart with Him." And as He so spake, there was thunder and lightning and an earthquake, and the heavens parted asunder and there appeared a bright cloud which bore Him up. And there came voices of many angels, rejoicing and singing praises and saying: "Gather us, O Priest, unto the light of the Majesty." And when they drew nigh unto the firmament, we heard His voice saying: "Depart hence in peace."[2]

To the same effect, as regards the day of the Ascension, is the statement of the angels to the women at the tomb, recorded in the *Gospel of Peter*, which dates from the second half of the second century:

"Wherefore are ye come? whom seek ye? not Him that was crucified? He is risen and is departed; but if ye believe it not, look in and see the place where He lay, that He is not here: for He is risen and is departed thither whence He was sent."[3]

[1] M. R. James, *The Apocryphal New Testament*, 1924, p. 519.
[2] James, *op. cit.*, p. 503.   [3] *Ibid.*, p. 93.

THE TEACHING OF THE ANTE-NICENE CHURCH

Two other works may be mentioned here, although they take us beyond the limits of the second century, viz. the *Testaments of the Twelve Patriarchs* and the *Letter of Jesus to Abgarus*. The former, if we may accept the persuasive thesis of de Jonge,[1] is to be dated between A.D. 190 and 225, and was written by an ordinary Christian, with little interest in exactness of dogmatic terminology, who made extensive use of Jewish traditional material. In the eighteenth chapter of the *Testament of Levi*, which consists of a hymn glorifying Christ, we read:

> And His star shall arise in heaven, as a king shedding forth the light of knowledge in the sunshine of day, and He shall be magnified in the world until His Ascension (ἀναλήψεως).[2]

To similar effect is the statement in the *Testament of Benjamin*:

> He shall arise from Hades, and shall pass from earth into heaven: and I know how lowly He shall be upon earth, and how glorious in heaven.[3]

This adds nothing to what we already know, but the importance of this work lies in the fact that it reflects the interests not of the theologian but of the ordinary Christian, and so indicates that belief in the Ascension was a definite element in the generally accepted *regula fidei*.

The *Letter of Jesus to Abgarus* originally formed part of the *Acts of Thaddaeus*, and was transcribed by Eusebius in his *Ecclesiastical History*.[4] In this epistle, which emanates from the third century, Jesus is represented as saying to the king: "I must fulfil all things for the which I was sent hither; and, having fulfilled them, be received up immediately to Him that sent me." That the Ascension could thus find expression in a local legend of the Middle East is proof positive of the universality of the belief.

In North Africa, too, it clearly formed part of the body of tradition transmitted in the Church. To this Tertullian bears witness when he states:

> The rule of faith is . . . that rule by which we believe that there is one, and only one, God, and that He is none other than the

---

[1] M. de Jonge, *The Testaments of the Twelve Patriarchs*, 1953.
[2] 18. 3.   [3] 9. 5.   [4] i. 13. 10.

81

Creator of the world, who produced all things out of nothing through His own Word, first of all sent down; that this Word is called His Son, and in the name of God was seen "in divers manners" by the patriarchs, heard at all times in the prophets, and last of all entered into the Virgin Mary by the Spirit and Power of the Father, was made flesh in her womb, and was born of her as Jesus Christ; thereafter He preached the new law and the new promise of the Kingdom of heaven, worked miracles; having been crucified, He rose again the third day, was taken up to heaven and sat down at the right hand of the Father, and sent in His place the power of the Holy Spirit to lead such as believe, and will come again in glory to take the saints to the enjoyment of everlasting life and of the heavenly promises, and to condemn the wicked to everlasting fire, after the resurrection of both these classes shall have happened, together with the restoration of their flesh.[1]

This passage obviously reflects Tertullian's polemical interests,[2] and in opposition to the various sects that he is attacking in this treatise, i.e. the *De Praescriptione* (*c.* 200), he emphasizes the oneness of God, the identity of Jesus with the Messiah of ancient prophecy, the reality of His human birth and the resurrection of the flesh. The exigencies of controversy equally influenced the majority of his references to the Ascension, which he does not so much seek to expound as to use as a weapon in his anti-heretical armoury.

In his *De Baptismo* (198-200), Tertullian has in view the attacks at Carthage of a certain Quintilla of the Cainite sect, who "has carried away a great number with her most venomous doctrine, making it her first aim to destroy Baptism".[3] In opposing this erroneous teaching, Tertullian has occasion to consider the difference between Christian Baptism and the baptism of John, and he brings in the Ascension to support his argument that the distinction lies in the gift of the Spirit which is conveyed by the former alone.

The Lord Himself said that the Spirit would not descend on any other condition but that He should first ascend to the Father. What the Lord was not yet conferring, the servant of course could not furnish. Accordingly in the Acts of the Apostles, we

[1] *De Praes.*, 13; cp. *De virg. vel.*, 1; *Adv. Prax.*, 2.
[2] J. N. D. Kelly, *Early Christian Creeds*, 1950, p. 87.   [3] 1.

find that men who had "John's baptism" had not received the Holy Spirit, whom they knew not even by hearing.[1]

Towards the end of this same treatise, Tertullian considers the times most suitable for Baptism, and, while admitting that "every day is the Lord's; every hour, every time is apt for Baptism", contends that the Pascha affords the most fitting occasion and next to that the period of Pentecost

> wherein too the Resurrection of the Lord was repeatedly proved among the disciples, and the hope of the advent of the Lord indirectly pointed to, in that, at that time, when He had been received back into the heavens, the angels told the apostles that "He would so come, as He had withal ascended into the heavens".[2]

In his *De Resurrectione Carnis* (210-12), which is a companion volume to the *De Carne Christi*, Tertullian opposes four Gnostic sects, those of Marcion, Apelles, Basilides and Valentinus, whose addiction to docetism has led them to deny the reality of Christ's flesh and of its Resurrection. The Ascension again provides Tertullian with a weapon in his onslaught on this position. These heretics affirm that all flesh and blood is excluded from the Kingdom of God, but

> Jesus is still sitting there at the right hand of the Father, man yet God—the last Adam, yet the primary Word—flesh and blood, yet purer than ours—who "shall descend in like manner as He ascended", the same both in substance and form, as the angels affirmed, so as even to be recognized by those who pierced Him. Designated, as He is, "the Mediator between God and man",[3] He keeps in His own self the deposit of the flesh which has been committed to Him by both parties—the pledge and security of its entire perfection. For as "He has given to us the earnest of the Spirit",[4] so has He received from us the earnest of the flesh, and has carried it with Him into heaven as a pledge of that complete entirety which is one day to be restored to it.[5]

A further tenet of these heretics is that the Resurrection has either taken place already in the case of certain individuals, being entirely spiritual in character, or that it will be accomplished immediately after death. On the basis of numerous

[1] 10.   [2] 19.   [3] 1 Tim. 2: 5.   [4] 2 Cor. 5: 5.
[5] *De Res.*, 51; in cap. 58 Tertullian uses the translations of Enoch and Elijah to the same effect, cp. *De Anima*, 50.

New Testament passages Tertullian shows that the Resurrection is to be closely linked with the Second Advent which has manifestly not yet taken place, for, he asks, "Who has yet beheld Jesus descending from heaven in like manner as the apostles saw Him ascend, according to the appointment of the angels?"[1]

The fifth and final book of the *Adversus Marcionem* would appear to have been completed *c.* 212, after the *De Resurrectione* to which it refers,[2] and some five years after the work was first begun. The author's concern is to refute the dualism existing according to Marcion between the God of the Old and the God of the New Testament, and it is with this end exclusively in view that he utilizes the Ascension. Arguing from the existence of spiritual gifts, Tertullian sets out to demonstrate that "these also were promised by the Creator through Christ". He contends that they have been bestowed in fulfilment of the prophecy of Joel, that Christ is their dispenser in accordance with the words of Isa. 11: 1-3, and then he continues:

> Now hear how he declared that by Christ Himself, when returned to heaven, these spiritual gifts were to be sent. "He ascended up on high", i.e. into heaven; "He led captivity captive", meaning death or slavery of man: "He gave gifts to the sons of men", i.e. the gratuities which we call *charismata*. . . . Since then the Creator promised the gift of His Spirit in the latter days; and since Christ has in these last days appeared as the dispenser of spiritual gifts . . . it evidently follows in connexion with this prediction of the last days, that this gift of the Spirit belongs to Him who is the Christ of the predicter.[3]

In another passage, still insisting that Christ and the prophets pertain to the same God, Tertullian quotes from 1 Thess. to the effect that at the Parousia the faithful will be caught up in the clouds to meet the Lord, and comments:

> Now as Christ has prepared for us this ascension into heaven, He must be the Christ of whom Amos spoke: "It is He who builds His ascent up to the heavens",[4] even for Himself and His people.[5]

Finally, expounding the Epistle to the Ephesians, which Marcion accepted albeit with a changed title, viz. to the

1 *De Res.*, 22.   2 *Adv. Marc.*, v. 10.   3 *Adv. Marc.*, v. 8.   4 Amos 9:6.   5 v. 15.

Laodiceans, Tertullian refers to the words "Father of glory" in 1: 17 and says:

> this is He whose Christ, when ascending to heaven, is celebrated as "the King of glory" in the psalm: "Who is the King of glory? The Lord of hosts, He is the King of glory."[1]

The *Scorpiace* was written during a period of persecution, most probably that of Scapula in A.D. 213, and it is a defence of martyrdom against the Gnostics who were arguing that such sacrifice of life was unnecessary and not required by God. Denial of Christ in this life was to them of no importance, since they taught that the individual would be afforded an opportunity of confessing Christ after death. Tertullian's reply to this latter point is that, assuming such an opportunity were to be vouchsafed, it could only be for those who were raised to heaven; but such a translation is only feasible if there has already been a confession of Christ in this life.

> Heaven lies open to the Christian before the way to it does; because there is no way to heaven but to him to whom heaven lies open; and he who reaches it will enter. . . . If you have ever read in David: "Lift up your gates, ye princes, and let the ever-lasting gates be lifted up; and the King of glory shall enter in"; if you have also heard from Amos, "Who buildeth up to the heavens His way of ascent, and is such as to pour forth His abundance over the earth", know that both that way of ascent was thereafter levelled with the ground, by the footsteps of the Lord, and an entrance thereafter opened up by the might of Christ, and that no delay or inquest will meet Christians on the threshold, since they have there not to be discriminated from one another, but owned, not put to the question but received in.[2]

In his *Adversus Praxean* (A.D. 213), Tertullian assails the Modalist or Patripassian heresy, which held that "the Father Himself came down into the Virgin, was Himself born of her, Himself suffered, indeed was Himself Jesus Christ".[3] Tertullian's concern therefore is to demonstrate that there is a distinction between the Father and the Son, and it is to this end that he employs the Ascension.

> It is the Son [and not the Father] who ascends to the heights of heaven, and also descends to the inner parts of the earth.

[1] v. 17.   [2] *Scorp.*, 10.   [3] 1.

"He sitteth at the Father's right hand"—not the Father at His own. He is seen by Stephen, at his martyrdom by stoning, still sitting at the right hand of God, where He will continue to sit, until the Father shall make His enemies His footstool. He will come again on the clouds of heaven, just as He appeared when He ascended into heaven. Meanwhile He has received from the Father the promised gift, and has shed it forth, even the Holy Spirit.[1]

Although Tertullian eventually went over to the Montanists and then became the founder of a sect, the so-called Tertullianists, which persisted at Carthage up to the time of Augustine, Cyprian, bishop of the same city, regarded him as his master, if we may believe the report of Jerome,[2] and did not let a day pass without reading his works. Cyprian too had his controversies which arose as the aftermath of the Decian persecution, but although they involved certain doctrinal issues they were primarily disciplinary in character. Since the Ascension had little direct bearing upon them, it has a subordinate place in Cyprian's thought. Thus in his *Ad Quirinum* (*Testimoniorum libri III*), one of his earliest works (A.D. 249), the second book of which is a compendium of Christology consisting of a large number of Scriptural passages arranged under appropriate headings, although there are separate sections devoted to the Resurrection[3] and to the Session,[4] the Ascension receives only a passing mention in the latter.[5] On the other hand, in the small tract *Quod idola dii non sint*, which is in the main an assembly of quotations from Latin Apologies compiled by Cyprian while yet a neophyte[6] (*c.* 246), there is the unambiguous affirmation that the prophets bore witness that

when He should have suffered, He should return again into heaven, to show the power of the divine majesty . . . then in a cloud spread around Him He was lifted up into heaven, that as a consequence He might bring to the Father man whom He loved, whom He put on, whom He shielded from death.[7]

Other references to the Ascension are only incidental[8] or implied,[9] except in a single passage in the *De Unitate* (A.D.

[1] 30.   [2] *De vir. ill.*, 53.   [3] ii. 25.   [4] ii. 26.
[5] Dan. 7: 13, 14 and Isa. 33: 10, 11 are cited.
[6] H. Koch, *Quod idola non sint: ein Werk Cyprians, Cyprianische Untersuchungen,* 1926, pp. 1-78.
[7] 14.   [8] e.g. *Ep.*, 3. 3.   [9] e.g. *Ep.*, 63. 18, 19; *De Lap.*, 12; *De Patent.*, 24.

251), where Cyprian uses it to stress the necessity of humility on the part of a confessor:

> let him be in his doings modest with discipline, so that he who is called a confessor of Christ may imitate Christ whom he confesses. For since He says: "Whosoever exalteth himself shall be abased, and he who humbleth himself shall be exalted", and since He Himself has been exalted by the Father, because as the Word, and the strength, and the wisdom of God the Father, He humbled Himself upon earth, how can He love arrogance, who even by His own law enjoined on us humility, and Himself received the highest name from the Father as the reward of His humility?[1]

In temperament Hippolytus is to be compared more with the fiery Tertullian than with the eirenic but firm Cyprian. Like the former he contended with the heretics of his day, and as Tertullian attacked the Modalists in his *Adversus Praxean*, so Hippolytus assailed them in his *Contra Noetum* (? A.D. 200), and made use of the Ascension to support his verbal offensive.

> "No man hath ascended up to heaven, but He that came down from heaven, even the Son of man which is in heaven." What then can he [i.e. Noetus] seek besides what is thus written? Will he say indeed that the flesh was in heaven? Yet there is the flesh which was presented by the Father's Word as an offering—the flesh that came by the Spirit and the Virgin, and was demonstrated to be the perfect Son of God. It is evident therefore that He offered Himself to the Father and before this there was no flesh in heaven. Who then was in heaven but the Word unincarnate, who was despatched to show that He was upon earth and was also in heaven?[2]

The assertion that the Incarnate Word offers His manhood to the Father in and through the Ascension is found repeated in a fragment of the lost homily *In Helcanam et Annam* to the effect that "He Himself first ascended to heaven and brought man as a gift to God".[3] Other references to the Ascension by Hippolytus are only incidental, as in his baptismal Creed[4] or in his early treatise *De Christo et Antichristo* (*c.* 200):

[1] 21.   [2] 4.   [3] *P.G.* 10. 864C.   [4] *Ap. Trad.*, xxi. 15 (ed. Dix).

He first completed the course, and was received into the heavens, and was set down on the right hand of God the Father.[1]

We learn, however, from a passage in the *De Psalmis*, preserved by Theodoret of Cyrus, that Hippolytus interpreted psalm 24 of the Ascension:

> He comes to the heavenly gates: angels accompany Him: and the gates of heaven were closed. For He had not yet ascended into heaven. Now first does He appear to the powers of heaven as flesh ascending. Therefore to these powers it is said by the angels, who are the couriers of the Saviour and Lord: "Lift up your gates, ye princes; and be lifted up, ye everlasting doors: and the King of glory shall come on."[2]

In making this application Hippolytus ranged himself with the orthodox exegetes and against the Naasseni who, in docetic vein, understood the psalm to prophesy a spiritualizing of Christ prior to His return to the heights.[3]

Hippolytus was a commentator rather than an original thinker: he was superficially brilliant but lacking in depth, and the Christology which he opposed to the heretics of his day was so subordinationist that it found its logical outcome in the extreme Arianism and Macedonianism of the succeeding century. It was with justification that Callistus dubbed him a ditheist,[4] thereby increasing further the personal animosity which Hippolytus felt towards him, and which led Hippolytus to set himself up as an anti-pope when Callistus succeeded Zephyrinus in A.D. 217. But if the personal factor was mainly determinative in producing the Hippolytan schism, it was a question of principle[5] that led Novatian, some three decades later, to assume the role of yet another anti-pope in opposition to Cornelius, whose lenient treatment of those who had lapsed in the Decian persecution of A.D. 250 conflicted with his own rigorist convictions. The *De Trinitate*, however, was written by Novatian before this breach took place, and it provides adequate grounds for his continued high reputation as a divine.

---

[1] 46; cp. *c. Noetum*, 18.   [2] *P.G.* 10. 609C.
[3] *Refut.*, 5. 8. 18 (*C.G.S.*, 92. 15).   [4] *Refut.*, 9. 12. 16 (*C.G.S.*, 240. 23).
[5] S. L. Greenslade, *Schism in the Early Church*, 1953, pp. 37-42.

The *De Trinitate* takes the form of an exposition of the rule of faith, which was evidently triadic. In expounding the second member, viz. that concerned with Christ, Novatian makes considerable use of the Ascension to support, on the one hand, the dual nature of the Incarnate Word and, on the other, His complete divinity. Drawing a distinction between the One who descended from heaven at the Incarnation and the One who ascended into heaven when the work of redemption had been completed, Novatian was able to demonstrate that Christ was both God and man:

> In the same manner as He was as man inferior to others, so as God He was greater than all. And in the same manner as He ascended as man into heaven, so as God He had first descended thence. And in the same manner as He goes as man to the Father, so as the Son in obedience to the Father He shall descend thence. So if imperfections in Him prove human frailty, majesties in Him affirm divine power. For the risk is, in reading of both, to believe not both but one of the two. Wherefore as both are read of in Christ, let both be believed, so that finally the faith may be true, being also complete.[1]

Further, on the basis of this same distinction, Novatian affirms the pre-existence of the Word and consequently the reality of His Godhead:

> It is He who "as a bridegroom goeth forth from His bride-chamber; He exulted as a giant to run His way. His going forth is from the end of the heaven, and His return unto the ends of it";[2] because, even to the highest, "no one hath ascended into heaven save He who came down from heaven, even the Son of man who is in heaven". And if this Word descended from heaven as a bridegroom to the flesh, in order that, by assuming flesh, He might as Son of man ascend thither whence as the Son of God He had descended, the Word—since by a mutual connexion flesh wears the Word of God, and the Son of God assumes frail flesh—ascending with the flesh which He had wedded to that place whence without flesh He had descended, resumed of necessity the glory which He is shown to have possessed before the foundation of the world, He is clearly proved to be God.[3]

Novatian laid such store by this argument that he employed it twice more in the course of his treatise.

[1] 11. [2] Ps. 19: 5. [3] 13.

If Christ is only man, why does He say: "What if ye shall see the Son of man ascending thither where He was before?" But He ascended into heaven, therefore He was there in that He returned thither where He was before. But if He was sent from heaven by the Father, He certainly is not man only; for man, as we have said, could not come from heaven. Therefore as man He was not there before, but ascended thither where He was not.[1]

"I know whence I came, and whither I go; ye know not whence I came and whither I go. Ye judge after the flesh."[2] Behold, He also says that He will return thither whence He bears witness that He came before, as being sent—to wit, from heaven. He came down therefore from whence He came, in the same manner as He goes thither from whence He descended. If Christ were only man He would not have come thence, and therefore would not depart thither, because He would not have come thence. Moreover, by coming thence, whence as man He could not have come, He shows Himself to have come as God.[3]

Novatian's sober theology, a not untypical product of the Western mind with its essentially practical character, fell short of the wide range of the Alexandrian speculation. Both Clement and Origen were interested in problems of an abstract nature, and although the latter was more Biblical than the former, both were so much under the influence of Platonism that they were better equipped to appreciate the ideal content of Christian truth than to expound a positive theology of redemption. For this reason the Ascension has little part in the philosophico-theological system they sought to create. Indeed, in the writings of Clement only one allusion is to be noted, viz. in the *Paedagogus* (c. 190), the second book of his trilogy, where the knowledge of the impending Ascension is said to have provided an incentive to the disciples to apprehend the truth from their Master before He left them.

The Lord, in the Gospel, spurs on His disciples, urging them to attend to Him, hastening as He was to the Father; rendering His hearers more eager by the intimation that after a little while He was to depart, and showing them that it was requisite that they should take more unsparing advantage of the truth than ever before, as the Word was to ascend to heaven.[4]

[1] 14.   [2] John 8: 14, 15.   [3] 15.   [4] *Paed.*, 1.5 (*P.G.* 8.264B).

The importance which Origen attached to the ecclesiastical tradition of doctrine ensured some mention of the Ascension, and indeed in the preface to his *De Principiis*, which he wrote at Alexandria between the years 220 and 230, he includes it among "the particular points (*species*)" which he asserts to have been "clearly delivered in the teaching of the apostles".[1] At the same time the Ascension was not spared that allegorization which Origen employed so zealously in his exposition of the Scriptures. So he declares, in his *de Oratione*, composed *c.* 233-34 after he had settled in Caesarea:

> Let us seek to understand in a mystical sense the words at the end of the Gospel according to John: "Touch me not, for I am not yet ascended to my Father", thinking of the Ascension of the Son to the Father in a manner more befitting His divinity, with sanctified perspicuity, as an ascension of the mind rather than the body.[2]

This should not be taken to mean that Origen did not believe that an Ascension had taken place, since he asserts in his *Contra Celsum* (246):

> We also have a great high priest, who by the greatness of His power and understanding "has passed through the heavens, even Jesus the Son of God",[3] who has promised to all that have truly learned divine things and have lived lives in harmony with them to go before them to the things that are beyond this world; for His words are: "That where I go, ye may be also."[4] And therefore we hope, after the troubles and strivings here, that we may come to the topmost heavens.[5]

Again,

> After His Ascension into heaven Christ made His holy apostles, men ignorant and unlearned, taken from the ranks of taxgatherers and fishermen, but who were filled with the power of His divinity, to itinerate through the world.[6]

Moreover, "the chief advent of the Holy Spirit is declared to men, after the Ascension of Christ to heaven".[7] The individual

[1] *De Prin.*, I, *praef.* 4. [2] *de Orat.*, 23.2. [3] Heb. 4: 14. [4] John 14: 3.
[5] 6.20; cp. 8.34. It is to be noted that in the succeeding chapters (6.21-23) Origen rejects the conception of seven heavens, although it had been accepted by Irenaeus; cp. Clement, *Strom.*, 4.159.2.
[6] *De Prin.*, 2.6.1. [7] *De Prin.*, 2.7.2.

believer himself is to ascend in due course "following Him who has passed into the heavens, Jesus the Son of God, who said: 'I will that where I am, there ye may be also' ".[1]

The Ascension is also used by Origen to emphasize the divinity of Christ, but his method differs from that of Novatian.

> If it be recorded that my Jesus was "received up into glory",[2] I perceive God's care for man; because God, who caused this to happen, commends in this way the Master to those who witnessed it, so that they might fight, not for human learning but for divine teaching, that they might devote themselves as far as possible to the God who is over all.[3]

Yet Origen moved far from the concrete realism of the New Testament writers, and it was his Hellenistic background that disposed him to favour the allegorical interpretation which has been quoted above. Convinced that God cannot be circumscribed locally and that the Son cannot therefore be deemed to move spatially when He is said to descend or ascend, he interpreted the Ascension, in a manner not unacceptable in the twentieth century, as concerned with spiritual exaltation rather than with physical motion. So he contends:

> When it is said that the Father of the saints is in heaven, we must not understand Him to be circumscribed and to dwell in heaven in bodily fashion; for God contained in this way will then be found less than heaven if heaven contains Him. We must believe that all things are contained and held together by Him, by the ineffable power of His Godhead. And in general we must interpret those passages which, in so far as they are taken literally, are thought by the more simple to assert that God is in a place, in conformity with large and spiritual ideas about God.[4]

Consequently the Ascension is not to be related to spatial categories:

> But the Word of God, coming down to us, and while He is still among men humbling Himself as touching His own proper dignity, is said to pass from this world to the Father, that we may also contemplate Him there in His perfection, returning to His own proper fulness after the emptying with which He emptied

[1] *De Prin.*, 2.11.6.   [2] 1 Tim. 3: 16.   [3] *c. Cel.*, 3.31.   [4] *de Orat.*, 23.1.

Himself among us, where we also with Him as our guide shall be fulfilled and delivered from all emptiness.[1]

Origen's Hellenism was not acceptable to all his contemporaries, nor to many in succeeding generations, and amongst his most distinguished opponents was Methodius (✝ 311), who was most probably bishop of Philippi in Macedonia.[2] Methodius, however, was not at first unsympathetic towards Origen,[3] nor was he himself free from Greek influence, since his *Symposium* is an imitation of Plato. In this work we find a single reference to the Ascension which indicates one of the grounds of Methodius' later antagonism. He speaks of "the undefiled and blessed flesh, which the Word Himself carried into the heavens, and presented at the right hand of God".[4] The extreme realism of this phraseology adumbrates the *De Resurrectione* in which he sought to refute Origen's theory of resurrection in a spiritual body and to defend the complete identity of the human body with the body of the resurrection.

Methodius was a master of style, being judged by Jerome to be a pleasing and elegant writer,[5] and what he achieved in Greek Lactantius accomplished in Latin, having, according to Jerome again, "a flow of eloquence worthy of Cicero".[6] His theology, however, was not commensurate with his diction, and hence Jerome's further statement: "would that he had been as ready to teach our doctrines as he was to pull down those of others."[7] It was in his *Divinae Institutiones*, begun c. A.D. 304 soon after he had resigned the chair of rhetoric at Nicomedia, that Lactantius sought to demonstrate the falsity of pagan religion. In the fourth book of this first attempt at a Latin *Summa*, he expounds his theory of true knowledge, showing how Christ has brought insight into the nature and being of God, and in the course of this survey he twice describes the Ascension, declaring that it was in fulfilment of prophecy.[8] In his *Epitome*, which is an abridged re-edition of the *Institutes* published some time after A.D. 314, Lactantius provides a convenient summary of these two passages:

[1] *de Orat.*, 23.2.
[2] Not of Olympus in Lycia; F. Diekamp, "Über den Bischofssitz des hl. Märtyrers und Kirchenvaters Methodius", *Theologische Quartalschrift*, 1928, pp. 285-308.
[3] Jerome, *Adv. Ruf.*, I.11. [4] 7.8. [5] *De vir. ill.*, 83.
[6] *Ep.*, 58.10. [7] *Ibid.* [8] 4.12, 21.

Then at length, on the fortieth day, He returned to His Father, being taken up in a cloud. The prophet Daniel had long before shown this, saying: "I beheld in a vision of the night, and behold, one like unto a son of man coming in clouds of heaven. And he came unto the Ancient of days, and those that were standing near presented him. And there was given him a kingdom, and honour, and authority; and all the peoples, tribes and tongues shall serve him; and his power is for everlasting, which will never pass away, and his kingdom shall never be brought to nought." Likewise David in the 109th psalm: "The Lord said unto my Lord, Sit at my right hand, until I put thine enemies as the footstool of thy feet."[1]

Lactantius's statements concerning the Ascension are not remarkable for their profundity, but in this he was not untypical of the ante-Nicene Fathers as a whole. There are indeed only three writers who have any special contribution to make: Irenaeus, who integrates it into his theory of Recapitulation; Novatian, who associates it so closely with the doctrine of the Incarnation; and Origen, who raises a doubt as to the propriety of a too literal interpretation of the Lucan account in Acts. Other references fall into two main groups. On the one hand, we find the Ascension frequently utilized for controversial purposes; on the other, we find it present without exception in all quasi-credal formulae, and if this latter adds little to our understanding, it is a necessary preparation for the crystallization of Christian belief in the succeeding Age of Conciliar Creeds.

[1] *Epitome,* 47.

5

THE AGE OF CONCILIAR CREEDS

TWO factors, above all others, dominated the life and thought of the Church in the fourth century. These were, on the one hand, the conversion of Constantine, with the consequent interest of the emperor in matters ecclesiastical, and, on the other hand, the protracted struggle against Arianism, with its accompanying heated theological debate. The conjunction of these two elements produced the wearisome succession of councils at which repeated attempts were made to affirm and to impose standards of orthodoxy: hence the many definitions of faith either promulgated by these assemblies to strengthen the position of their constituent members or recited by individuals to demonstrate their doctrinal integrity.

Our previous references to quasi-credal formulae in the ante-Nicene Church would dispose us to expect that the Ascension would have its place in these conciliar creeds, and such indeed is the case—the Ascension is not lacking in a single one. Whether we consider the creed of the Council of Nicea[1] (A.D. 325) or those of the Dedication Council at Antioch in 341,[2] or the Homoean "blasphemy" of Sirmium of 359,[3] or that of the Synod of Constantinople in the following year[4]—in all we find mention of the Ascension. A similar result issues from an examination of the confessions of faith of such men as Alexander of Alexandria,[5] Eusebius of Caesarea,[6] Marcellus of Ancyra,[7] Theophronius of Tyana,[8] Epiphanius of Cyprus,[9] Theodore of Mopsuestia,[10] and even Arius himself[11]—all profess a belief in the Ascension into the heavens.

Yet, although uniform in their testimony, these creeds do

[1] J. N. D. Kelly, *Early Christian Creeds*, 1950, pp. 215f.
[2] Athanasius, *de Synod.*, 22, 23, 25.   [3] *Ibid.*, 8.   [4] *Ibid.*, 30.
[5] Kelly, *op. cit.*, pp. 188f.   [6] *P.G.* 20.1537B.
[7] Epiphanius, *Pan. haer.*, 72.3.   [8] Athanasius, *de Syn.*, 24.
[9] *Ancoratus*, 118f.   [10] Kelly, *op. cit.*, p. 187.   [11] *Ibid.*, p. 189.

witness to a difference of terminology. The majority employ an active form—"He ascended", ἀνελθόντα—but a few have the passive—"He was taken up", ἀναλημφθέντα. Later theologians were to see in these two usages an important theological distinction and to apply the first to the Godhead of Christ and the second to His humanity. Initially, one might have expected the Arians to favour the passive form, since it could be patent, where the distinction just drawn is not observed, of a subordinationist interpretation. Arius himself, however, had the active in his confession of faith, while Alexander, his bishop at Alexandria (313-28) and first opponent, had the passive. Yet ἀνελθόντα does require a word of explanation. Why was it generally adopted in preference to one or other of the Scriptural terms?

A comparison of the various creeds reveals that in all, save possibly two,[1] where ἀνελθόντα is found, it is preceded, in the clause relating to the Incarnation, by κατελθόντα. On the other hand, in those few creeds where the passive is found, viz. that of Alexander, the Fourth Creed of Antioch and those of Sirmium and Constantinople (360), κατελθόντα is lacking. This suggests that ἀνελθόντα has been adopted to maintain a credal balance between the descent and the ascent, and indeed in one formulary, viz. the so-called Second Creed of Antioch, this balance is specially emphasized so that one reads not merely κατελθόντα but κατελθόντα ἄνωθεν, and the correspondence with ἀνελθόντα is, as it were, underlined. Thus these creeds suggest the interpretation of the Ascension as the completion of the divine economy of salvation—a theme which we shall notice frequently in the later sermons.

Although these creeds in their references to the Ascension are free from any Arian influence, either negative or positive, the Ascension itself was not spared a place in the controversy. Anything and everything in the Scriptural record which might conceivably suggest the subordination of the Son to the Father was pressed into service by the anti-Nicene party. Thus Acts 2: 36, where Peter affirms that as a consequence of the Ascension God has made Jesus "both Lord and Christ", was interpreted to mean that only after the Ascension did the Son of

[1] See J. G. Davies, "An Addition to the Reconstituted Creed of Jerusalem", *Vig. Christ.*, IX, 1955, pp. 218-21.

God begin to be Lord.[1] Again, Phil. 2: 9, with its allusion to the exaltation of Christ, was understood to indicate an advancement or promotion and therefore a prior inferiority.[2]

Athanasius' references to the Ascension are determined exclusively by the exigencies of this controversy. He is concerned not to expound but to defend, and not so much to defend the Ascension in itself as the consubstantiality of the Son with the Father. He does so by affirming that the exaltation of Christ is to be understood of His humanity.

The term in question, "highly exalted", does not signify that the essence of the Word was exalted, for He was ever and is "equal with God",[3] but the exaltation is of the manhood. Accordingly this is not said before the Word became flesh, that it might be plain that "humbled" and "exalted" are spoken of His human nature; for where there is humble estate, there too may be exaltation; and if because of His taking flesh "humbled" is written, it is clear that "highly exalted" is also said because of it. For of this was man's nature in want, because of the humble estate of the flesh and of death. Since then the Word, being the Image of the Father and immortal, took the form of the servant, and as man underwent for us death in His flesh, that thereby He might offer Himself for us through death to the Father; therefore also, as man, He is said, because of us and for us, to be highly exalted, that as by His death we all died in Christ, so again in the Christ Himself we might be highly exalted, being raised from the dead and ascending into heaven, "whither the forerunner, Jesus, is entered for us, not into the figures of the true, but into heaven itself, now to appear in the presence of God for us".[4] But if now for us the Christ is entered into heaven itself, though He was even before Lord and framer of the heavens, for us therefore is that present exaltation written . . . that we may be exalted in Him, and that we may enter the gates of heaven, which He has also opened for us, the forerunners saying: "Lift up your gates, O ye rulers, and be ye lift up, ye everlasting doors, and the King of glory shall come in." For here also the gates were not shut on Him, as being Lord and Maker of all, but because of us is this too written, to whom the door of paradise was shut. And therefore in a human relation, because of the flesh which He bore, it is said of Him: "Lift up your gates", and "shall come in" as if a man were entering; but in a divine

[1] Athanasius, c. Arianos, 2.15.   [2] Ibid., 1.40.
[3] John 5: 18.   [4] Heb. 6: 20; 9: 24.

relation, on the other hand, it is said of Him, since "the Word was God",[1] that He is the "Lord" and "King of glory".[2]

Another aspect of the Arian teaching with which Athanasius had to cope comes to the fore in his letter to Adelphius, bishop of Onuphis. Some of them apparently denied not only the divinity of Christ but also the reality of His human nature,[3] and he represents them as saying: "We do not desire the Word to be made flesh, lest in it He should become our Mediator to gain access to Thee, and so we inhabit the heavenly mansions. Let the gates of the heavens be shut lest Thy Word consecrate for us the road thither through the veil, viz. His flesh." In his answer, Athanasius again makes use of the Ascension:

> Why, the blessed Stephen saw in the heavens the Lord standing on God's right hand, while the angels said to the disciples: "He shall so come in like manner as ye beheld Him going into heaven." And surely if the flesh is inseparable from the Word, does it not follow that these men must either lay aside their error, and for the future worship the Father in the name of our Lord Jesus Christ, or, if they do not worship or serve the Word who came in the flesh, be cast out on all sides?[4]

Nevertheless, the Ascension is not an important factor in Athanasius' theological thought, partly no doubt because of its misuse by the Arians, but not entirely so, since in one of his earliest works, when Arianism was not in his purview, he applied to the Crucifixion an interpretation which would have been more suitably employed of the Ascension. The pericope in question is to be found in the *De Incarnatione* (c. A.D. 318), where Athanasius seeks to answer the enquiry: why did Christ suffer death in no other way than on a cross? He replies that as the lower atmosphere is the realm of the devil, it was necessary for Christ to die in the air.

> For thus being lifted up, He cleared the air of the malignity both of the devil and of demons of all kinds, as He says: "I beheld Satan as lightning fallen from heaven";[5] and He made a

---

[1] John 1: 1.
[2] *c. Arianos*, 1.41; cp. 1.45. The same theme is expounded in the Pseudo-Athanasian Fourth Discourse, *c. Arianos*, 4.6, 7.
[3] *Ep.*, 60.1 (*P.G.* 26.1072).   [4] *Ibid.*, 60.5.   [5] Luke 10: 18.

new opening of the way up into heaven, as He says once more: "Lift up your gates, O ye princes, and be ye lift up, ye ever-lasting doors."[1]

This is manifestly a form of the Classical theory of the atonement, but one cannot help thinking that it might have gained in depth and coherence if Athanasius had represented the Ascension, rather than the Crucifixion, as that feature of the atoning act which "cleared the air of the malignity of the devil". At the same time, it must be acknowledged that Athanasius' main concern in this passage is to demonstrate the reason for death by crucifixion and that he is quite capable elsewhere of applying Ps. 24: 7 not to the Crucifixion, as here, but, as we have seen above, to the Ascension.[2] Moreover, while in his commentary on the Psalms, Ps. 68: 18 is also interpreted of the Crucifixion,[3] Pss. 24,[4] 47[5] and 110[6] are all referred to the Ascension, which he unquestionably upheld, witness his *Expositio Fidei*:

> in which humanity He was crucified and died for us, and rose from the dead, and was taken up into the heavens . . . (and showed us) also a way up to the heavens, whither the humanity of our Lord, in which He will judge the quick and the dead, entered as precursor (πρόδρομος) for us.[7]

Amongst those who opposed Athanasius in his defence of the Nicene faith, more from lack of understanding of the issues involved than from any deeply held convictions, was Eusebius of Caesarea. Indeed, he played a prominent part in the Council of Antioch (330), which deposed Eustathius, an active anti-Arian, and he was a member of the Synod of Tyre (335), which meted out similar treatment to Athanasius himself. Although a brilliant pioneer as an historian, Eusebius was no theologian. This is exemplified by his treatment of the Ascension, which in the *Demonstratio Evangelica* he is content to describe by exact quotation of the Acts' account with no comment whatsoever.[8] Elsewhere in the same treatise, he does no more than apply to the Ascension those psalms which one may say were now customarily associated with it, viz. 24,[9] 47[10]

[1] 25. [2] *c. Arianos*, 1.41. [3] *P.G.* 27.297. [4] *Ibid.*, 27.141.
[5] *Ibid.*, 27.217. [6] *Ibid.*, 27.461. [7] *Ibid.*, 25.201B. [8] 6.18.
[9] 7.1; *Comm. in ps. xxiii* (*P.G.* 23.220). [10] 6.2.

and 110,[1] and in one passage[2] he echoes unmistakably the teaching of Origen, whom he had sought to defend in an Apology, written in collaboration with the presbyter Pamphilus:

> In the 17th psalm it is written: "And he lowered the heavens and descended, and it was dark under his feet. And he rode upon Cherubim, and flew, he flew upon the wings of the winds"; wherein there is a prophecy of His Ascension from earth to heaven. And when there is a fit opportunity I will show that we must understand the descent and ascent of God the Word not as of one moving locally, but in the metaphorical sense which Scripture intends in the use of such conventional terms.[3]

The "Athanasius of the West" is the title with which Hilary of Poitiers is frequently invested; and with good reason, for his opposition to Arianism was untiring and led eventually to his exile to Asia Minor. It was there, during 356-59, that he wrote his great work *De Trinitate*, a treatise more often mentioned with approval than studied with assiduity. Yet for its originality and profundity of thought it merits the closest attention, and not least with respect to the doctrine of the Ascension contained therein. Hilary, like Novatian before him, appreciated the close relation between the Incarnation and the Ascension, and hence his teaching on the latter cannot be fully understood apart from his Christology, which he elaborated with considerable daring.

Christ, according to Hilary, was perfect God[4] and perfect man;[5] one Person possessing two natures. But how, he is concerned to ask, was such a union possible? How could the manhood co-exist with the Godhead in one Person? In his reply Hilary adumbrates the kenotic theory of Christology and takes his starting point from Phil. 2: 6, 7. The Son of God emptied Himself of the divine form in order that He might exist in the servant's form of man[6] because

---

[1] 5.3. In 4.15 and 7.1 he uses Ps. 110 of the eternal co-session of the Son with the Father.

[2] Two other statements of Eusebius relating to the Ascension are considered below, pp. 193f., 198.

[3] 6.9. In 6.1 he quotes Ps. 18: 9-11, commenting: "it presents darkly the return to divine glory."

[4] *De Trin.*, 9.4, 14, 51.

[5] *Ibid.*, 10.21; *Tr. in ps. cxxxviii*, 3.

[6] *De Trin.*, 9.38; *Tr. in ps. lxviii*, 25.

He could not descend from God into man, except by emptying Himself, as God, of the form of God. But when He emptied Himself, He was not effaced so as not to be; since then He would have become other in kind than He had been. For neither did He, who emptied Himself within Himself, cease to be Himself; since the power of His might remains even in the power of emptying Himself; and the transition into the form of a servant does not mean the loss of the nature of God, since to have put off the form of God is nothing less than a mighty act of divine power.[1]

It is not easy to determine exactly what Hilary understood by the "form of God", but if we define it as His "glory" we shall probably be not far from his meaning.[2] Hilary lays such stress upon this self-evacuation or self-renunciation of glory that he can even affirm that it involved a disturbance of the divine unity,[3] in so far as there was in Christ a created nature, viz. His manhood, which was sundered by an infinite distance from God the Father, though indissolubly united with the divinity of His Son. Only when the manhood had been exalted into harmonious association with the Godhead of the Father and of the Son would this partial separation and breach come to an end. Thus the goal of the Incarnation is the elevation of the manhood, and this involves both a process and a consummation. The process consists of the increasing submission of the Godhead to the infirmities and inequality of the manhood; the consummation consists of the restoration of the glory of the Son, when it becomes, as it had been before, the same as that of the Father, and of the sharing of that glory by His humanity.[4] It is at this point that the importance of the Ascension in Hilary's system of thought becomes apparent, since the Ascension is itself the exaltation.[5] So he affirms:

He who has been born as man and suffered all the afflictions of our flesh has gone up on high to our God and Father to receive

[1] *De Trin.*, 12.6.
[2] J. A. Dorner, *The Person of Christ*, I, ii, 1870, pp. 407-9; E. W. Watson, *Nicene and Post-Nicene Fathers*, IX, 1899, pp. lxxi-lxxiii.
[3] *De Trin.*, 9.38.
[4] *Tr. in ps. ii*, 27; *liii*, 14; *cxxxviii*, 19.
[5] Hilary also speaks of the Resurrection as the means of glorification (*De Trin.*, 11.42; *Tr. in ps. liii*, 5) and would appear, like Paul, to regard Resurrection and Ascension as two elements in one single process.

His glory as man our representative.[1] For the nature of the earthly body does not secure this Ascension except by being transformed into celestial glory.[2]

Thus, if the flesh were united to the glory of the Word, the man Jesus Christ could abide in the glory of God the Father, and the Word made flesh could be restored to the unity of the Father's nature, even as regards His manhood, since the assumed flesh had obtained the glory of the Word. Therefore the Father must reinstate the Word in His unity, that the offspring of His nature might again return to be glorified in Himself: for the unity had been infringed by the new dispensation, and could only be restored perfect as before if the Father glorified with Himself the flesh assumed by the Son.[3]

Consequently, while the Ascension refers primarily to the humanity,[4] in virtue of the unity of the two natures it must also refer to the Godhead which is thereby reinstated in the unity of the Father, for there can be no division in the one Person of Christ.

Whether, therefore, dead or buried, descended into Hades or ascended into heaven, all is one and the same Christ: as the Apostle says: "Now this 'He ascended', what is it but that He also descended to the lower parts of the earth? He that descended is the same also that ascended far above all heavens, that He might fill all things." How far then shall we push our babbling ignorance and blasphemy, professing to explain what is hidden in the mystery of God? "He that descended is the same also that ascended." Can we longer doubt that the man Christ Jesus rose from the dead, ascended above the heavens and is at the right hand of God? We cannot say His body descended into Hades, which lay in the grave. If then He who descended is one with Him who ascended; if His body did not go down into Hades, yet really arose from the dead and ascended into heaven, what remains except to believe in the secret mystery, which is hidden from the world and the rulers of the age, and to confess that ascending or descending He is but One?—One Jesus Christ for us, Son of God and Son of man, God the Word and man in the flesh, who suffered, died, and was buried, rose again, was

[1] *De Trin.*, 1.33.
[2] *Tr. in ps. cxxxviii*, 22. Hence Ps. 57: 5 refers to the Ascension (*Tr. in ps. lvi*, 6).
[3] *De Trin.*, 9.38.   [4] *Ibid.*, 11.14.

received into heaven, and sitteth at the right hand of God; who possesses in His one single self, according to the divine plan and nature, in the form of God and in the form of a servant, the human and divine without separation or division.[1]

But this Ascension affects all men, according to Hilary, who, commenting on Matt. 5: 14—"a city set on a hill cannot be hid"—states:

He calls the flesh which He had assumed "a city", because as a city is formed of a variety and multitude of inhabitants, so in Him, through the nature of the body which He had taken on Himself, an assembling together, so to speak, of the whole human race is contained. . . . Therefore it cannot now be hid because it has been placed in the heights of the most exalted God and has been lifted up to the wonder of His works to be contemplated and understood by all.[2]

An equally staunch opponent of Arianism in the West was the great Ambrose of Milan, whose *De Fide* was undertaken at the request of the Emperor Gratian when he was about to go to the East to aid his uncle Valens in repelling a Gothic invasion (378). Ambrose begins the fourth book of this work by affirming that while it is a matter for marvel that human knowledge has not submitted itself to the words of Scripture, it is not surprising that it has failed to comprehend Christ, since even the angels without revelation would be ignorant of the mystery of Godliness. He continues:

And so when the Lord rose again, and the heights of heaven could not bear the glory of His rising from the dead, who of late, so far as regarded His flesh, had been confined in the narrow bounds of a sepulchre, even the heavenly hosts doubted and were amazed. For a Conqueror came, adorned with wondrous spoils, the Lord was in His holy Temple, before Him went angels and archangels, marvelling at the prey wrested from death, and though they knew that nothing can be added to God from the flesh, because all things are lower than God, nevertheless bearing the trophy of the Cross . . . and the spoils borne by the everlasting Conqueror, they, as if the gates could not afford passage for Him who had gone forth from them . . . , sought

---

[1] *De Trin.*, 10.65.   [2] *In Matt.*, iv.12 (*P.L.* 9.935).

some broader and more lofty passage for Him on His return—
so entirely had He remained undiminished by His self emptying. . . . Enoch had been translated, Elijah caught up, but the
servant is not above his Master, for "No man hath ascended
into heaven, but he who came down from heaven"; . . . Enoch
then was translated, and Elijah caught up; both as servants,
both in the body, but not after resurrection from the dead, nor
with the spoils of death and the triumphal train of the Cross
had they been seen of angels. And therefore the angels, descry-
ing the approach of the Lord of all, first and only vanquisher of
death, bade their princes that the gates should be lifted up,
saying in adoration: "Lift up the gates, such as are princes
among you, and be ye lifted up, O ye everlasting doors, and the
King of glory shall come in." Yet there were still, even among
the host of heaven, some that were amazed, overcome with
astonishment at such pomp and glory that they had never yet
beheld, and therefore they asked: "Who is the King of glory?"
Others again—those, to wit, who had been present at His rising
again, those who had seen or already recognized Him—made
reply: "It is the Lord strong and mighty, the Lord mighty in
battle" . . . and back again came the challenge of them that
stood astonished: "Who is that King of glory? For we saw Him
having neither form nor comeliness; if then it be not He, who
is that King of glory?" Whereto, they which know, answer:
"The Lord of hosts, He is the King of glory." Therefore, the
Lord of Hosts, He is the Son.[1]

Having thus described the Ascension in Scriptural terms,
Ambrose is ready to make the application, proving against
the Arians the omnipotence of the Son:

How then do the Arians call Him fallible, whom we believe to
be the Lord of hosts, even as we believe of the Father? How
can they draw distinctions between the sovereign powers of each,
when we have found the Son, even as also the Father, entitled
"Lord Sabaoth"? . . . Therefore, since He who ascended was
the Son, and again, He who ascended is the Lord of Sabaoth
(i.e. the Lord omnipotent), it surely follows that the Son of God
is omnipotent.[2]

Returning to the attack, Ambrose further asserts:

It is expedient for thee that thou shouldest believe that He has
ascended and is sitting at the right hand of the Father; for if

[1] *De Fide*, 4.5, 6, 8-10, 11-14.   [2] *Ibid.*, 4.14.

in impious thought thou detain Him among things created and earthly; if He depart not for thee, ascend not for thee, then to thee the Comforter shall not come, even as Christ Himself hath told us: "For if I go not away, the Comforter will not come unto you, but if I depart, I will send Him unto you."[1]

In his *De Spiritu Sancto*, also written at the request of Gratian (381), Ambrose repeats this same theme, and speaks of the grace of the Spirit:

which the Lord Jesus shed forth from heaven, after having been fixed to the gibbet of the Cross, returning with the triumphal spoils of death deprived of its power, as you find it written: "Ascending up on high, he led captivity captive, and gave good gifts to men." . . . And since captive breasts certainly could not receive Him, the Lord Jesus first led captivity captive that our affections being set free, He might pour forth the gift of divine grace.[2]

But perhaps Ambrose's most noteworthy contribution to the history of the doctrine lies in certain scattered and undeveloped statements which were to be expanded later by his disciple Augustine. "Christ's purpose in the Incarnation", according to Ambrose, "was to pave for us the road to heaven. Mark how He says: 'I ascend to my Father and your Father, to my God and your God.' "[3] When the Son of God was incarnate, He took universal human nature in which all individuals are subsumed[4]—"He took *us* in that flesh."[5] Hence His death is our death: His Resurrection our resurrection, and His Ascension our ascension, "for it was not merely one man but the whole world that entered in the Person of the All-redeemer".[6] So then "in Him we sit at the right hand of the Father, not in the sense that we share His throne, but that we rest in the Body of Christ."[7]

The position of Cyril of Jerusalem in the Arian controversy is not entirely clear.[8] If in his early career he seems to have been something of a semi-Arian, later he would appear to

---

[1] *De Fide*, 4.24.   [2] I.66.   [3] *De Fide*, 3.51.
[4] cp. the same idea propounded by Hilary, p. 103.   [5] *Expos. ps. cxviii*, 10.14.
[6] *De Fide*, 4.7.   [7] *Ibid.*, 4.135.
[8] J. Lebon, "La Position de saint Cyrille de Jérusalem dans les Luttes provoquées par l'Arianisme", *Rev. d'Hist. Eccl.*, XX, 1924, pp. 181-210, 357-86.

have realized that, mathematically at least, this also involved his being a semi-Nicene. Yet whatever the final verdict on his position may be, in regard to the Ascension he sided definitely with the orthodox party, since he emphatically states:[1]

> Let us not endure those who falsely say that it was after His Cross and Resurrection and Ascension into heaven that the Son began to sit on the right hand of the Father. For the Son gained not His throne by advancement, but throughout His being (and His being is by an eternal generation) He also sitteth together with the Father.[2]

The fourteenth Catechetical lecture, in which Cyril discourses on the Ascension, was delivered on a Monday, but as the lessons appointed for the preceding Sunday had "included the account of our Saviour's going up into the heavens", and as Cyril had already delivered a sermon on that theme, he provides no more than a summary of his exposition on the grounds that his hearers will presumably remember what he has already said. This homily would seem to have comprised three sections, to the first of which we may give the title: "The Ascension as the fulfilment of prophecy"; to the second: "The possibility of the Ascension"; and to the third: "The Ascension to be differentiated from the translations of Enoch and Elijah." Under the first head, he cites Pss. 24, 47 and 68, together with Amos 9: 6. Under the second, he says:

> For when they [i.e. the Jews] speak against the Ascension of the Saviour as being impossible, remember the account of the carrying away of Habakkuk:[3] for if Habakkuk was transported by an angel, being carried by the hair of his head, much rather was the Lord of both prophets and angels, able by His own power to make His ascent into the heavens on a cloud from the Mount of Olives. Wonders like this thou mayest call to mind, but reserve the pre-eminence for the Lord, the Worker of wonders; for the others were borne up, but He bears up all things.[4]

Under the third head, he argues:

> Remember that Enoch was translated, but Jesus ascended: remember what was said yesterday concerning Elijah, that Elijah

---

[1] Whether or not the Mystagogical Lectures are Cyrilline (W. J. Swaans, "A propos des 'Catéchèses Mystagogiques' attribuées à S. Cyrille de Jérusalem", *Muséon*, LV, 1942, pp. 1-43), there is little reason to doubt his authorship of the Catechetical Lectures.
[2] *Catech.*, xiv.27.   [3] Bel and the Dragon, 36.   [4] *Catech.*, xiv. 25.

was taken up in a chariot of fire, but that the chariots of Christ "are ten thousandfold even thousands upon thousands":[1] and that Elijah was taken up towards the east of Jordan, but that Christ ascended at the east of the brook Cedron: and that Elijah went "as into heaven"[2] but Jesus "into heaven": and that Elijah said that a double portion in the Holy Spirit should be given to his holy disciple, but that Christ granted to His own disciples so great enjoyment of the grace of the Holy Spirit, as not only to have Him in themselves but also, by the laying on of their hands, to impart the fellowship of Him to them who believed. And when thou hast thus wrestled against the Jews,—when thou hast worsted them by parallel instances,—then come further to the pre-eminence of the Saviour's glory, viz. that they were the servants, but He the Son of God.[3]

Cyril is emphatic that this return to the Father does not imply His absence from the Church on earth; He is present in the Spirit,[4] since He "went up into heaven and fulfilled the promise",[5] i.e. of sending the Spirit from on high.

These lectures were delivered by Cyril in the Martyrium,[6] the vast basilica which was believed to have been erected over the place where the relics of the true Cross had been discovered, and he was conscious of the pedagogical value of the Holy Places; he did not therefore miss the opportunity of saying:

When Jesus had finished His course of patient endurance, and had redeemed mankind from their sins, He ascended again into the heavens, a cloud receiving Him up; and as He went up angels were beside Him, and angels were beholding. . . . In fact, He, who was crucified here on Golgotha, has ascended into heaven from the Mount of Olives on the east.[7]

An equal interest in the sacred sites is manifested by Jerome, and he could write to Marcella, the wealthy patrician widow whose house on the Aventine he had made his centre during

[1] Ps. 68: 17.
[2] This is the first instance of the use of this apologetic exegesis of 2 Kings 2: 11, which is repeated *ad nauseam* in the later homilies; it rests upon the fortuitous presence in the LXX of the word ὡς.
[3] *Catech.*, xiv.25.
[4] xiv.30.
[5] xvii.13.
[6] The Mystagogical Lectures were delivered in the Anastasis, i.e. the building enshrining the tomb of Christ.
[7] iv.13, 14.

his stay in Rome, urging her to visit the Holy Places, including the Mount of Olives whence Christ had ascended.[1] He could describe too the grand tour of Paula, the heiress of the Gens Aemilia, and how she came to Olivet "from which the Saviour made His Ascension to the Father".[2] Jerome, however, although domiciled in the East, remained a Latin writer *par excellence*, but his understanding of the Ascension was less original than that of Hilary, more prosaic than that of Ambrose and less penetrating than that of Augustine. His reaction to the Scriptural statement that God has raised us up with Christ and made us to sit with Him in the heavenlies[3] is if anything to explain it away. To him, this passage from Ephesians refers to the future consummation and he argues that it is the practice of Scripture to refer to something as past or present while it is yet future, and that this is possible because of the foreknowledge of God. But at the same time, he suggests that this statement may be understood spiritually of the present, since we have received the earnest of the Spirit and since where our treasure is there our heart is also, hence while in the flesh we have our conversation in heaven and so may be said to sit with Christ in the heavenlies.[4] But if Jerome lacked theological profundity, he was by no means devoid of scholarly perspicacity, and so we find him noting that Ps. 68: 18 is quoted in Eph. 4: 8 in a version different from that of the original, the *accepit* of the latter having been changed to *dedit*. His explanation is that what the psalm foretold has now been fulfilled.[5]

Yet as an expositor Jerome tended to keep very closely to the text, and avoided any kind of speculation. This is exemplified by a further series of statements which superficially may appear to refer to the Ascension. The first one reads as follows:

> The Lord's Day, the day of Resurrection, the day of Christians, is our day. Wherefore it is also called the Lord's Day, because on it the Lord ascended as a victor to the Father.[6]

It would seem from this that Jerome believed the Ascension to have taken place on Easter Day; but as elsewhere he does

---

[1] *Ep.*, 46.13. [2] *Ep.*, 108.12. [3] Eph. 2: 6. [4] *In Ep. ad Eph.*, i.2 (*P.L.* 26.499).
[5] *Ibid.*, ii.4 (*P.L.* 26.530).
[6] *In die dominica Paschae* (G. Morin, "S. Hieronymi Presbyteri tractatus novissime reperti", *Anecdota Maredsolana*, III/2, p. 418).

speak of the forty days,[1] one is led to question whether in fact this is the correct interpretation to be placed on the passage just cited.

The words "ascended . . . to the Father" are quite clearly an echo of Our Lord's saying to Mary Magdalene in the garden, recorded in John 20: 17. How Jerome understood this need not be in doubt, since he has left at least three separate expositions of it. They are these:

Do not touch Me: you do not deserve to touch Me whom you seek in the tomb. Do not touch Me, whom you think to be such and do not believe to have risen. Do not touch Me, for to you I have not yet ascended to my Father: when to you I shall have ascended to the Father, then you will deserve to touch Me.[2]

This is the meaning: "Whom you seek dead, you do not deserve to touch alive. If you think that I have not yet ascended to the Father, but have been taken away by the deceit of men, you are unworthy of my touch."[3]

This is the meaning: "You do not deserve to cleave to my footprints nor to adore as Lord and hold His feet, whom you do not think to have risen. For to you I have not yet ascended to my Father." But the other women who touched the feet[4] confessed the Lord and desired to cleave to His footsteps, whom they were assured had ascended to the Father.[5]

A comparison of these passages indicates that the words "ascended to the Father" were understood by Jerome to refer to the Resurrection. One notes the parallelism between "whom you seek in the tomb . . . you do not believe to have risen", and "for to you I have not yet ascended to my Father": between "whom you seek dead, you do not deserve to touch alive" and "if you think I have not yet ascended to the Father". Thus the "ascending to the Father" of which Jerome speaks is the Resurrection,[6] and the explanation of his use of the phrase is that he found it in the fourth Gospel.[7] But observant

---

[1] *Epp.*, 59.5; 120.7. [2] *Hom. in Ioh. Evang.* I, 1-14 (Morin, *op. cit.*, p. 392).
[3] *Ep.*, 120.5. [4] Matt. 28: 9. [5] *Ep.*, 59.4.
[6] V. Larrañaga, *L'Ascension de Notre-Seigneur dans le Nouveau Testament*, 1938, pp. 528-31.
[7] Because he could use the phrase of the Resurrection, he could also apply to Easter Day Pss. 24: 7-10 and 118: 19 (Morin, *op. cit.*, p. 416).

though he was, Jerome did not appreciate that the Johannine pericope implied a different chronology of the Ascension from that which he and his contemporaries had accepted. Indeed, the prevailing attitude to the Bible and its inspiration allowed of no contradiction in Holy Writ and Jerome, by interpreting John 20 in this way, was unable to see any.[1] Hence when one of his correspondents indirectly focused attention upon it, he refrained from giving a reply in the terms proposed. It was his friend Marcella who put to him the question:

> Whether after the Resurrection the Lord continued with His disciples for forty days and was never elsewhere or whether He secretly ascended to heaven and descended and nevertheless did not deny His presence to the apostles?[2]

Jerome, while implying that his answer to the first part was in the negative, directed her attention away from the second part to the consideration of the omnipresence of the Divine Son.

> If you consider God, the Son of God, concerning whom is the statement, and He it is who made it: "Do not I fill heaven and earth? saith the Lord" . . . immediately you will not doubt that even before the Resurrection God the Word so indwelt the Lord's body that He was in the Father and encompassed the circle of heaven and was present to all. . . . He was therefore at one and the same time both with the apostles for forty days and with the angels and in the Father and at the far bounds of the sea.

By the time that Jerome was writing this answer to Marcella in Bethlehem, c. 395, the Arian controversy was fast dying down within the Empire; other controversies were to come, and in one of them, which centred in the teaching of Origen, Jerome himself played a not insignificant part. One of his principal opponents was his erstwhile friend Rufinus (✝ 410), whom at one time Jerome had desired to be conveyed to him as swiftly as Philip was transported to the eunuch,[3] and to

---

[1] Jerome has been followed at the present day by P. Benoit ("L'Ascension", *Revue Biblique*, LVI, 1949, pp. 198-203) who seeks to distinguish between an exaltation on Easter Day and a visible Ascension forty days later, the former being the occasion of Christ's entry into glory, the latter of His final departure. This is unconvincing because Luke, and the other New Testament writers, quite evidently regarded the Ascension as the occasion of Christ's entry into glory.
[2] *Ep.*, 59.5.   [3] *Ibid.*, 3.

whom in heated antagonism he later referred as "the Grunter". But on the subject of the Ascension they had no occasion to cross swords, and Jerome would have found no fault with Rufinus's summary of the doctrine in his *Commentarius in Symbolum Apostolorum*, even though it reveals an Origenist appreciation of the problem it involves:

He ascended into heaven, not where the Word of God was not before (for He was always in heaven and remained with the Father) but where the Word made flesh had not sat before.[1]

He concludes therefore that the title "King of glory" in Ps. 24 must be taken to refer to the flesh ascending, and the captivity of Ps. 68 to fallen humanity, while the gifts of the same psalm indicate the descent of the Spirit.

A similar exegesis is found in the writings of Didymus the Blind of Alexandria (+ 395), another Origenist of whom both Rufinus and Jerome had been pupils. Thus he interprets Ps. 24 of the Ascension[2] and Ps. 68,[3] although he argues that the latter may also be referred to the Crucifixion, as Athanasius had applied it before him. Of Ps. 110, he says:[4]

"The Lord", i.e. the Father, "said to the Lord," the Son, who had completed the economy, risen from the dead and ascended into heaven, "Sit thou at my right hand, etc." Paul declared that these words had been fulfilled after the Ascension, when he affirmed of Jesus: "when he had made purification of sins, sat down at the right hand of the Majesty on high, etc."[5] And again: "To which of the angels did he say at any time: Sit thou on my right hand?"[6]

Didymus then goes on to assert, with typical Origenist emphasis, that the right hand is not to be understood in terms of space, but refers to the equality of the Son with His Father in His sovereignty.

Origen continued to exercise his influence in this particular throughout the patristic period, but he made little or no contribution to the thought of the three outstanding figures as regards the doctrine of the Ascension in this age of Conciliar

---

[1] 31.
[2] *P.G.* 39.1297.
[3] *Ibid.*, 39.1445.
[4] *Ibid.*, 39.1537.
[5] Heb. 1: 3.
[6] Heb. 1: 13.

Creeds, viz. Athanasius, Hilary and Ambrose. We shall have occasion to notice, in the next lecture, the mark of the teaching of the last of this trio upon his disciple Augustine, whose homilies on the Ascension are the earliest extant in Latin. Among Greek writers, Cyril of Jerusalem, as we have seen, is the first recorded to have delivered a sermon on the Ascension, but of this only a summary remains; for the first complete Greek Ascension address we must turn to the years after the inclusion in the Church's Calendar of a feast specially devoted to the celebration of that event.

6

THE FIRST SERMONS

ONLY incidental attention was paid to the Ascension by the writers that we have considered hitherto. As part of the rule of faith it could not be omitted; as an argument for or against the orthodox position it could not be entirely disregarded, but since it in no sense occupied the forefront of debate no attempt was made to expound it in detail.[1] But now a new factor began to operate which served in part to counteract this neglect. Consequent upon the changed relationship between Church and State, effected by the conversion of Constantine, a fresh emphasis was placed upon the Church's Calendar as a means of sanctifying human life in time.[2] The Calendar was conceived no longer eschatologically but historically, i.e. as consisting of a series of commemorations of past events. This inevitably directed attention to the separate incidents in the life of Our Lord, and, amongst these, to the Ascension.

Thus the observance of the feast of the Ascension[3] meant that henceforth, at least on that one day in the year, the homilist, having his theme provided for him, was certain to expound the subject of the Ascension. "Count forty days", prescribes the *Apostolic Constitutions*, a Syriac compilation dating from 375-400, "from the Lord's Day to the fifth day of the week, and celebrate the Feast of the Ascension of the Lord, whereon He finished all His dispensation and constitution, and returned to that God and Father that sent Him, and sat down at the right hand of power, and remains there until His enemies are put under His feet."[4]

[1] Hilary is the only possible exception.
[2] G. Dix, *The Shape of the Liturgy*, 1945, p. 333.
[3] It is customary to assert that Ascension Day was not observed until the latter part of the fourth century; the evidence seems to me to warrant a different conclusion, viz. that it was in existence from the first decades (see Appended Note I, "The Observance of Ascension Day", below p. 192).
[4] 5.19; cp. 5.7; 8.33.

1. *The Early Greek Homilists*

Whether or not to Chrysostom belongs the honour of having preached the earliest Ascension Day sermon to have survived cannot be determined,[1] since while it is probable that it belongs to the year 392, the date of a sermon by Gregory of Nyssa, also delivered on an Ascension Day, is not certain, although it would seem to belong to the closing years of his life as it has no hint of the controversies in which he had been previously engaged.

Gregory, one of the great Cappadocian trio,[2] had an acute and speculative mind which does not reveal itself at its best in this homily.[3] There is too much of the rhetorician, a profession adopted by Gregory before he entered the ministry, and too little of the theologian; too much concern for the elegantly turned phrase and too little for sober doctrinal exposition. Its theme is the contribution made by the Psalms to our understanding of the Ascension, but Gregory contents himself with quoting psalms 24 and 68, adding no more than the traditional exegesis, to the effect that the former refers to the celestial powers as they welcome the triumphant King of glory and the latter to captive human nature liberated from the thraldom of sin. Indeed, Gregory has more of value to say incidentally of the Ascension elsewhere in his works. So he is concerned to maintain that the exaltation refers to the manhood,[4] and, in Origenist vein, that no motion in space can be predicated of the Deity.[5] In the second book of his *Contra Eunomium* (*c.* 383), he cites Jesus' logion to Mary at the tomb[6] and comments:

In these words He sums up the whole aim of His dispensation as man. For men revolted from God and "served them which by nature were no gods"[7] and though being the children of God became attached to an evil father, falsely so-called. For this cause the Mediator between God and man, having assumed the

---

[1] J. Sirmond (*Opera Varia*, I.1728, cols. 39-56) prints a Latin version of a sermon which he ascribes to Eusebius of Caesarea and entitles *De Resurrectione et De Ascensione*. The author is not Eusebius of Caesarea—though possibly Eusebius of Emesa—and the work has nothing to do with the Ascension, being more correctly styled *De Resurrectione* when reprinted by Migne (*P.G.* 24.1093-1114).

[2] Neither Basil of Caesarea, Gregory's brother, nor Gregory of Nazianzus, has much to tell us of the Ascension; cp. Greg. Naz., *Carmina*, 1.11.220-1.

[3] *P.G.* 46.689-93. [4] *c. Eunom.*, 6.4. [5] *Ibid.*, 12.1. [6] John 20: 17. [7] Gal. 4: 8.

firstfruits of all human nature, sends to His brethren the announce-
ment of Himself not in His divine character, but in that which
He shares with us, saying: "I am departing in order to make by
my own self that true Father, from whom you were separated,
to be your Father, and by my own self to make that true God
from whom you had revolted to be your God; for by that firstfruits which I have assumed, I am in myself presenting all
humanity to its God and Father." Since then the firstfruits made
the true God to be its God and the good Father to be its Father,
the blessing is secured for human nature as a whole, and by
means of the firstfruits the true God and Father becomes Father
and God of all men. Now "if the firstfruits be holy, the lump also
is holy".[1] But where the firstfruits, Christ, is (and the firstfruits
is none other than Christ), there also are they that are Christ's,
as the apostle says.[2]

This same image of the firstfruits[3] also finds a place in
Chrysostom's sermon, which certainly surpasses that of Gregory;
indeed, the large number of spurious Ascension addresses attributed to Chrysostom testifies to his pre-eminence as a preacher.
"His words", wrote Suidas in his Lexicon, concerning "John
of Antioch surnamed the Golden Mouth", "resounded more
loudly than the cataracts of the Nile. Since the world began,
no one else has ever possessed such gifts as an orator." In the
sermon on the Ascension we find several of those characteristics
which earned John so great a reputation. There is his use of
lively imagery rather than of theoretical argument: there is
his easy and diffuse manner which does not overtax the listener:
there is his sober and thorough exegesis, eschewing the excess-
ive allegorism of the Alexandrian school for the more literal
approach of the Antiochene.

Chrysostom begins[4] with a graceful allusion to the martyrs,
an exordium prompted by the fact that he is preaching in the
martyrium of Romanesia, in the vicinity of Antioch. He then
affirms that the present festival is notable because it marks the
reconciliation of the human race with God. This fact provides
grounds for wonder, since hitherto God and man had clearly
been at enmity the One with the other.

[1] Rom. 11: 16.
[2] c. Eunom., 2.8.
[3] It was also used of the Ascension by Epiphanius (Panarion, 51.31).
[4] P.G. 50.441-52.

But we who appeared unworthy of earth have been led up to-day into the heavens: we who were not worthy of the pre-eminence below have ascended to the Kingdom above: we have scaled the heavens: we have attained the royal throne, and that nature, on whose account the Cherubim guarded paradise, to-day sits above the Cherubim. But how did this great marvel take place? How were we who had quarrelled, who had shown ourselves unworthy of earth and had fallen below from our origin—how were we taken up to such a height? How has the strife been brought to an end? How has the wrath been removed? How?

The answer, according to Chrysostom, lies in the Mediatorship of Christ through whom reconciliation has been effected.

And to-day is the foundation of these benefits, for as He assumed the firstfruits of our nature, so He took them up to the Lord.

The preacher then launches into one of those illustrations that he so delights to employ.

For as it happens in a field full of corn, when a man takes a few ears of corn and makes a small sheaf and offers it to God, he blesses the whole cornfield by means of this sheaf, so Christ has done this also, and through that one flesh and firstfruits has made our race to be blessed. But why did He not offer the whole of nature? Because that is not the firstfruits if He offers the whole, but if He offers a little, preparing the whole to be blessed by the smaller amount.

Chrysostom next refers to Lev. 19: 23, 24, which enacts that the fruit of a new tree is not to be taken until the fourth year, consequently it is not just the *first* fruits but the first *good* fruits that are to be offered to God. So our human nature "was not offered, even if it was the first, but that was freed from sin (in Christ) and was therefore offered up, for this is the firstfruits."

And these things refer to our flesh which He offered. So He offered the firstfruits of our nature to the Father and so the Father admired the gift, and on account of the worth of the offerer and the blamelessness of that which was offered, He received it with His own hands and placed the gift next to Him, and said: "Sit thou on my right hand." To which nature did

God say: "Sit thou on my right hand"? To that which heard:
"Dust thou art, and unto dust shalt thou return."[1]

So, Chrysostom informs us, the angels rejoiced, for if there
is joy in heaven over one sinner that repents, how much more
joy is there when "the universal nature was brought into
heaven through the firstfruits". The angels indeed rejoiced at
the Incarnation: they showed themselves again at the Resurrection and for a third time at the Ascension. Their presence
on this last occasion, according to Chrysostom, who here rests
heavily on the Acts' account, was necessary for two reasons:
first, to soothe the disciples' sorrow at the departure of their
Lord by declaring His return, and, second, to assure them that
this Ascension was indeed into heaven itself.

Elijah was taken up "as if" into heaven, for he was a servant;
but Jesus into heaven, for He was Lord. The one in a fiery
chariot, the other in a cloud. For when it was necessary for the
servant to be called, a chariot was sent, but when the Son, a
royal throne, and not simply a royal throne, but the Father's.
For concerning the Father Isaiah says: "Behold, the Lord sitteth
upon a light cloud."[2] Since the Father sits upon a cloud, He
sends the cloud for the Son. And when Elijah ascended, he left
his cloak to Elisha; but when Jesus ascended, He left spiritual
gifts to His disciples, not making one prophet but a myriad of
Elishas, much greater and more illustrious than he.

The sermon concludes with a fine and sustained exhortation to practise righteousness that at the Second Coming we
might be found worthy to be taken up by the Lord.

In the second of his Homilies on the Acts of the Apostles,[3]
delivered in 400 or 401, when he had left Antioch and become
bishop of Constantinople, Chrysostom repeated many of the
same points that he had made in this sermon some eight years
before, viz. the contrast between the translation of Elijah and
the Ascension of Christ, which we have already observed in
Cyril of Jerusalem: the royal dignity implied by the appearance of the cloud, and the reasons for the angels' presence.
His exposition of this last point includes a new and interesting
distinction drawn between the Resurrection and the Ascension.

---

[1] Gen. 3: 19.   [2] Isa. 19: 1.   [3] *P.G.* 60.28-30.

117

In the Resurrection they saw the end but not the beginning, and in the Ascension they saw the beginning but not the end. Because in the former it had been superfluous to have seen the beginning, the Lord Himself who spake these things being present and the sepulchre showing clearly that He was not there; but in the latter they needed to be informed of the sequel by the words of others.

Also worthy of note is Chrysostom's further distinction between Ascension and assumption, of which Athanasius had in part laid the foundation.

Moreover the angels did not say: "whom ye have seen taken up", but "going into heaven". Ascension is the word, not assumption. The expression "taken up" belongs to the flesh. . . . Of the expressions, some are adapted to the conception of the disciples, some agreeable with the divine majesty.

In his *Expositio in psalmum xlvi*[1] Chrysostom draws the same distinction:

"God ascended with a shout." It does not say "He was taken up" but "He ascended", showing that He ascended without being led by anyone else, but He Himself travelled along this way. For Elijah did not go like Christ but was led by another power, because human nature could not traverse a strange road. But the Only-begotten ascended by His own power.[2]

A like interest in terminology is revealed in a second sermon on the Ascension,[3] assigned to Chrysostom but more correctly to be described as "of doubtful origin",[4] although in breadth of treatment it is not entirely unworthy of its attribution.

While they were watching He was taken up: He was parted from them and was borne up into heaven and a cloud received Him up: and as they were looking into heaven He went. He was received up: He was taken up: He was borne up: He entered: for Jesus did not enter into a holy place made with hands, but into heaven itself, now to appear before God.[5] And

[1] *P.G.* 55.213-14.
[2] Chrysostom interprets the "shout" as a reference to Christ's triumph, in so far as He overcame sin and death, and affirms that He carried up the trophy (τρόπαιον), viz. our human nature.
[3] *P.G.* 52.773-92. [4] O. Bardenhewer, *Patrology*, 1908, p. 332. [5] Heb. 9: 24.

not only entered but passed through: "For", says Paul, "we
have a great high priest who passed through the heavens", Jesus.[1]
He went up: He ascended: He was taken up: He went: He
passed through. Take note. He ascended as having authority in
order that the saying of the prophet might be fulfilled: "God
ascended with a shout."[2]

But the most interesting idea developed by this homilist lies
in the parallelism he draws between the earnest of the Spirit
who descended from heaven and the earnest of human nature
that was taken up into heaven; both are pledges of salvation.[3]
"Above His body, below His Spirit for us." He then proceeds
to argue that as a man and his wife are united and so become
one kin (γένος), so

> when the flesh of Christ was taken up, through that flesh the
> whole Church became of the same kin as Christ; Paul was
> Christ's kinsman, Peter, every believer, all of us, every godly
> person. Wherefore Paul says this: "Being therefore the kin of
> God".[4] . . . Paul thus affirms the existence of a kinship. And
> again elsewhere: "We are a body of Christ and severally limbs
> of his flesh."[5] On account of the flesh which He took up, we are
> His kinsmen; we therefore have this pledge above, i.e. the body,
> which He took from us, and below the Holy Spirit with us. And
> behold the wonder! I do not say that the Holy Spirit came down
> from heaven and is no longer in heaven, and that having changed
> places the body is in heaven and the Spirit on earth, but that
> the Spirit is with us and everywhere and above. "For whither",
> it is said, "shall I go from Thy Spirit?"[6] And why dost thou
> wonder if the Spirit is with us and above, and the body of Christ
> is above and with us? Heaven has the holy body and earth
> received the Holy Spirit: Christ came and brought the Holy
> Spirit; He went up and took our body. . . . We have therefore
> the pledge of our life in heaven; we have been taken up with
> Christ.

The sermon ends, as does Chrysostom's own, by directing
attention to the Second Advent and with an exhortation to
righteousness that we might be found worthy at His coming.

[1] Heb. 4: 14.   [2] Ps. 47: 5.
[3] Tertullian was the first to formulate this theme, *De Res.*, 51, cited above,
p. 83.
[4] Acts 17: 29.   [5] 1 Cor. 12: 27.   [6] Ps. 139: 7.

Pursuing the subject of Chrysostom's *Spuria*, we find a further ten homilies on the Ascension ascribed to him, all dating from the first half of the fifth century. One of these[1] is no more than a cento compiled from Chrysostom's works, and incorporating large sections from the authentic Ascension sermon and the Second Homily on Acts. Thus there is the distinction between the translation of Elijah and the Ascension of Christ: the contrast between the fallen condition of humanity and the glory to which it has been exalted in Christ: the image of the firstfruits and the concluding exhortation to righteousness, which is however based not upon the Parousia but on the response in gratitude that the believer should make to all that Christ has achieved for him. The various sections are skilfully combined, and throughout there sounds the keynote of festive joy, so much so that on occasion the homilist bids his hearers to "leap" and even to join him "in a choral dance":

> For to-day our firstfruits ascended up to heaven, and taking up the flesh from us took possession of His Father's throne, in order that He might work reconciliation for His servants, destroy the old enmity and bestow freely upon the men of earth the peace of the powers above. For to-day he makes available to us a feast in honour of victory over the devil, He makes available the prizes, the crowns and the glory. . . . Stand amazed therefore, beloved, at the ingenuity of thy Master, and glorify Him who gives such things freely to thee; for the distinction of the gift surpassed the magnitude of the loss. See, we who were excluded from paradise have even been taken up into heaven itself: we who have been condemned to death have even been given immortality: we who were quarrelsome and despicable have even been counted worthy to be called sons, and not sons only but also heirs, and not heirs only but also coheirs with Christ. . . . Now the sting of death has been removed: now the victory of Hades has been destroyed: now the power of death has been brought to an end: now the enmity has been terminated: now the incessant war has ceased: men have been made like the angels. For the Lord of all has ascended, reconciling the Father to the generation of man. And that He ascended for this reason, hear what He says: "It is expedient for you that I go away, for if I go not away the Comforter will not come unto you." And as a sign of reconciliation He promises to give us the coming of the Paraclete . . . who was sent down to lead us into all truth.

[1] *P.G.* 52.793-96.

Our next sermon[1] bears traces of Chrysostom's style, but is doubtless unauthentic. Its sole merit lies in its brevity: it adds nothing to our understanding of the doctrine and perhaps the only feature worthy of note is to be found in the opening sentences, which reveal one of the ways in which the preacher, who, as frequently in these early sermons, announced no text, sought to captivate the interest of his congregation from the outset.

There are three inexpressible wonders not known from the beginning of time, which surpass the powers of nature, while they themselves remain calm and undisturbed—for a triple stranded cord is not quickly rent asunder. These are: the travail of an unwedded mother; the Resurrection from a three days' Passion; the Ascension of the flesh into heaven. For time knows that the barren bring forth, but not without marital intercourse: it knows that the dead are raised, but not unto eternal life: it knows that a prophet was taken up, but not into heaven, i.e. "as if", not into the true heaven.

There is, however, one of these sermons[2] that does adhere fairly closely to one Scriptural passage, viz. 1 Tim. 3: 16. Its author expounds each phrase in turn and at length comes to the words: "He was received up in glory." The effect of this event upon mankind is to mitigate the punishments they have suffered hitherto at the hands of God.

The earth awaited a Mediator who would make peace above and below. Of whom Paul said: "He is our peace, who destroyed the enmity in his flesh."[3] How many now are there more lascivious than the Sodomites? The air does not pour out fire upon them as previously. For the earth has received a Mediator of peace, and He went forth to the human race. How many now are more villainous than the generations of Noah? The heaven does not submerge them with a flood. How many are more ferocious than Cain? And God does not punish them as He punished Cain. For whenever He is provoked by us, seeing the firstfruits upon the joint throne, He is reconciled. Whenever He is stirred to anger by the intemperance of those below, seeing the sinless humanity at His right hand, He is placated. Whenever the race below deals wickedly and arouses His wrath, the

[1] *P.G.* 52.791-94. [2] *P.G.* 61.711-12. [3] Eph. 2: 14, 15.

kinsman of our race, sitting with Him, soothes His fury. Explaining this to thee, Paul says: "Christ is at the right hand of God and maketh intercession for us."[1]

Thus the Ascension is the necessary prelude to the intercession. He concludes, somewhat lamely, by affirming the reality of the Ascension, and quotes again the text upon which he has mainly based his address:

"Great is the mystery of godliness; He was seen of angels, believed on in the world, received up in glory." To Him be the glory for ever and ever. Amen.

The three following sermons need not detain us long. The first[2] is remarkable for its irrelevancies, and all that it has to say germane to our subject consists in the brief affirmation that through the Ascension human nature has been enthroned in heaven. The second,[3] which in some manuscripts is also assigned to Eusebius of Alexandria,[4] is equally reticent about the event it purports to commemorate; its author has a penchant for stringing together Scriptural quotations with little regard for context, so, e.g. he tells us that after forty days Jesus went to the Mount of Olives and delivered a final message to His disciples consisting of John 20: 21; Matt. 28: 19; Mark 16: 15; Matt. 10: 8; Luke 6: 28; and John 13: 35! His other remarks are confined to an exhortation to imitate Christ and to the statement that although Christ has ascended,[5] we must not grieve since He has not left us orphans,[6] but has sent the Holy Spirit to us. The third sermon[7] is described by its editor as *inepti Graeculi opus*—a work of tasteless little Greek. The sole feature of its contents of any interest is the emphasis upon the coeternity of the Son.

To-day our Master Christ ascended to the Father's throne. To-day He who was incarnate sat down with the Father; not that He was previously separated from Him, nor that He now sits with Him for the first time, for He always rested in the bosom of the Father, alone containing the Father and alone contained by the Father. For "I", He said, "am in the Father, and the

---

[1] Rom. 8: 34. [2] *P.G.* 62.727-30. [3] *P.G.* 64.45-48. [4] *P.G.* 86.422.
[5] He cites John 20: 17. [6] John 14: 18. [7] *P.G.* 52.801-2.

Father in me."[1] And the Word was in the Father and the Word was on earth, not descending and leaving the Father's bosom empty, nor ascending into heaven and leaving the earth empty of His presence; but both living along with men and sitting together with the Father, and both sitting together with the Father and not separated from men. For "behold", He says, "I am with you always, even unto the end of the age."[2]

The four sermons that remain of Chrysostom's *Spuria* have one thing in common, in addition to their being each an Ascension homily, and that is that they all reflect the Christological controversies of the fifth century, three of them bearing traces of the Nestorian and one of the Eutychian debate.

The first one[3] is clearly anti-Nestorian, and its author is therefore concerned to emphasize the unity of the two natures in Christ. To this he devotes much of his time, and so we find him declaring:

> It was not one who was seen by the prophets and another who passed His time with the apostles: nor one who was in the bosom of the Father and another who was judged under Pilate: nor one who was fixed to the Cross with nails and another who was borne by the Cherubim: nor one who was wrapped in a napkin by Joseph and another who grasps creation in the palms of His hands: nor one who was laid in the tomb and another who is hymned by the Seraphim: but He who is seated by the side of the Father and who in the womb of the Virgin was born without seed.

His teaching on the Ascension is confined to an elaboration of the theme that this feast celebrates the overthrow of the devil, who has hitherto held man in bondage. It commemorates the victory of "the Lord strong and mighty in battle"[4] who has harrowed Hell and set free the captives. "Every Christian festival", he says, "condemns the devil, but this one especially."

> The day of the Lord's Ascension makes the devil lament, but the faithful to brighten with joy. For now the pleasant spring comes forth and the beautiful young buds grow up: the vine shoots appear heavy with fruit: the olive trees come into flower: the fig trees bear early fruits: the closely sown fields are stirred by the west wind, imitating the billows of the sea: all things rejoice

[1] John 14: 11.   [2] Matt. 28: 20.   [3] *P.G.* 52.797-800.   [4] Ps. 24: 8.

with us at the Lord's Ascension. Come now and I will sing you the words of David, which he himself proclaimed for us on account of the Lord's Ascension: "O clap your hands, all ye people, shout unto God with the voice of triumph; the Lord has gone up with the sound of a trumpet"[1] to where He was. He has been received up whence He had not been separated. For He who descended is He who ascended above the heavens.

Our next sermon[2] is most probably by the same unknown author whose anti-Nestorian polemic we have just been considering. Since the heresy he has here in view, viz. Eutychianism, is not one which divides the two natures in Christ but so absorbs the manhood in the divinity that only one nature is said to persist, the homilist endeavours to demonstrate their duality. This sermon has a further interest in so far as it provides an excellent example of the type of allegorical exegesis of Scripture which was fast becoming the norm in the Church, despite the counter efforts of the Antiochene school. On both these counts then—its anti-Eutychianism and its exegetical method—it is a work worthy of citation in a more or less complete form, and only those few sections will be summarized that have no direct bearing on either of these two points.

Joyful is each festival of Christ's economy, and gladdening the hearts of the faithful. Joyful, too, is to-day's festival. Why it is joyful, we will show in what follows.

In six days, as it is written, God made all His works and rested the seventh day. Wherefore upon each of these days it was the good pleasure of the Word of God to seek and to save those that were perishing, and to become man; and according to the number of the days of creation, He has given us the feasts of His economy.

The first, we learn, is the Nativity; the second the Epiphany; the third the Crucifixion; and the fourth the Resurrection.

The fifth festival is the holy Ascension of the Lord into the heavens, which we now make our diligent study. It is the fifth of the festivals as it took place on the fifth day of the week. Wherefore we ought to keep the feast because on this day Christ

[1] Ps. 47: 1, 5.　　[2] P.G. 52.799-802.

led up the firstfruits of our nature, i.e. the flesh, into the heavens. Wherefore the apostle also said: "he raised us up with him, and made us to sit with him in the heavenly places in Christ Jesus."[1] Whence the author and inventor of all evil, the devil, on account of the tumour of pride and the cloud of arrogance, fell down, thither by the greatness of His beneficence Christ has restored man who had been cast out from paradise by the devil's most evil counsel. The present festival is therefore worthy of all honour.

The homilist then, in parenthesis as it were, tells us that the other two festivals, to make up the count of seven, are the descent of the Spirit which is the sixth, and seventh the day of resurrection which we all await. He continues:

Having therefore shown forth the seven festivals, let us return to the present one. We have an account of the present festival, I refer to the Ascension of Christ into the heavens, for David has said: "He bowed the heavens also and came down, and thick darkness was under his feet."[2] He thus clearly signified the coming of the Word from heaven to earth. He says that thick darkness was under His feet, signifying the clothing of the divinity by the flesh, so that His coming was unknown to many on account of the humility and meekness. For again the same prophet says: "Lord, thy way was in the sea, and thy paths in the great waters, and thy footsteps were not known."[3] For if they had known, the apostle says, "they would not have crucified the Lord of glory".[4] And again he says: "He rode upon a cherub; he flew swiftly upon the wings of the wind."[5] He says "upon a cherub", because when He was in the heavens with the Father He was borne upon the cherubim, and when He tarried with men on earth He did not in any way vacate the cherubic and heavenly throne. By "wings of the wind" he speaks darkly of the cloud upon which He also ascended, as it is written in the Acts of the Apostles: "and a cloud received him from their sight".[6] And below it adds: "as they were gazing into heaven as he went" wondering and ecstasy and a confused murmuring fell upon the apostles, for they were by nature mortals and not accustomed to beholding things of this kind; they were perplexed in mind.

But someone will say that Peter and James and John had previously seen the Transfiguration. They did indeed see previously the Lord transfigured and a cloud overshadowing Him,

---

[1] Eph. 2: 6.   [3] Ps. 77: 19.   [5] Ps. 18 :10.
[2] Ps. 18: 9.   [4] 1 Cor. 2: 8.   [6] Acts 1: 9.

but they did not see the cloud wrapt up into the air and the Master taken up into the heavens. That was a miracle and this was a miracle, but the one was more formidable than the other. This is more sublime than that, yet the power and mystery of the one God performed both. Then Moses and Elijah appeared to those with Peter speaking to Him; but now the cherubic throne, i.e. the invisible power, standing upon the hidden cloud, snatched away the Lord while He was talking with His servants. Then Peter boldly answered: "Lord, it is good for us to be here: and let us make three tabernacles; one for thee, and one for Moses, and one for Elijah."[1] Now indeed not one of the disciples can utter a word nor open his mouth, but stricken with great fear they were confounded. But the Scripture adds: "and behold, two men stood by them in white apparel; which also said." Nor was this superfluous for these men being dressed in white is an indication of a great festival. But what did they say? "Ye men of Galilee, why stand ye looking into heaven? The vast miracle terrifies you; have you forgotten when He said: 'I go to my Father and your Father, and to my God and your God'?[2] Was it not on account of this that He said to you: 'I leave you not orphans'[3] and again: 'My peace I give unto you, my peace I leave with you'?[4] Did He not promise the Paraclete, i.e. the Spirit, to you? This Jesus who has been taken up into heaven shall so come in like manner as ye beheld him going into heaven. So He will come with the clouds of heaven, with glory and much power: so He will come in His season when about to judge the world in righteousness. For the Father gave Him all judgment. Do you not remember that when He was with you, He said: 'All authority hath been given unto me in heaven and on earth'?"[5] Then the apostles came to themselves and returned, praising and blessing God and awaiting the divine gift, i.e. the advent of the Holy Spirit. And so was fulfilled that which is said in the Psalms: "God went up with a shout; the Lord with the sound of the trumpet."[6]

Clearly the prophet there signified the duality of the natures in the economy in Christ. To the same effect, Thomas also, after the Resurrection of the Lord, felt His side and cried: "My Lord and my God."[7] "God went up with a shout; the Lord with the sound of the trumpet." "With a shout" because with an incessant voice they send up the thrice holy hymn to God, and how He was received up on the cherubic throne we have shown before. "With the sound of the trumpet", i.e. of an archangel,

[1] Mark 9: 5.   [2] John 20: 17.   [3] John 14: 18.   [4] John 14: 27.
[5] Matt. 28: 18.   [6] Ps. 47: 5.   [7] John 20: 28.

proclaiming His Ascension into the heavens. But also the Holy
Spirit, to those powers above, proclaimed with a ruling voice:
"Lift up the gates, O ye powers, and be ye lift up, ye everlasting
doors, and let the King of glory come in."[1] But the powers say:
"Who is this King of glory?" To whom the Spirit: "The Lord
strong and mighty; the Lord mighty in battle." For He overcame the enemy; He armed Himself against the tyranny of the
devil in a human body, and extinguished his fiery darts, and
being nailed to the Cross, and having tasted death, being immortal, He spoiled Hades, and, being manifested as a victor,
rose from the dead. Then, having converted the erring sheep,
behold He comes up bearing him upon His shoulders to the
ninety and nine who had not gone astray, who were in the
mountains, i.e. who were feeding in the heavens. "The Lord
strong and mighty; the Lord mighty in battle." And again he
says: "The Lord of the powers, he is the King of glory." The
powers, therefore, as they had heard their Lord, cried out the
word of glory with one accord and received the Lord with joy
and led Him to the highest throne. And that was fulfilled which
was spoken by David: "The Lord saith unto my lord, Sit thou
at my right hand, until I make thine enemies the footstool of
thy feet."[2] O heretics [to which nature was this addressed, was
it not to] that flesh assumed from us and animated from the
holy Virgin? Let them be ashamed therefore that confess one
nature in Christ. For it is evident that the divine nature was
joined eternally to the Three of majesty. May Christ our God
count us all worthy of His eternal Kingdom, to whom be the
glory and the power with the undefiled Father, together with
the Holy Spirit for ever and ever. Amen.

The Eutychian controversy succeeded the Nestorian, to
which it was indeed largely a reaction, but we must now return
in time to the period of the latter to examine the last two
Ascension sermons attributed to Chrysostom. These are to be
found in the *Codex Berolinensis 77*, and have recently been
edited for the first time by P. C. Baur.[3] Their editor maintains that they both belong to the period of Christological
debate immediately prior to the Council of Ephesus, which
met in 431, and further, that both stem from the Antiochene

[1] Ps. 24: 7.
[2] Ps. 110: 1.
[3] "Drei Unedierte Festpredigten", *Traditio*, IX, 1953, pp. 101-26. One of these
three sermons is not concerned with the Ascension.

school of theology. One of them he considers to be possibly by Nestorius himself, although, as he admits, this ascription cannot be more than tentative.

To Nestorius, if he be the author,[1] the Ascension is the crown of all the Church's festivals, since it is the festival of Christ's victory.

> For now the Master has taken up the firstfruits of our bodies. Now we celebrate the Lord's Ascension by which He has placed our nature in the heavenlies. For He raised up His temple which God had indwelt and, when He passed over the great expanse of air, took with Him His own vesture, filling all things by His divine nature.

So that nature which is of the same stock as our own, and which was the covering of the invisible Godhead, has been taken up by that Godhead into the heavenlies, and the purpose of this is "in order to make heaven passable to those upon earth". Hence this festival proclaims the success of the mission of the Son on man's behalf.

The second Antiochene sermon[2] has in view the Jewish opponents of Christianity who, amongst other things, denied the Ascension. The homilist therefore argues, on the one hand, that twelve witnesses should be sufficient for any one, especially for the Jew who accepts the ruling that "at the mouth of two witnesses, or at the mouth of three witnesses, shall a matter be established",[3] and, on the other hand, that the Ascension is prefigured in the Old Testament.

> Let us hear therefore what Daniel said, prophesying concerning the Lord's Ascension: "I saw", he says, "and behold, there came with the clouds of heaven one like unto a son of man."[4] For the Second Advent shall also be like the Ascension which is previous to it, as also the Book of Acts signifies. . . . Notice carefully, I beg, how the prophet wisely makes known the hypostases. "Behold", he says, "there came with the clouds of heaven one like unto a son of man, and he came even to the ancient of days." Let us also notice what is the conclusion of the prophecy: "And to him", it says, "there was given dominion, and glory, and a kingdom." Notice carefully to whom it says dominion was given:

---

[1] "Drei Unedierte Festpredigten", *Traditio*, IX, 1953, pp. 116-19.
[2] *Ibid.*, pp. 122-24.   [3] Deut. 19: 15.   [4] Dan. 7: 13.

not to the Word who always was with God the Father, for He has dominion for ever, but to the ensouled body from the Virgin which was united to Him; for He is God and perfect man. To him there was given "dominion, and glory, and authority, and a kingdom" according to the economy of the flesh.

This festival then is the occasion of the presentation to the Father of the firstfruits of that nature which had been assumed. It is the occasion of the offering to the Father of the sacrifice for the whole world. It is the occasion when man, "who had been banished from paradise through the disobedience of Adam, through the Second Adam has gone up not to the paradise of earth but into heaven itself".

The uncompromising opponent of the Antiochene school and of Nestorius in particular was Cyril of Alexandria. No sermon of his on the Ascension survives, but from scattered references there would seem no reason to suppose that on this subject at least he differed from Nestorius. Indeed, his comments on Ps. 47[1] are all but identical with the principal ideas we have noted in the two preceding homilies.

When He had completed the economy for us, He ascended into the heavens to God the Father, being, as it were, the firstfruits of humanity renewed unto incorruption, for in Christ we have been made rich. . . . He ascended into the heavens in order to appear before the face of God for us. But there was in heaven a strange spectacle, man distinguished with the glory belonging to God and elevated above all expectation. It was therefore necessary for the powers above to be instructed by the Holy Spirit that He who was God by nature, even the Word of God, had been made man.

It is then, according to Cyril, the Incarnate Word who is glorified in heaven. As man He is one with us; as Son He is consubstantial with the Father. As man He appears before the face of God for us in order to bring us in Himself to God; as Son He sits at the right hand of the Father to bestow the glory of adoption on all humanity. We can therefore say, with the author of Ephesians, that we also are seated in the heavenlies in Christ Jesus, since what belongs to the Son has become the

[1] *P.G.* 69.1053. He also interprets Ps. 24 (*ibid.*, 845) and Dan. 7: 13 (*P.G.* 70.1461) of the Ascension, but refers Ps. 68 (*P.G.* 69.1152) to the Crucifixion.

endowment of His human nature in which we are included.[1]
Cyril was not the first nor was he the last to oppose Nestori-
anism. Amongst those who had preceded him and had indeed
played no small part in inaugurating the controversy was
Proclus, bishop designate of Cyzicus and afterward bishop of
Constantinople (434-46). On Lady Day, 429, Proclus delivered
a panegyric "on the Virgin mother of God",[2] which was in
effect an attack upon the teaching of Nestorius's domestic
chaplain, Anastasius. Nestorius defended his subordinate's
views, which he shared, in a series of sermons, and it was the
circulation of these that brought Cyril into the fray. Amongst
Proclus's own sermons there is one preached on Ascension
Day.[3] It contains, as might be expected, an explicit affirmation of the Theotokos position, but its main theme is the contrast between the pitiful condition of man, fallen through the
transgression of Adam, and the glorious inheritance now
opened to him through the Ascension of the second Adam.

> Blessed be God! The nature of creation is divided into heaven
> and earth; yet to-day the grace, which unites that which is
> divided, does not permit me to see the division. For who will
> say that heaven and earth are divided when they see my image
> reigning both below and above? But below we are still tyran-
> nized by corruption and wasting away in graves we give joy to
> the devil; yet whenever he looks up into the heavens, he lays
> aside his joy, seeing above the resurrection root of the dead
> below. He sees Him, whom he delivered to the Cross below,
> clothed in a body in the heavens and he is distressed with fear,
> not understanding the power. Oh what profit outweighing loss!
> Having lost paradise, we have gained heaven. Having been
> brought down, we have been led up into heaven,[4] and we stand
> higher on account of the transgression. Wounded within para-
> dise, we have found healing without. Having been killed by the
> tree of life, we have been made whole by the Christ-killing tree:
> having been sunk in the port, we have returned to life in the
> waves of the sea. Where is thy mischief, pirate? The Cross which

---

[1] *In Ioh. Evang.*, 14.2, 3 (*P.G.* 74.181-84); *In Ep. ad Heb.*, 9.24 (*ibid.*, 985).

[2] *P.G.* 65.679-92.

[3] *P.G.* 65.833-37. Photius, who transcribed the exordium, attributed it to Nilus (*P.G.* 79.1497-1500). I have shown reason elsewhere for regarding this as a mis-attribution and for accepting the authorship of Proclus ("Proclus and Pseudo-Nilus", *H.T.R.*, XLIX, 1956, pp. 179-81).

[4] The lacuna is supplied from Photius (*P.G.* 79.1497D).

thou didst make fast by the pilot has become the rudder of ship-wrecked nature, and it steers us to the heavenly harbour.

The bishop continues to stress the darkness of the Cruci-fixion and the glory of the Ascension "when the bodily nature was elevated" in the presence of the angelic hosts, "until He was received into the Father's bosom who had never departed from the Father". So this festival is an occasion for rejoicing.

Therefore, sing a strain, O earth, instead of a dirge. That nature on whose behalf thou wast troubled has been translated into heaven; thy kindred has been transplanted into the heavenlies. Look up to-day into the air to the second Adam: gaze into the heavens which greets thine own.

The same keynote of joy sounds throughout a fragment of a second sermon[1] for Ascension Day which has been preserved by Photius.[2] Its main interest lies in the typological use of Enoch and Elijah, who are said to "have sketched the mystery of immortality" and so to have provided mankind with a hope of resurrection which has at last been realized through Christ. Human nature now "reigns together with the Godhead. . . . The Creator has raised creation on high together with His divinity, and has settled it in the Father's bosom."

The same exegesis of the Enoch passage, viz. that his trans-lation was to provide hope for the "athletes of godliness" in the period before the Resurrection of Christ, is found in the writings of Theodoret of Cyrus[3] (423-58), who also taught that through the Ascension "our firstfruits" was taken up into heaven.[4] Theodoret had been a fellow student with Nestorius and entered the lists against Cyril and his supporters, only to be deposed eventually by the adherents of the opposite heresy, Eutychianism, who packed the Robber Synod at Ephesus (449) under Cyril's successor at Alexandria, Dioscorus. Amongst those who acquiesced in this sentence was Basil of Seleucia in Isauria; he was later, at Chalcedon, to change sides and concur

---

[1] P.G. 79.1500-1. There is a third fragment (ibid., 1500), but its contents are insignificant.

[2] Photius ascribes this extract also to Nilus, but it is probably from the pen of Proclus; see my article, H.T.R., loc. cit.

[3] Quaest. select. in Gen., 45 (P.G. 80.145).

[4] In ps. xxiii (P.G. 80.1033-36). Ps. 68 is also applied by him to the Ascension (ibid., 1388).

in the condemnation of Eutyches. To Basil there belongs in all probability a sermon on the Ascension which has been preserved amongst the writings of Athanasius.[1] It bears evident marks of that lack of simplicity and naturalness and that profusion of rhetorical ornament for which Photius was content to censure him.[2] So Basil declares:

> He who was mocked by the Jews sits at the right hand of the Father above the cherubim and is hymned by throngs of angels. He who had His head crowned with Jewish thorns is bound with a diadem of divine dignity. How often has the lyre of David sounded, predicting these things by the divine afflatus. "The Lord saith unto my lord, Sit at my right hand, until I make thine enemies the footstool of thy feet." Now indeed these musical notes have become realities, and what once, in songs, he desired to see, to-day he sees in deed; and heaven became conducive to melodies when it took on its back Him who is remembered by the minstrel.

Then, after painting a picture of the fall of man and the triumph of the devil, still in sophistic vein, Basil continues:

> God showed mercy upon the erring image in creation. What does He do therefore? He fashions again a second Adam, out of nature raising up a patron of nature; and borrowing earth from a Virgin, He gives shape to a new embryo according to a truer image in Himself. He fashions and it remains, and constructing a garment in the womb, as in a royal chamber, He clothes the image in order to veil the nudity of the image. For He displayed Him stronger than deceit and superior to sin; immortal even after death; a deliverer from the tombs who was in a tomb; and crowning Him with immortality, He brought Him back to-day to the heavens, bestowing a decoration upon the whole creation, i.e. the firstfruits of nature.

At last, it seems, we are to hear about the Ascension—but no! the bishop turns next to Enoch and Elijah, and, like Proclus and Theodoret, interprets their translations as being the means of preserving hope to mankind under sentence of death. He then directs the attention of his hearers to a problem which, to judge from the number of times it was discussed,

---

[1] *P.G.* 28.1091-1100. [2] *Bibl.*, ed. Hoeschelius, 1653, col. 377.

both before and after Basil, presented a constant difficulty, viz. how to reconcile the statement in the Fourth Gospel that no one has ascended into heaven save He who descended from heaven with the Old Testament record of Elijah's ascension. Basil rests his answer, like Cyril of Jerusalem, upon a literal interpretation of the LXX rendering of this incident, which states that Elijah was taken up "as" (ὡς) into heaven, i.e. not into the heaven of heavens itself; therefore "the servant has not equal honour with the Master". But Basil has not yet finished with typology.

God commands the writer Moses to become the depicter of creation and He orders Him to imitate the Creator through the Tabernacle, so that the external form of the Tabernacle might be a copy of the earth and the things on the earth, but the inner portion of the Tabernacle, cut off by curtains. . . . He assigned to that part which is not visible. And so ordering the image of heaven and earth to be outlined by figures, and rendering the innermost sanctuary inaccessible to men, He appoints a way into the most sacred parts for the high priest alone; and so He brought it about that the entrance of the high priest might be a figure of the Ascension into heaven; then the people, seeing heaven open in a figure, and only the high priest venturing to penetrate into the inviolate parts, might grow accustomed to the spectacle and not be made hostile to the wonders. Of these things Paul, the teacher of the world, reminded the Jews, declaring by letter: "Now these things having been thus prepared, the priests go in continually into the first tabernacle, accomplishing the services; but into the second the high priest alone, once in the year. But Christ having come a high priest of the good things to come, through the greater and more perfect tabernacle, not made with hands, that is to say, not of this creation, nor yet through the blood of goats and calves, but through his own blood, entered in once for all into the holy place, having obtained eternal redemption. For Christ entered not into a holy place made with hands, like in pattern to the true; but into heaven itself, now to appear before the face of God for us."[1] Thus God knew both how to confound the unbelieving with types and to confirm wonders by wonders. So Christ went up into heaven: so He fulfilled the types by the work of truth. It was necessary therefore to join the Ascension to the Resurrection of the Saviour and for the victor over Hades to occupy heaven.

[1] Heb. 9: 6, 7, 11, 12, 24.

Basil concludes his piece of not insignificant oratory with a description of the Ascension and a proclamation of the Second Coming.

In view of his personal history, Basil was probably a wise man to eschew mention of Christology in this sermon. Diadochus, on the other hand, bishop of Photice in Epirus (c. 450), made his Ascension sermon,[1] which is the last of these early Greek homilies to be reviewed in this section, the occasion for a sustained attack on the monophysite teaching.

The homily is skilfully constructed in two halves with a short bridge section between them. The first part is devoted to affirming the fact of the Ascension with the aid of copious citations from the Psalms, leading to the conclusion: "He was taken up and exalted above the heavens, wholly Lord, for having descended first to earth He ascended into the heavens." Diadochus then states that the meaning of these prophetic words which he has quoted has been drawn out by the apostles under the inspiration of the Holy Spirit, and in particular the nature of the Incarnation. So, in the second part of his discourse he proceeds to utilize the Ascension, like Novatian in the West two centuries before him, to prove, against Eutychianism, the twofold nature of the one Person. Scripture states that:

He was taken up and that He ascended in order that we might believe that He is both God and man in one Person ($\dot{\epsilon}\nu$ $\mu\iota\hat{q}$ $\dot{\upsilon}\pi o\sigma\tau\acute{a}\sigma\epsilon\iota$). On account of His divinity He ascended, and on account of the body He is said to have been taken up, i.e. assumed. Wherefore this ought to be noted by everyone that He who descended is the same as He who ascended far above the heavens that He might fill all things with His goodness.[2] . . . Wherefore the prophets proclaimed the Lord and did not mix the form of His Incarnation into one nature ($\phi\acute{\upsilon}\sigma\iota\nu$), as certain suggest, but uttered some words apposite to God, concerning His divinity, and others appropriate to man, concerning His body, in order that they might clearly teach that He who ascended . . . is of the Father; but that He who was of the Virgin remains man, being one in form and one in Person ($\dot{\epsilon}\nu$ $\dot{\upsilon}\pi o\sigma\tau\acute{a}\sigma\epsilon\iota$). For the incorporeal, giving Himself a form by the assumption of the flesh, visibly ascended whence invisibly He had descended to be made flesh. . . . As God He supports all things by His will; as

[1] P.G. 65.1141-48.　　[2] Eph. 4: 10.

man He was supported by the cloud in order that He might not deny the laws of the nature which He had taken. Wherefore the saints shall be caught up into the cloud, as the divine Paul taught us[1] when the expected Lord comes upon a cloud. For that which is fitting to God when He became incarnate on account of the body is also fitting to those who are being deified on account of the riches of His grace, when God wishes to make men gods. Let no one suppose therefore that the denseness of human nature, which we saw the holy Word of God unite to Himself, that this will be changed into the resplendent and glorious substance of God, since indeed the truth of both natures subsisted in Him unconfused. But it was not in order to make His form visible that the glorious Lord was incarnate, but in order that by His participation He might destroy for ever the evil disposition sown in us by the serpent. So the Incarnation of the Word changed the disposition but not the nature, in order that we might be deprived of the memory of evil and be clothed with the love of God. Not that we might be changed into what we were not, but that we might be renewed with glory to that which we were. Now to Him be the glory and the power, to Him who descended invisibly from heaven and ascended visibly into heaven, who was before the ages and is now and ever shall be. Amen.

2. *The Early Latin Homilists*

Amongst the early Latin homilists Augustine of Hippo unquestionably has pride of place. His pre-eminence rests not only upon the fact that his Ascension sermons are the first extant, but also upon the profundity of theological thought that they contain. Preaching was an activity in which Augustine displayed considerable zeal, often addressing the people on five successive days and sometimes twice in one day. He was indeed the Chrysostom of the West, although the oratorical style of these two men differed considerably. Where Chrysostom was diffuse, Augustine was brief: where the one indulged in digressions and the use of lively imagery, the other adhered closely to a well-defined theme, avoiding examples and similes and depending for his effect upon unadorned simplicity and logical power. The result is that while Chrysostom is patent of summary without loss, Augustine is so succinct that frequently only full quotation will do justice to his content.

[1] 1 Thess. 4: 17.

Augustine's teaching on the Ascension[1] centres in four main points, to which he returns again and again. These are: first, the interpretation of John 3: 13;[2] second, and closely connected with this, the doctrine of *totus Christus*, the whole Christ, consisting of Head and members, the latter participating in the former's Ascension in virtue of their unity; third, the nature of the bodily Ascension, and, fourth, the significance of the number forty in reference to the period between the Resurrection and the Ascension.

Augustine considers the first point, viz. the meaning of John 3: 13, in an early work, *De Agone Christi*, written in 396 or 397.

> Let us not listen to those who deny that our Lord raised His body with Him into heaven, and refer to what is written in the Gospel: "No man hath ascended into heaven, but he that descended out of heaven", and say that because the body did not descend from heaven, it could not have ascended into heaven. For they are without understanding, since the body did not ascend into heaven, because the Lord ascended but the body did not ascend, but was raised into heaven, being raised by Him who ascended. For if anyone descended, the grace of the Lord unclothed from the heights when He descended clothed Himself, and being clothed ascended again, and we say rightly: "No man hath ascended into heaven except He who descended." Let us not consider the clothing which He raised with Himself, but we say that He alone ascended who was clothed.[3]

This theme is connected by Augustine with the *totus Christus* conception in his third homily on the Ascension.[4]

> For to-day, as you hear, brethren, our Lord Jesus Christ ascended into heaven. Let our hearts ascend with Him. Let us hear the apostle's words: "If then ye were raised together with Christ, seek the things that are above, where Christ is, seated on the right hand of God. Set your mind on the things that are above, not on the things that are upon the earth."[5] For when He

[1] The number of Augustine's Ascension sermons is too great and their interrelationship too complex to be compressed into a footnote; they are set out in Table F on p. 190.

[2] In only one Ascension sermon (Lambot, *Rev. Bénéd.*, LI, 1939, pp. 25-27) does Augustine interpret Phil. 2: 6-11. He regards "emptied Himself" as synonymous with "taking the form of a servant" and adds "the kenosis involved acceptance of humiliation not loss of sublimity".

[3] 25 (*P.L.* 40.304).   [4] *Sermo* 263 (*P.L.* 38.1209-12).   [5] Col. 3: 1, 2.

ascended, He did not depart from us; so we ourselves are now
with Him there, although that which is promised us has not yet
been accomplished in our bodies. He has now been exalted above
the heavens. But the perfect and angelic habitation in the
heavenlies is not to be despaired of by us on that account, because He said: "No man hath ascended into heaven, but he that
descended out of heaven, even the Son of man, which is in
heaven." But this is said on account of the unity by which He
is our Head and we are His body. When He ascended into
heaven, we were not separated from Him. He who descended
from heaven does not grudge us heaven, but proclaims: "Be my
members, if you wish to ascend into heaven."[1] By this therefore
we are strengthened; by this we are enflamed in all our prayers.
Let us meditate upon earth on the fact that we are reckoned
together in heaven. . . . Let no one be disturbed by the deceitful
heretics as to how the Lord descended without a body when
He ascended with a body, as if this were contrary to the words:
"no man hath ascended into heaven, but he that descended out
of heaven." How, they say, can the body which did not descend
from heaven ascend into heaven? But this refers to a Person[2]
and not to the bodily appearance of a person. He descended
without the covering of a body; He ascended with the covering
of a body. Yet no one, save He that descended, ascended. For
if He joined us to Himself as His members, so that He might be
the same when we had been conjoined with Him, how much
more should that body, which He assumed from the Virgin, be
unable to have a distinct personality in Him? . . . So no one,
except Christ, has ascended into heaven, because no one, except
Christ, has descended from heaven; albeit He descended without a body and ascended with a body, and we shall ascend, not
by our virtue but by our union with Him. "For the twain shall
become one flesh. This mystery is great: but I speak in regard
of Christ and of the church."[3] Wherefore He Himself says: "So
that they are no more twain, but one flesh."[4]

In his fifth sermon on the Ascension,[5] Augustine reiterates
in a sentence the same teaching: "The going before of the

1 cp. Augustine's teaching that the individual believer will undergo not only
resurrection but also ascension, Guelf. XX (G. Morin, *Miscellanea Agostiniana*,
I, 1930, p. 506).
2 cp. *Biblioth. Casin.*, II.76 (Morin, *op. cit.*, pp. 413-15).
3 Eph. 5: 31, 32.
4 Matt. 19: 6.
5 *Sermo* 265 (*P.L.* 38.1218-24), preached at Carthage, Ascension Day, 418.

Head is the hope of the members."[1] And again, in *Sermo* 294, *De Baptismo parvulorum contra Pelagianos*:[2]

All who are reborn ascend into heaven through the grace of God: and "no man hath ascended into heaven, but he that descended out of heaven, even the Son of man, which is in heaven". Whence this? Because all who are reborn are made His members. Both Christ alone born of Mary is one Christ, and the Head with the body is one Christ. He wishes therefore to say this: "No man has ascended except He who descended. Christ therefore has ascended. If thou wishest to ascend, be in the body of Christ. If thou wishest to ascend, be a member of Christ." "For as the body is one, and hath many members, and all the members of the body, being many, are one body; so also is Christ."[3]

The same teaching is affirmed by Augustine in his 91st sermon:[4]

Dost thou wish to ascend? Hold fast Him who ascends. For thou canst not raise thyself by thyself. Because "No man hath ascended into heaven, but he that descended out of heaven, even the Son of man, which is in heaven." If no one has ascended except He who descended, and moreover He Himself is the Son of man, our Lord Jesus, dost thou wish to ascend? Be a member of Him who alone has ascended. For the Head with the rest of the members is one man. And since no one can ascend except he who had been made a member in His body, the saying is fulfilled: "No man hath ascended but he that descended."

Finally, before we leave Augustine's teaching on the *totus Christus*, there is this passage from *Sermo* 144,[5] which contains in a small compass the pith of his doctrine:

How then is Christ alone [in His Ascension]? Is it not because Christ with all His members is one, just as a head with its body? But what is His body save the Church? As the apostle Paul says: "Now ye are the body of Christ, and severally members thereof."[6] When therefore we had fallen and on account of us He had descended, what is this "no man hath ascended but he

---

[1] *P.L.* 38.1219.
[2] *Sermo* 294.10 (*P.L.* 38.1341).
[3] 1 Cor. 12: 12.

[4] 6 (*P.L.* 38.570).
[5] 4 (*P.L.* 38.789-90).
[6] 1 Cor. 12: 27.

that descended" save that no one ascended except that which is made one with Him and, as it were, united as a limb in the body of Him that descended? So He said to His disciples: "apart from me ye can do nothing."[1] On the one hand He is one with the Father, and on the other one with us. He is one with the Father because there is one substance of Father and Son. He is one with the Father because "being in the form of God, he did not think it a thing to be grasped to be on an equality with God". But He was made one with us because "he emptied himself, taking the form of a servant".[2] He was made one with us according to the seed of Abraham in whom all nations shall be blessed; which, when he recalled it, the apostle said: "He saith not, And to seeds, as of many; but as of one, And to thy seed, which is Christ."[3] And because we also belong to that which is Christ, having been incorporated together and holding to the Head, Christ is one; and because he also says to us: "then are ye Abraham's seed, heirs according to promise."[4] For if the seed of Abraham is one and that one seed of Abraham is only to be understood of Christ, we also are the seed of Abraham; the whole therefore, i.e. the Head and the body, is one Christ.

Our third point for consideration is the nature of the bodily Ascension—a subject which Augustine treats with care and fitting reticence in his *De Fide et Symbolo*, another early work, written in 393.

It is wont to give offence to certain parties, either impious Gentiles or heretics, that we should believe in the assumption of an earthly body into heaven. The Gentiles, however, for the most part, set themselves diligently to ply us with the arguments of the philosophers, to the effect that there cannot possibly be anything earthly in heaven. For they do not know our Scriptures, nor do they understand how it has been said: "It is sown a natural body; it is raised a spiritual body."[5] For it is not expressed thus, as if the body were turned into spirit; inasmuch as at present too our body, which is called animal (*animale*), has not been turned into soul and become soul (*anima*). But by a spiritual body is meant one which has been made subject to spirit in such wise that it is adapted to a heavenly habitation, all frailty and every earthly blemish having been changed and converted into heavenly purity and stability. . . . But the question as to where and in what manner the Lord's body is in

[1] John 15: 5. [2] Phil. 2: 6, 7. [3] Gal. 3: 16. [4] Gal. 3: 29. [5] I Cor. 15: 44.

heaven is one which it would be altogether over curious and superfluous to prosecute. Only we must believe that it is in heaven. For it pertains not to our frailty to investigate the secret things of heaven, but it does pertain to our faith to hold elevated and honourable sentiments on the subject of the dignity of the Lord's body.[1]

The fourth point on which Augustine expressed himself not infrequently relates to the forty-day period of the Resurrection appearances. In his fourth sermon on the Ascension,[2] which otherwise contains nothing of interest, he discourses on the appropriateness of the number forty, referring to the time that the ark was on the waters, that Moses spent on the holy mount, that the Israelites wandered in the wilderness and that Jesus fasted in the desert. In his *Quaestionum in Heptateuchum libri septem*[3] (*c.* 419), he alludes again to Moses and to Jesus' fast, adding Elijah's journey in the wilderness and the forty days' moratorium allowed the Ninevites for repentance. In his third Ascension homily[4] he finds allegory even in numbers: Christ came to fulfil the Law in which there are ten commandments; there are also four corners of the earth whither the grace of Christ must spread, *ergo* $10 \times 4 = 40$.

Finally, we need to note the distinction that Augustine makes between the Resurrection and the Ascension—a distinction emphasized particularly in his first[5] and third[6] Ascension homilies. He begins the former, which is mainly devoted to the subject of hope, with the statement: "The Resurrection of the Lord is our hope; the Ascension of the Lord is our glorification." He begins the latter with the words:

> The glorification of our Lord Jesus Christ, when He rose and ascended, is completed. We have celebrated His Resurrection at the Pascha; to-day, we celebrate His Ascension. Each day is a festive occasion for us. For He rose in order to display to us an example of resurrection, and He ascended in order to protect us from above.

[1] *De Fide et Symb.*, 6 (*P.L.* 40.187-88).
[2] *Sermo* 264 (*P.L.* 38.1212-18).
[3] I.169 (*P.L.* 34.594-95).
[4] *Sermo* 263.4 (*P.L.* 38.1211-12).
[5] *Ibid.*, 261 (*P.L.* 38.1202-7), preached at Carthage on Ascension Day, May 14, 397.
[6] *Ibid.*, 263 (*P.L.* 38.1209-12). The second Ascension homily (*Sermo* 262—*P.L.* 38.1207-9) has little to say of the Ascension beyond affirming its occurrence.

The renown of Augustine, like that of Chrysostom, was such
that a number of further Ascension sermons were published
under his name, although they did not emanate from his
hand. Amongst those that will be considered later[1] is one of
which Faustus of Riez was the author, and another that was
written by Caesarius of Arles. There are two others which are
also attributed to Fulgentius of Ruspe[2] (468-533), though
neither he nor Augustine would seem to have been responsible
for them. There remain three more, of which the first[3] is undistinguished; the second[4] is mainly devoted to the theme that
the Ascension completes the work of redemption; the third[5]
alone merits any attention. Its author, probably not Augustine,[6]
has imbibed much of the great Doctor's thought, and his first
section is no more than an expansion of the theme of hope
with which Augustine's own first Ascension homily is concerned.[7] His second section finds us also on familiar ground:

Now our Head has raised us up in His body; where He is the
members are also. Because where the Head went before the members followed after. He is the Head: we are the members. He is
in heaven: we are on earth. Is He, as it were, far from us? If
you ask space, He is far away; but ask love, He is with us. For
if He were not with us He would not have said in the Gospel:
"Lo, I am with you alway, even unto the end of the world."[8]
If He is not with us, we lie when we say: "The Lord be with
you." Did He not proclaim from heaven, when Saul was per-
secuting not Him but His saints, His servants (or, I may say,
His family, His members): "Saul, Saul, why persecutest thou
me?"[9] Behold I am here in heaven, and thou art on earth, and
thou persecutest me. Why me? because thou persecutest my
members. I am there through my members. . . . He therefore
by whom heaven and earth were made, on account of him whom
He had fashioned from the earth, descended to earth and raised
up earth to heaven.

[1] See below, pp. 145, 155.
[2] Augustine, *Sermones* 180, 181 (*P.L.* 39.2085-87) are identical with Fulgentius,
Sermones 48, 49 (*P.L.* 65.914-16). The second is insignificant; the first has the
interesting comment: "May Thy death be our ransom money, Thine Ascension
our pledge (*pignus*), lest altogether swallowed up by grief, we, whom Thou hast
raised from the pains of hell, should be overwhelmed" (915).
[3] *Sermo* 178 (*P.L.* 39.2083-84).
[4] *Ibid.*, 179 (*P.L.* 39.2084-85).
[5] *Ibid.*, 395 (*P.L.* 39.1716-17).
[6] Note the extended use of similes in the first section.
[7] *Sermo* 261 (*P.L.* 38.1202-7).   [8] Matt. 28: 20.   [9] Acts 9: 4.

The mantle of preaching, in Latin at least, and on the subject of the Ascension in particular, fell next upon Maximus, bishop of Turin in Northern Italy. Over two hundred of his homilies and sermons remain,[1] and indeed we know more of his thought than we do of his life, since the only two certain facts are that he was present at a synod of Milan in 451 and in November 465 assisted at a Roman synod. His style is energetic and robust, and though at times his language is unnecessarily ornate, his use of certain vivid metaphors is perhaps the most important of his contributions to the doctrine of the Ascension. This is evident from the first homily[2] we shall review, of which the main burden is the development of two images of the ascending Christ. The first is derived from Ps. 103: 5: "thy youth is renewed like the eagle." There is a three-point analogy between the eagle and Christ, according to Maximus. The eagle soars up to the skies, so Christ has penetrated the heights of heaven. The eagle disdains the filth of earth and enjoys the wholesomeness of the pure upper air, so Christ has left the dregs of earthly sin and has mounted up to that most holy place where the pure life is enjoyed. The eagle frequently swoops down and bears off as spoils that which belongs to another, so Christ has descended and taken up man who had been the captive of the devil. This reference to spoils and captives leads to the second image, used originally by Ambrose, viz. that of a victor's triumphal procession.

"He ascended", it says, "on high; he led captivity captive." How well the prophet describes the Lord's triumph. It was customary, as they say, for the procession of the captives to precede the chariot of the triumphal kings, but the glorious captivity did not precede the Lord when He went into heaven and was not led before the conveyance but itself conveyed the Saviour. For by a certain mystery, while the Son of God carried up the son of man to heaven, captivity itself both carried and was carried. But it says: "He gave gifts to men." This is the sign of victory, for after a triumph the victor always bestows gifts, and sitting upon his throne presents that which produces delight to the slaves. So Christ the Lord, after His triumph over the devil, sitting at the right hand of the Father, to-day bestowed gifts upon His

---

[1] A number have been much corrupted by later copyists.
[2] *Hom.* 60 *de Temp.* (*P.L.* 57.367-70).

disciples, not gold coins nor silver but heavenly gifts of the Holy Spirit.

So the Ascension marks the completion of Christ's redemptive work; then

> He received the government of the earth and the eternal rule of heaven, as He said Himself: "all things have been delivered unto me of my Father in heaven and earth".[1] . . . He has gathered man . . . and has made the exile from paradise a citizen of heaven. Wherefore, beloved, our rejoicing should be great, because those whom the tempter expelled, the Saviour has lifted up, and those whom the service of the devil had conquered, the grace of Christ has set free.[2]

The next sermon[3] to come from the pen of Maximus is notable for its brevity and for the compactness of its argument. He begins:

> The mystery of the Lord's Ascension, dear brethren, has ordained to-day's festival. Let us rejoice that the Only-begotten of God came to earth for the redemption of all and let us be glad that He entered heaven for our immortality. For this is the truth of our saving faith that we believe in His Passion and do not deny His glory. Nor indeed is the essence of the miracle such that He who came from heaven returned to heaven, but that He brought to the Father the manhood which He had assumed from the earth. . . . The earth rejoices when it sees its Redeemer reigning in the heavens; heaven is glad because it has not lost its God which it had, and has received the manhood which it had not. The earth rejoices at the Son of God having descended from heaven, but heaven is glad no less at the Son of man having ascended from the earth. "He sits", it says, "at the right hand of the Father." This was necessary, beloved, in order that the flesh of man, which, when sin was in authority, had been captivated for a long time, might receive the freedom of living there whither sin could not penetrate. Therefore the Saviour ascended to the Father in order that He might gain possession of the authority which was His due and that an inviolate faith of promised immortality might remain for us.

---

[1] A combination of Matt. 11: 27 and 28: 18.
[2] *Sermo* 44 *de Temp. (P.L.* 57.623-26).
[3] *Ibid.,* 45 *de Temp. (P.L.* 57.625-26).

The sermon concludes with an emphasis on the distinction between Elijah and Christ[1] and an exhortation to rejoice in the ascended Lord. An exposition of Ps. 24, in the manner now customary, is the chief feature of the following sermon,[2] but two statements add to our knowledge of Maximus's doctrine, viz.:

> Having fought in man and having conquered through man, Christ made him the inhabitant of heaven and the Lord of earth. . . . Christ went before now to open heaven to mortals. These gates will stand open, beloved, for the faithful and will always stand open, which, death having been overcome and the devil conquered, the Saviour, going before, opened when He returned to the Father.

To these we may add two further points from other sermons. First, Maximus regarded the descent of the Holy Spirit as proof positive of the Ascension of Christ to the Father.[3] Second and finally,[4] Maximus interpreted the cloud of the Lucan account as the vehicle of the divine presence and equated it with the cloud on the Mount of Transfiguration.[5]

Although Maximus lived through turbulent times, his sermons on the Ascension give no hint of the doctrinal controversies which were currently wracking the East and from which the West could not stand aloof. Leo I equally, in his two Ascension sermons, does not seek to make capital of the occasion for the doctrinal position he upheld and which was endorsed by the acceptance of his *Tome* at Chalcedon. However, in the

---

[1] cp. *Hom.* 113 *de Sanctis* (*P.L.* 57.518).

[2] *Sermo* 46 *de Temp.* (*P.L.* 57.625-28).

[3] *Hom.* 62, 63 *de Temp.* (*P.L.* 57.377, 378).

[4] *Sermo* 47 *de Temp.* (*P.L.* 57.627-30) is not by Maximus. It is also, without good reason, ascribed to Leo I (*P.L.* 54.499-500. It is to be noted that the text in this volume of Migne is complete and thus supplies the lacunae in the version printed in *P.L.* 57). This sermon by an unknown hand contains two statements worth recording. "First Christ descended in order that He might be made the companion of our nature; now He ascended in order that He might make us participators in His glory." "The High Priest has ascended the holy of holies as our precursor, and sits at the right hand of His Father to confirm by His example the hope of us His members, whither the lowly flock might follow where it believes its shepherd to have gone before. For so the Lord promised to His apostles, saying: 'Where the body is, thither will the eagles also be gathered together' (Luke 17: 37). For He calls the eagles holy who desire to depart and be with Christ."

[5] *Hom.* 61 *de Temp.* (*P.L.* 57.373-74). Maximus refers to Matt. 17: 5; Ps. 105: 39 and Exod. 13: 21.

first[1] of them, which is mainly concerned with the forty days, he cannot deny himself a reference to the primacy of Peter, a theme near to his heart, although in the final paragraph he shows himself capable of concise theological definition in a style which is at once elevated and solemn.

> Since then Christ's Ascension is our uplifting, and the hope of the Body is raised whither the glory of the Head has gone before, let us exult, beloved, with worthy joy and delight in the loyal paying of thanks. For to-day not only are we confirmed as possessors of paradise, but have also in Christ penetrated the heights of heaven, and have gained still greater things through Christ's unspeakable grace than we had lost through the devil's malice. For us, whom our virulent enemy had driven out from the bliss of our first abode, the Son of God has made members of Himself and placed at the right hand of the Father.

The second sermon[2] nowhere attains this clarity of expression, and consists largely of an exhortation to moral endeavour and of an extended statement that through the Ascension our faith is completed, strengthened and refined.

Where Leo hesitated to bring in anti-heretical polemics, the British-born Faustus, who in 452 became bishop of Riez in Provence, did not display the same reticence. His sermon on the Ascension, now recovered from amongst the writings of Augustine,[3] is no more than a diatribe against Monophysitism. It is to this end that he makes use of the Ascension, asserting that in it we see clearly not one nature but two, viz. the manhood which was elevated and the Godhead which elevated.

The decades immediately following the institution of an Ascension Day festival were without doubt the Golden Age in the history of the doctrine. The meeting of the Council of Chalcedon in 451 and the end of the episcopate of Leo in 461 mark a watershed in this as in so many other particulars. The teaching of the preceding period came to its full fruition in Chrysostom among the Greeks and Augustine among the Latins—later theologians were to find in their writings a rich storehouse from which to extract their own expositions of belief.

---

[1] *Sermo* 73 (al. 71) (*P.L.* 54.394-96).
[2] *Ibid.*, 74 (al. 72) (*P.L.* 54.397-400).
[3] *Ibid.*, 176 *de Temp.* (*P.L.* 39.2081-82).

Yet, illustrious though the first homilists were, their formulation of the doctrine was marred by two principal defects. On the one hand there was the dominating influence of the Lucan account, and on the other the belief in the resurrection of the flesh.

The latter conception, which would perhaps be better described as one of reanimation rather than of resurrection, had a long history, reaching back into the second century. When Tertullian could say that our Lord's words: "the very hairs of your head are all numbered",[1] indicate that every single one will be restored to man on the day of resurrection,[2] a crass carnality, as distinct from the materialism which is proper to incarnational Christianity, was fast becoming the basis of Christian hope in the after-life, despite the legitimate protests of an Origen. Such an understanding of the nature of the resurrection body inevitably affected the formulation of the doctrine of the Ascension, and hence the many references to the "body", to the "flesh" or to the "covering" which Christ took with Him into heaven. We who cannot accept such an interpretation must perforce reinterpret the teaching of the Fathers, so valuable for its flashes of insight, and see in the Ascension, not the transportation of an earthly frame to a localized heaven but the consummation of the process, including death and Resurrection, whereby the manhood, i.e. the human organism, of the Son of God was transformed while still retaining its identity.

[1] Matt. 10: 30.   [2] *De Res. Carn.*, 35.

7

LATER GREEK AND LATIN WRITERS

DURING the century which elapsed after the inclusion in the Church's Calendar of the festival of the Ascension, the attention directed to the significance of that event, as we have seen from our survey in the last lecture, was not inconsiderable. Indeed, much more of importance doctrinally was produced in those comparatively few years than throughout the whole of the next millennium. That this is so, even when due allowance has been made for the chance survival of documents, may be gauged from the incidental and insignificant statements relating to the Ascension which stand in the letters, sermons, commentaries and doctrinal compendia of which there is no dearth in these centuries. The initial impetus given to the study of the doctrine thus quickly lost its momentum: the Ascension remained an article of faith; it was scarcely an object of absorbing interest.

1. *Greek Writers*

This neglect of the doctrine of the Ascension may be illustrated in the East from the writings of Procopius of Gaza, the Christian sophist whose life falls in the period 465 to 528, and who made his native Syrian city a centre of oratorical display. We find in his works only one reference worthy of note to the Ascension, viz. in his commentary on Genesis. Discussing the translation of Enoch, Procopius says:

> Notice again how on the seventh day God rested from the creation of the world, and in the seventh generation God took Enoch as firstfruits of the rational nature for a symbol of the consummation.[1]

He then proceeds to speak of Elijah as a second type of the Ascension, at the same time emphasizing that as neither Enoch

---

[1] *P.G.* 87.264C.

147

nor Elijah died, unlike Christ, they cannot be called the first born of the dead.

A similar lack of interest is revealed by Sophronius, who was consecrated bishop of Jerusalem (634-38) some hundred years after the time of Procopius. There is extant a collection of his Anacreontic odes, written in the style of Anacreon, a lyric poet of Teos in Ionia (559-478 B.C.), in praise of the feasts of the Church. The nineteenth[1] poem is devoted to the Ascension, but contains little or nothing of a doctrinal nature, being concerned with a description of the churches, including the Church of the Ascension, which had been built to enshrine the Holy Places.[2]

There may, however, possibly belong to this period a complete sermon[3] on the Ascension which has been preserved amongst the works of Epiphanius of Salamis (367-403). It was certainly not from his pen, but it may emanate, though one cannot say this with complete assurance, from his namesake who occupied the same see in the latter half of the seventh century. Whoever the author may be, it is a lively address— perhaps almost too lively to belong to this period—and it is spiced with daring metaphor and direct speech ascribed both to Christ and the devil.

Where are those who are captivated by the horse-race and love the swiftness of charioteers? Come, behold a marvellous race: the Creator of the world carried upon a human chariot, not driving in disorder on earth but riding sublimely courses high in the air, and speeding to reach the heavenly turning point in the race course, and overthrowing powerfully Beliar as He rushes by.

Christ is the Good Shepherd who left the ninety and nine sheep, i.e. the angels, in the celestial mountains and sought the erring sheep, i.e. mankind, and brought him back to the heavenly refuge as a gift to His Father, saying:

[1] *P.G.* 87.3811-16.

[2] The *Triodium*, which contains some unoriginal remarks about the Ascension, (*P.G.* 87.3968), is falsely ascribed to Sophronius and is the composition of Joseph the hymnographer in the ninth century.

[3] *P.G.* 43.477-86. The author is also concerned to assert the distinction between the ascensions of Christ and Elijah, a distinction which was apparently being denied by certain Jewish opponents.

"Father, I have found that sheep that had gone astray, the very one whom the deceitful serpent had beguiled by cunning tricks, and showed evil ways and contaminated the purity of divine knowledge with the common filth of idolatry."

To-day the devil laments his inferior state, looking at our body raised into the heavens. To-day sin has been dismissed like smoke through the assumption of Christ Jesus. To-day the devil wails, saying: "What shall I do, unhappy one? . . . The Son of Mary has deceived me. I did not know that God was hidden in a human body . . . I wished to pursue Him and drag Him down as a lead weight; I wished to seize Him and nudge Him with my elbow secretly. What shall I do? He has driven me from every place. He has slung me down into the earth like a little stone. Falling upon the ground I thought to hide in the waters, but finding me hidden in the streams of Jordan like a dragon, He gripped me and flogged me."

This makes enjoyable reading, but it adds nothing to our understanding of the Ascension except to have re-emphasized that, for this author at least, the Ascension is part of the atoning act and on that account may be hymned as marking the final victory against the powers of evil.

But the tendency of the East at this time was against original thought, and even John of Damascus, whose intellectual brilliance amidst the dullness of his contemporaries gives him considerable pre-eminence, was in the main an encyclopaedist, garnering the ecclesiastical wisdom of the past. At first in the service of the Caliph at Damascus, John abandoned that career to enter the monastery of St. Saba near Jerusalem in the twenties of the eighth century. It was here that he produced his famous *De fide orthodoxa*,[1] but we may search it in vain for any extended reference to the Ascension. In his *Carmina*, however, a collection of odes in the new style introduced by Andrew of Crete (✝ c. 720), which earned John the title of one of the princes of Greek hymnography, there is a complete poem on the subject of the Ascension.[2] Yet its technical skill is more to be admired than its doctrinal content, and all we learn of the Damascene's belief is that to him the Ascension was the occasion of the glorification of Christ, of the exaltation of human nature, and of the offering of redeemed creation to the Father.

[1] *P.G.* 94.517-1228.   [2] *P.G.* 96.844-45.

A century and a half of almost complete silence brings us to Leo Imperator, also known as Philosophus or Sapiens, who ruled the Eastern Empire until his death in 911. In an area where the Church had long been under the domination of the State, Leo was not the first wearer of the purple to make an incursion into theology. The result is neither more nor less undistinguished than the achievements of those who made theology their whole-time activity. His eleventh discourse[1] is devoted to the Ascension, and after affirming that through the Resurrection immortality has been vouchsafed to man, he continues:

> But not only did He raise up that which had fallen, but He also set it upon a joint throne. . . . For to-day the Only-begotten Son, having fulfilled [His mission], leaves His abode as man with those below and ascends to the Father who had sent Him, bearing the firstfruits and mediatorship which He took as flesh from us. For to-day our dust is taken up on the shoulders of the cherubim and being received within the inner place is set upon the royal throne.

Leo then informs us that there is no action of the Saviour which is without a hidden, spiritual meaning. "What then", he asks, "may be learned from this?" Unfortunately, this promise of better things to come is not fulfilled, for, after quoting the Lucan account and referring to Ps. 24: 7, he concludes lamely with an ungraphic description of the ascent into the heavens.

It is refreshing after this to turn to the writings of Theophanis Ceramei,[2] archbishop of Taormina in Sicily. Though he is no exception to the general contemporary practice of reproducing the ideas of his predecessors, in this instance of Gregory of Nazianzus, he does so intelligently, developing them and adding some few contributions of his own.[3]

> The present festival is brilliant and distinguished, and this foremost feast provides material for consideration. For this is the crown of the mysteries of Christ; this is the completion of our salvation. To-day the nature of man has been established on the

[1] *P.G.* 107.113-20.
[2] His dates are disputed, but he was probably a contemporary of Leo Imperator.
[3] *Hom.* 39 (*P.G.* 132.744-64).

throne above the heavens. To-day the ancient enmity of the rational nature has been destroyed, and a union of angels and men has been effected. To-day the substance of humanity has been raised above the dignity of incorporeal beings and has become a participator in the divine dignity. To-day the intellectual Powers keep festival and behold with amazement earth united with heaven.

After this brief but relevant introduction, Theophanis turns to the Scriptural record of the Ascension, as it is found in the Lucan writings, commenting upon it verse by verse until he reaches the reference to the cloud. Then, following Gregory of Nazianzus,[1] he asserts:

But the cloud was the Holy Spirit;[2] for it is impossible for a perceptible cloud to pass beyond the upper air, where the moisture is naturally consumed by the heavenly fire. But as He descended by the Spirit, when Gabriel spoke thus to the Virgin: "The Holy Ghost shall come upon thee",[3] so He ascended accompanied closely by the Spirit.

Theophanis then considers the question: why was the Ascension delayed for forty days? His answer, again derived in part from Gregory,[4] is not without ingenuity.

We know of three begettings of Christ upon earth: the first of the most holy Mother; the second in Jordan by means of the water; the third, the regeneration from the dead according to which He became the first born of all creation.[5] In the first generation, she took Him, after forty days, as the first born and presented Him in the Temple before the Lord and offered sacrifice according to the commandment of the Law.[6] In the second generation, which was by Baptism, He was led up by the Spirit into the wilderness and for forty days He overcame all temptations, and showed Himself stronger than the tempter and began to preach the Kingdom of God. Similarly therefore, after the third generation, I mean the resurrection from the dead, after forty days He was taken up to the temple above the heavens and

[1] *Orat.*, 39.17.
[2] In *Hom.* 40 (*P.G.* 132.779A) Theophanis declares that the cloud which led the Israelites in the wilderness was the Holy Spirit. In *Hom.* 59 (*ibid.*, 1037A), he says that the cloud which descended on the mount of Transfiguration was also the Holy Spirit and (1039A) similarly the cloud at the Ascension.
[3] Luke 1: 35.   [4] *Orat.*, 40.2.   [5] Col. 1: 15.   [6] Luke 2: 22.

brought our nature, spotless in Him, to God the Father, inasmuch as He had conquered the ruler of this world and had become superior to all principalities and powers.

Theophanis' next section is concerned with the witnesses of the Ascension. These, according to him, fall into three groups: the eleven apostles; Mary and many of the Seventy, including Nathanael the Canaanite who, it is argued, must have been present—otherwise he would not have seen the fulfilment of Jesus' promise to him: "Ye shall see the heaven opened, and the angels of God ascending and descending upon the Son of man";[1] and the angels themselves, who confirmed the faith of the Apostles and welcomed Him into the heavens with the words of Ps. 24. But, asks Theophanis, why was it that the angels had to enquire the identity of this King of glory?

> They knew that He was about to ascend to the heavenlies after the completion of His economy, and that He was to be received by the heavenly gates and would sit down. Or what else does that Gospel parable show: He wishes that we should be "like unto men looking for their lord, when he shall return from the marriage feast"?[2] For evidently He hinted at the angels sitting by the heavenly gates and looking for the Lord when He would descend on account of the mystic marriage when He united the Church to Himself. Of the future Ascension therefore the angels were not ignorant: but that He should come with a body, this put them at a loss.

Theophanis concludes with an exhortation on the theme: "Thither in heart and mind let us ascend."

In his 49th Homily, which is on the words of John 1: 43 read on the feast of St. Philip, Theophanis returns again to the promise to Nathanael of which he had treated in his Ascension sermon.

> We assert therefore that He says the heavens have been opened on account of the unhindered ascent of man to God which Christ gave freely to us when He exalted our substance into the heavens. For the entrance of sin interposed a partition and a middle wall between God and men. This the Lord removed, having freely given us a way of ascent into the heavens. Immediately therefore

---

[1] John 1: 51.   [2] Luke 12: 36.

He deified the flesh by the union and offered immortality by
the Resurrection and made us worthy of perfect reconciliation
with the Father by the Ascension which He called the opening
of heaven.[1]

We can appreciate the piquancy of Theophanis' approach
the more if we compare it with the manner of those who treated
the subject later. Thus all that Oecumenius, bishop of Tricca
in Thessaly (c. 995) can find to say, in his commentary on
Acts, is that the cloud demonstrates the equality of the Son
with the Father. "For it is said concerning the Father: 'A cloud
and darkness are round about him.' "[2] The historian Michael
Glyca, whose *Annales* were written in 1118, can do no more
than reproduce the thought of his predecessors:

> If thou wishest to learn this, for what reason He remained forty
> days, not more nor less, upon the earth after His Resurrection
> from the dead, behold the great Epiphanius will briefly solve
> this mystery for thee: "After His birth, Christ lay in a manger;
> He was swathed in swaddling clothes, and after forty days He
> was taken to the holy Temple and, according to the law of Moses,
> was presented to God. Also when He had become the first born
> of the dead, He remained forty days and so He was exalted to
> Jerusalem which is above and appeared before the face of God
> for us."[3]

Another historian, Nicephorus Callistus, who belongs to the
first half of the fourteenth century, contents himself with re-
peating this same statement.[4] Even Gregory Palmas, metro-
politan of Thessalonica, in the fifties of the same century,
cannot escape from the doldrums into which Greek theology
as a whole had entered. He has left us two sermons on the
Ascension, both concerned more with the overcoming of sin
and the practice of virtue than with the Ascension itself. In
the first,[5] after listing a number of types, including Habakkuk,
he asserts that Christ "both rose and ascended for us, preparing for us resurrection and ascension to endless ages". In the
second,[6] he makes the same point: "Whosoever before death
crucifies sin by repentance and the citizenship of the Gospel,

[1] *P.G.* 132.893B, C.
[2] Ps. 97: 2. *P.G.* 118.52D.
[3] *Ann.* III (*P.G.* 158.425A, B).
[4] *H.E.*, 1.38 (*P.G.* 145.743D).
[5] *Hom.* 21 (*P.G.* 151.276-85).
[6] *Hom.* 22 (*P.G.* 151.285-96).

he alone after the general resurrection will be taken up in the clouds to meet the Lord in the air." His eschatology therefore, as that of many before him, comprised not only a general resurrection but also an ascension of all the faithful. The only other matter of interest is found in the first sermon, where he interprets Dan. 7: 13 to have a twofold reference to both the Ascension and the Parousia.

This is a disappointing record of theological activity, but the Ascension was not alone in its lack of adequate examination. After the middle of the fifth century Greek theology entered upon a period of decay; the earlier creative vigour had waned and scholars were content with excerpts, summaries and compilations. The task of the theologian was conceived to be not the pursuit of new insights into the nature and meaning of revealed truth but the cataloguing of the intellectual labours of former days. The acme of independent theological production had been reached, so it was believed; all that remained was the task of systematization. The Sixth General Council of 680 had formulated the limits of dogmatic thought for the Greeks, and this *ne plus ultra* attitude lay like a dead hand on all future speculation. The Ascension was and remained an accepted article of belief, but if one wanted to know what was meant by it, one had to consult the pronouncements of an earlier age.

2. *Latin Writers*

The decay of theological learning that characterized the Greek East during this period was also visible in the West. There is the same tendency to rest content with the achievements of the past and the same concern not to contribute to but merely to hand on the treasures of a bygone era. This tenacious fidelity to the inheritance from former times was due not a little to the disintegration of Roman civilization and the incursions of the Northern and Eastern tribes. But even the Carolingian Renaissance, consequent upon the gradual stabilization of political and social life, was ecclesiastical rather than theological. The works, too, which emanated from the great reformed monastic houses of the tenth and eleventh centuries were more devotional than doctrinal, while the contributions of the intellectual movement in which Abelard and Anselm played so important a part are to be sought elsewhere than in their teaching on the subject of the Ascension. A brief survey of the vicissitudes of that doctrine during this period will serve to confirm the accuracy of these generalizations.

Caesarius of Arles was one of those who revealed an essentially practical nature throughout the forty years of his episcopate (503-43). The aim of his many sermons was simply to inculcate the true Christian life in his flock, to incite them to a desire for good works and to stimulate them to pursue the good without relaxation of effort. It would be a mistake to minimize the doctrinal content of his utterances, for under the rule first of the Visigoths and then of the Ostrogoths, both semi-Arian in belief, Caesarius had incessantly to defend and expound the orthodox trinitarian faith.[1] But his sermon on the Ascension[2] is nevertheless very typical of his genius; the doctrine is basic but subservient to his practical end.

> Our Saviour, beloved brethren, has ascended into heaven: let us therefore not be disturbed on earth. Let the mind be there and here: there will be peace. In the meantime, let us ascend with Christ in heart; when the day of His promise shall have come, we shall also follow in the body. Yet we ought to know, brethren, that pride has not ascended with Christ, nor avarice, nor luxury, nor any fault of ours has ascended with our Physician. And so, if we desire to ascend after the Physician, we ought to lay aside faults and sins.

Already, in these opening sentences, Caesarius's concern for everyday Christian living is evident, and the sermon develops accordingly with an emphasis on the need for humility, in its second section, and for purity in its third and fourth. But this exhortation rests upon a firmly held understanding of the Ascension. "The Resurrection of the Lord", says Caesarius, quoting Augustine,[3] "is our hope; the Ascension of the Lord is our glorification." And again:

> Christ Himself is to you the way and the homeland (*patria*); the way according to His manhood, the homeland according to His

---

[1] cp. M. Dorenkemper, *The Trinitarian Doctrine and Sources of St. Caesarius of Arles*, 1953.

[2] Falsely ascribed to Augustine (*Sermo* 177; *P.L.* 39.2082-83); critical text, *Sermo* 21 in *Sermones*, ed. G. Morin, *Corpus Christianorum*, *S.L.*, 104, pp. 837-40.

[3] See above, p. 140.

Godhead. If you run faithfully, you go through Him and you
will attain to Him.

The practical bent manifested by Caesarius was equally
characteristic of Gregory the Great, and the sermon[1] which
he delivered on Ascension Day 591, in St. Peter's, within a
year of his consecration, shows his concern to recommend vir-
tuous living to his hearers amidst the contemporary political
chaos with its strong inducement to moral decadence. He used
the occasion to present an argument for chastity which is
nothing if not fanciful, but it was sufficiently acceptable to be
reproduced frequently by later homilists.

Gregory begins by distinguishing between Enoch and Elijah
on the one hand and Christ on the other. Where Enoch was
before the Law and Elijah under the Law, Christ was both
under the Law and after it, in so far as He fulfilled it: where
His precursors were taken up, Christ ascended by His own
power: where His heralds did not enter heaven itself, Christ
ascended to the Father's throne. Thus there is a progression
to be noted from the types to the antitype, and this progression,
according to Gregory, is to be seen also in the sphere of chastity.

> For Enoch indeed had a wife and sons; Elijah had no wife, nor
> is it stated that he had sons. Consider therefore how, through
> the passage of time, the pureness of sanctity had developed, be-
> cause it is openly revealed through the servants who were trans-
> lated and through the Lord who ascended. For Enoch was
> translated having been begotten by coitus and having begat by
> coitus. Elijah was taken up having been begotten by coitus but
> not having begat by coitus. The Lord indeed was assumed having
> neither begat by coitus nor having been begotten by coitus.

Equally fanciful, though sufficiently characteristic of both
the exegetical practices and the mnemonic devices which homilists were adopting to be worthy of note is Gregory's account
of the five "leaps" or bounds of our Lord. Quoting and applying to the Ascension 2: 8 of the Song of Songs: "Behold he
cometh, leaping upon the mountains, skipping upon the
hills", Gregory continues:

> Do you wish, my dear brethren, to know of His leaps? He came
> from heaven into the womb: from the womb He came into the

---

[1] *Hom.* 29, *in Evang., Lib.* II (*P.L.* 76.1213-19).

manger: from the manger He came to the Cross: from the Cross
He came into the tomb: from the tomb He returned into heaven.[1]

But perhaps Gregory's most interesting statements, doctrinally, are those that occur in his discussion of the question why
the angels appeared dressed in white at the Ascension when
they had not done so at the Nativity. White is the colour of
joy, and it was therefore not worn at the Nativity,

> because when the Lord was born the Godhead was seen humbled;
> when the Lord ascended the humanity was exalted. For white
> robes are more fitting exaltation than humiliation. At His assump-
> tion therefore the angels ought to have been seen in white robes
> because while in the Nativity the Godhead appeared humiliated,
> in His Ascension the manhood was displayed sublimated.

So the Ascension is an occasion for great rejoicing:

> For that nature, to whom it was said. "Dust thou art, and unto
> dust shalt thou return",[2] has entered into heaven to-day.

Gregory concludes by returning to his moralistic theme and
bidding his flock to ascend in heart and mind whither Christ
has gone before.

Amongst Gregory's correspondents was Isidore of Seville
(600-36), who was on terms of intimate friendship with the
pope. Isidore succeeded his brother Leander in the arch-
bishopric, and since the conversion of the Visigoths to orthodoxy had already been achieved, Isidore conceived his primary
task to be not the defence of the faith but the counteraction
of barbarism by the diffusion of education and learning. To
this end he set himself to garner the knowledge of former ages,
and produced works which were genuine compendia of entire
libraries. The influence of these encyclopaedic compilations on
the European mind during the Middle Ages cannot be over-
estimated, but he was erudite rather than original and contributed little to that which he preserved. This is clearly
indicated by his teaching on the Ascension which is summarized
in the first book of his *De Ecclesiasticae Officiis*.[3]

[1] Gregory derived this from Ambrose, although omitting the latter's further
leap into Jordan (*De Isaac et Anima*, 4.31, *P.L.* 14.513; *In Expos. in ps. cxiii*,
Sermo, 6.6, *P.L.* 15.1269-70). It may be that this exegesis was influenced by Wis.
18: 14, 15.
[2] Gen. 3: 19.   [3] 33 (*P.L.* 83.768).

The solemnity of the Lord's Ascension is thus celebrated because on this day, after the victory over the world and after the return from Hades, Christ is commemorated as having ascended into the heavens, as it is written: "Ascending on high, he took captivity captive; he gave gifts to men." This festival is celebrated throughout the course of the years in order that the manhood of the assumed flesh ascending to the right hand of the Father might be recalled, whose body we believe to be in heaven, in such fashion as when He ascended and the angel's voice proclaimed it, saying: "He shall so come in like manner as ye beheld him going into heaven", i.e. with the same form and substance of flesh, to which flesh He truly gave immortality and did not withdraw its nature. But the right hand of the Father at which the Son is believed to sit is not corporeal—to think which of God would be impious—but the right hand of the Father is perpetual bliss which is promised to the saints in the resurrection, i.e. to the universal Church which is the Body of Christ; so His left hand is to be understood to refer to the misery and eternal punishment which shall be given to the ungodly.

The Venerable Bede was no less erudite, and his learning was equalled only by his piety: indeed, he studied assiduously every branch of human thought—philosophy, the arts and the sciences. His sermon on the Ascension,[1] which belongs to the closing years of his life (730-35), reveals his careful observation coupled with that fanciful exegesis that had become endemic in Biblical scholarship. Thus he notes that Enoch was the seventh from Adam and proceeds to explain the number as a prefigurement of the sevenfold gift of the Spirit which Christ was to bestow as a consequence of His Ascension. Again, Bede remarks that Enoch's age, 365 years, corresponds with the days of the solar year; the translated Enoch was therefore the perfect type of the ascended Christ who is the true Sun, being the light of the world. Misplaced though this ingenuity may be, it led him to make one statement that is not without theological importance. He declared that the Ascension was the ground of the Sacraments. We find this thesis, which unfortunately is not expanded, in his discussion

---

[1] *Hom.* II.9 (*P.L.* 94.174-81; critical text in *Corpus Christianorum, S.L.,* 122, 280-89). *Hom.* III.63 (*P.L.* 94.429-32) is the same as *In Marc.* (*P.L.* 92.299-302) and contains nothing of interest. Bede's hymn on the Ascension (Hymn 6— *P.L.* 94.624-26; reprinted in *C.C., op. cit.,* 419-23) skilfully combines quotations from Ps. 24 with the Latin metre.

of the parallelism between Elijah and Christ. As the former left his cloak, with which he had been clothed, to his disciple Elisha, so the latter left His disciples the Sacraments of the humanity He had assumed that thereby they might be sanctified.

If it is remarkable to find a man of such literary ability appearing in so remote a corner of England, his geographical isolation prevented his having an effect comparable with that, on the continent, of Isidore, whose enduring influence is to be seen in the writings of Rabanus Maurus.

The passage quoted above from Isidore's *De Ecclesiasticae Officiis* stands unchanged in Book II of the *De Clericorum Institutione*[1] composed by Rabanus in 819. Rabanus, who was a disciple of Alcuin at Tours, later archbishop of Fulda and finally bishop of Mainz, belonged to the second generation of the Carolingian Renaissance, but his works indicate that, however much that movement led to a quickening of Church life, its influence upon theology was slight; it only accentuated the dependence upon the past which was already a deeply rooted characteristic of theological studies.[2] Thus Rabanus' first sermon on the Ascension[3] is largely a reproduction of the sermon by Caesarius that we have just considered, with a hint of Augustine thrown in, viz.: "Because the Ascension of Christ is our advancement, and whither the glory of the Head has gone before, thither the hope of the body is directed, let us exult with becoming joy." Rabanus' four other homilies relating to the Ascension, two delivered on the vigil[4] and two on the day itself,[5] contain nothing that is new, and are little more than exhortations to moral endeavour. Haymo of Auxerre,[6] however, to whom the homilies once assigned to Haymo of Halberstadt are now to be attributed,[7] approved of them sufficiently to adopt two of them as his own, Homilies 94 and 95

---

[1] II.40 (*P.L.* 107.353). This same section also reappears verbatim in *De Divinis Officiis*, 24 (*P.L.* 101.1225), falsely attributed to Alcuin; it is probably an eleventh-century compilation.

[2] J. de Ghellinck, *Littérature Latine au Moyen Age*, 1939, p. 148.

[3] *Hom.* 21 de Fest. (*P.L.* 110.42-43).

[4] *Hom.* 44, 45 in Evang. (*P.L.* 110.226-31).

[5] *Hom.* 46, 47 in Evang. (*P.L.* 110.231-36).

[6] *fl.* 840-65.

[7] J. de Ghellinck, *Le Mouvement Théologique du XIIe Siècle*, 1948, p. 34.

of Haymo being identical with Homilies 45 and 46 of Rabanus Maurus.[1]

Even the one Ascension sermon[2] of Haymo's own contriving that has survived is little more than a transcription of Gregory the Great's homily, reproducing his distinction between Christ and His precursors and his specious recommendation of chastity.

Next in the succession of Ascensiontide homilists is Rather (890-974), born at Liège, educated at the abbey of Lobbes, of which he became abbot, and ending his stormy career as bishop of the see of Verona. Pessimistic in outlook, with a veneer of humanism, he was a biting censor of contemporary morals, and his two Ascension sermons, the one delivered in 963[3] and the other in 968,[4] are dissertations on ethical conduct which contribute nothing to the history of the doctrine. Atto, bishop of Vercelli[5] (fl. 934-60), and Odilo, abbot of Cluny[6] (994-1054), are equally practical and equally unenlightening —moralism is in the ascendancy.

The title of the principal work of Werner, abbot of St. Blois († 1126), gives a clear indication of the character of its contents, viz. *Libri Delflorationum ex Melliflua diversorum Patrum.* Chapter 35 of the first book[7] is divided into two parts, the second of which consists of a sermon on the Ascension. It is in the first part, however, that Werner discusses the distinction between the types and prototypes, i.e. between Enoch and Elijah and Christ, and he borrows much from Gregory the Great, including the latter's fanciful commendation of chastity. The sermon itself begins with the statement that this festival marks the completion of Christ's victory, and it continues:

> To-day a new way, of which the apostle speaks,[8] has been in-augurated because through the flesh of Christ the entrance to heaven, through which no flesh previously had passed,[9] has been opened. To-day the opening of the book has been accomplished,

[1] Rabanus Maurus, *Hom.* 45, 46 *in Evang.* (*P.L.* 110.228-31; 231-33) are identical with Haymo, *Hom.* 94, 95 *de Temp.* (*P.L.* 118.536-40; 540-42).

[2] *Hom.* 96 *de Temp.* (*P.L.* 118.542-49).   [3] *Sermo* 8 (*P.L.* 136.734-40).

[4] *Sermo* 9 (*P.L.* 136.740-45).   [5] *Sermo* 10 (*P.L.* 134.845-46).

[6] *Sermo* 8 (*P.L.* 142.1011-14).   [7] *P.L.* 157.970-76.   [8] Heb. 10: 20.

[9] cp. the teaching of Petrus Alphonsus, a converted Spanish Jew, baptized 1106; in his *Dialogi* 11 (*P.L.* 157.650-57) he is concerned to argue that Jesus' body could have been exalted to heaven as it had been transformed through death and Resurrection.

which no one could open except the Lamb that had been slain,[1] when its mysteries are revealed together with those which are found concerning Christ in the Law and the Prophets. To-day also has been completed and consummated the dispensation of His humanity. First the Omnipotent descended in order to become a participant in our nature, then He ascended in order to make us participants in His glory. He descended to exalt us: He ascended to make us ascend with Him.

The peroration, in which Werner discusses the reasons why the Holy Spirit was not immediately given after the Ascension, was copied by Honorius of Autun in his *Elucidarium*[2] (✝ c. 1145). While in his *Speculum Ecclesiae*, Honorius's treatment of the Ascension[3] reproduces the metaphor of a Roman triumph, first elaborated by Maximus of Turin.[4]

Not even the great Bernard of Clairvaux (1090-1153) could escape the prevailing "isms" of the age, viz. archaism, plagiarism and moralism, to which may be added, as a fourth note, irrelevancy.[5] Thus of his five Ascension sermons, the first[6] has no reference to the Ascension; the second[7] is strongly reminiscent of Caesarius of Arles; the third[8] is devoted to the subject of purity, the fourth[9] to faith and the fifth[10] to the renunciation of evil ways. That Christ is the firstfruits and that He is the way to heaven comprises the sum total of his doctrine.

The reforming movement, which Bernard did so much to foster, soon spread to England, where the first Cistercian house was established at Rievaulx, the Rye valley, in the year 1132. Its third abbot, who entered the house within a year of its foundation, was Aelred (1110-66); and as, in accordance with the *Consuetudines*, he was obliged to preach to his community in the chapter house at least twelve times a year on the greater feasts of the Church, the number of occasions on which he spoke of the Ascension must have been considerable, but only

---

[1] Rev. 5: 9.

[2] I.25 (*P.L.* 172.1128). The authenticity of the *Elucidarium* was vindicated by J. Endres, *Honorius Augustodunensis*, 1906, pp. 22-25.

[3] *P.L.* 172.955-60.

[4] See above, p. 142.

[5] cp. Goffridus (✝ 1132), *Sermo* 6 (*P.L.* 157.258-62); this is an Ascension homily, but is concerned exclusively with the Last Judgment.

[6] *P.L.* 183.299-301.   [7] *P.L.* 183.301-4.   [8] *P.L.* 183.304-9.

[9] *P.L.* 183.309-16.   [10] *P.L.* 183.316-24.

two of these Ascension Day sermons have been preserved.[1] The abbot obviously prepared his homilies with great care, following the principles laid down by Guibert of Nogent in his didactic treatise on the art of preaching;[2] but since his aim was to edify and instruct in the ways of the spirit rather than to expound and clarify the articles of belief, his contribution belongs more to the history of devotion than to that of doctrine. Thus Aelred sought to explain how his monks might ascend in spirit and to this end, in both Ascension sermons, he lays emphasis on the need for renunciation and for the practice of humility and love. Such doctrinal comment that he does make is confined to the reiteration of Augustine's leading theme, so in the first sermon:

> To-day He wished to display in Himself, when ascending into heaven, that blessedness which we await, in order that we might be certain that we who are His members might ascend whither He who is our Head has ascended;

and in the second sermon:

> by the Ascension the whole Christ (*totus Christus*), that is the Head with the body, betook Himself to the heavenly Jerusalem.

Also worthy of note is the detailed way in which Aelred works out the typological correspondence between Elijah and Christ.

> We read in the Book of Kings that when Elijah was taken up in the fiery chariot, he left his cloak to Elisha, and the spirit of Elijah was doubled in Elisha. Elijah the prophet signifies our Lord, and Elisha signifies the apostles of the Lord and the disciples. The taking up of Elijah into the air signifies the Ascension of our Lord. But because Elijah was only a man, he needed the assistance of another. Our Lord, who was true God, ascended into heaven by His own power, as the evangelist says: "And it came to pass, while he blessed them, he was parted from them, and was carried up into heaven."[3] The cloak of Elijah signifies the holy Church, as the holy patriarch Jacob said concerning our Lord: "He hath washed his garments in wine, and his cloak

[1] *Sermo* 13 (*P.L.* 195.283-90) and "*In Ascensione Domini*" recently edited by C. H. Talbot, *Sermones Inediti B. Aelredi Abbatis Rievallensis*, 1952, pp. 100-4.
[2] *P.L.* 156.21. [3] Luke 24: 51.

in the blood of grapes",[1] because through His own blood He cleansed the Church. When Elijah ascended in the chariot he left his cloak to Elisha, and when our Lord ascended into heaven, He commended His Church to His disciples.

Aelred continues to point the parallelism by affirming, as Augustine had done before him,[2] that the double gift of the spirit to Elisha refers to the giving of the Spirit in John 20 and Acts 2.

This artifice of finding an exact concord between the Old and New Testaments was carried to extremes by Peter of Celles († 1187) and Garnier of Langres († 1198). The latter's Ascension sermon[3] is no more than an intricate study of innumerable Old Testament characters on an allegorical basis; the three sermons belonging to the former are, however, even more remarkable for their fantasy. The text for the first one[4] is taken from 2 Kings 2: 23, where the children mock Elisha with the words: "Go up, thou bald head." The application of the first word—*ascende*—to Christ presents no difficulty, but the second—*calve*—requires considerable invention of which, however, Peter proves himself not incapable.

Thou bald head, from whose brow the razor of the malignant Jews shaved the hairs when it put all the disciples to flight; thou bald head, in whom the prince of this world found nothing; thou bald head, who had not where to lay the head . . . etc.

It is a pity that such ingenuity should have been so misdirected, but it is evident again in the other two sermons,[5] which each have the text Job 39: 27: "Doth the eagle mount up at thy command, and make her nest on high?"—needless to say, the eagle is taken to signify Christ and the nest the throne of God.

In the writings of Peter of Blois († 1204) this allegorization is kept within more reasonable limits. Like Aelred, Peter occupied himself mainly with the spiritual life, and consequently his Ascension sermon[6] directs the attention of his hearers to the ascended Christ who is our treasure and to whom, since

---

[1] Gen. 49: 11.
[2] *In Ioh. Ev. Tract.*, lxxiv.2.
[3] *Sermo* 20 (*P.L.* 205.700-4).
[4] *Sermo* 50 (*P.L.* 202.785-88).
[5] *Sermones* 51, 52 (*P.L.* 202.788-91; 791-94).
[6] *Sermo* 23 (*P.L.* 207.627-30).

where our treasure is there is our heart also, we must ascend in mind. At the same time Peter has certain pertinent remarks to make. He begins by quoting Dan. 7: 13, 14, which he interprets as a reference to the Ascension.[1] He then continues:

> For He descended in order to ascend, and in order to draw us with Him as He ascended. "When I shall have been lifted up from the earth, I will draw all men unto myself."[2] God is infinite and He can neither increase nor ascend. Therefore in order that He might increase, He became a little lower than the angels; but He ascended in order that in His Ascension He might transcend the dignity of the angels. Indeed the humanity and generosity of Christ were revealed by His Nativity; His power and glory were revealed by His Resurrection. But we are to rejoice especially in His Ascension by which the way of life has been opened for us, faith has been strengthened, our trust has been made firm, in order that we might go whither our Head has preceded, that the Head may not be without His members.

The Ascension, according to Peter, proves the Resurrection.

> For who would believe the Resurrection unless the Ascension had proved it? . . . The flesh of Christ could not have ascended into heaven unless the virtue of the Resurrection had glorified it and rendered it immune and free from every burden of mortality.

The recurring echo of Augustine which we hear in this sermon also sounds in the homilies of Radulphus Ardens,[3] whose career is now placed at the end of the twelfth century.[4] So he affirms that the apostles "hoped whither their Head had ascended before, the inferior members might ascend with Him", and, following Augustine again,[5] he expounds the symbolism of numbers, arriving at the forty days of the Resurrection appearances by multiplying the ten commandments by the four evangelists.

[1] Hugh of St. Victor († 1140) makes the same application in his Ascension homily (*Sermones Centum*, 69; *P.L.* 177.1114-19).

[2] John 12:32.

[3] *Hom.* 68, 69 (*P.L.* 155.1917-22; 1922-27).

[4] B. Geyer, "Radulphus Ardens und das *Speculum Universale*", *Theologische Quartalschrift*, XCIII, 1911, pp. 63-89.

[5] See above, p. 140.

Alanus *de Insulis* (✝ 1203), called *doctor universale*, one time abbot of Larivoir in Champagne and later bishop of Auxerre in Burgundy, is equally Augustinian. In his anti-Albigensian treatise, *De Fide Catholica contra Haereticos*,[1] he states:

> When Christ said of Himself: "No man hath ascended into heaven, etc.", this is so to be understood that our definition of the whole does not exclude the part. So that if I say: "only you, Socrates", Socrates's body is not excluded. Wherefore, if I say: "Socrates is rational", his soul is not excluded. Similarly, if it is said: "No man hath ascended, etc.", which is said of Christ alone when He ascended into heaven, this does not exclude His spiritual Body, i.e. His Church.

Absalom, *abbas Sprinckirsbacensis* (*fl. c.* 1210), although he belonged to the Order of the Canons Regular of Augustine, is less beholden to his patron for his teaching on the Ascension than the majority of his contemporaries, but he shares their addiction to moralism and irrelevancy. Two[2] of three Ascension sermons are not really concerned with the Ascension at all, and the third[3] soon becomes an exhortation to practise purity and contemplation; but before this he does make one notable statement on the necessity of the humanity being elevated to heaven, although even here he is indebted to the Venerable Bede. He argues that the human nature was taken up because Christ, though in two natures, is one Person.

> So that those natures which had such an ineffable union between them could undergo no division in majesty or power. For that the human nature had the same power as the Word is testified in the Gospel: "All power hath been given unto me in heaven and on earth."[4] According to the exposition of the Venerable Bede that was not said of the divinity which is coeternal with the Father, but of the humanity which had been assumed . . . so that He who assumed and that which was assumed are one Person in the Trinity.

Helinand of Perseigne, another Cistercian (✝ *c.* 1227), reverts to Augustine for his teaching.

> Consider how liberally He has communicated His dignity to us so that He might make us reign with Him in heaven and might

[1] I.18 (*P.L.* 210.321).
[2] *Sermones* 32, 33 (*P.L.* 211.187-93; 193-99).
[3] *Sermo* 31 (*P.L.* 211.182-87).
[4] Matt. 28: 18.

sublimely dispose us at His right hand now in His Body, who is our Head.[1]

Surprisingly enough, there is scarcely a hint of Augustine's influence in the sermons of Martin, presbyter of Legio in Spain (✝ 1203)—surprising since to Martin belongs the dubious honour of having composed the longest Ascension sermon extant: it comprises a hundred and fourteen columns in Migne's *Patrologia Latina*.[2] It is a mosaic of digressions, for Martin could not deny himself the pleasure of pursuing every red herring that he drew across his own path. So he begins with a long discussion upon the nature of the Church, which is followed by an equally long exposition of those passages in Hebrews that refer to the heavenly high priesthood of Christ; this leads him next to a survey of Old Testament sacrifices as types of the sacrifice of the Lamb of God. Then, taking now a verse from the spurious ending of Mark and now one from the final chapter of Luke and the first of Acts to form a harmony, he comments on each single one with the Resurrection as his main interest; he also quotes the Matthean baptismal formula and so launches into an account of Baptism which he couples with an attack on the Jews for their failure to come to the saving waters. At long last he reaches the Ascension itself and discusses the distinction between Enoch, Elijah and Christ, interprets Dan. 7: 13 of the Ascension and refers Ps. 24 both to the lifting up of the gates of Hades at the *descensus* and to the lifting up of the gates of heaven at the Ascension. Martin then provides a dissertation upon the Second Advent and the Last Judgment, and, of course, cannot avoid considering in detail the general resurrection, the bliss of heaven and the torments of the damned. The one statement in this prolix address which is worth noting is to be found in the section relating to the Epistle to the Hebrews:

That eternal high priest once in the year, on the day of Atonement, entered the holy of holies, i.e. when the dispensation of the Incarnation, of the Nativity, of the Passion and Resurrection had been completed, He entered the heavens, entering into the

[1] *Sermo* 15 (*P.L.* 212.595-611). *Sermo* 14 (*P.L.* 212.591-95) is also an Ascension sermon, but consists of a paean of praise of the fact of redemption.
[2] *Sermo* 30 (*P.L.* 208.1085-1198).

Father by means of the manhood, from whom He had never departed by means of the divinity, in order to make it an atonement for the human race and to intercede by means of the humanity for all those who believe in Him.[1]

Martin concludes, most fittingly, with the words:

Now, beloved brethren, if it seem good, the prolixity of this sermon may be restrained, lest it appear to produce hypercriticism in those who read, as well as in those who listen.[2]

These words may also serve as a not altogether unsuitable coda to this lecture, which has revealed that the theological sterility of the East was shared by the West. If any credit belongs to this age, it is not that of pioneering fresh areas of thought but of preserving the treasures of the past, in forming a necessary link in the tradition of the deposit of the faith and in keeping alive a belief in the Ascension as an integral part of the redemptive act of God in Christ.

[1] *P.L.* 208.1126D.
[2] By contrast the accompanying sermon (31, *P.L.* 208.1197-1204) is far more to the point, and although it adds nothing to its predecessor of which it reproduces several passages, it is at least free from the irrelevancies which mar *Sermo* 30.

8

HE ASCENDED INTO HEAVEN

THE Scriptures, according to John Chrysostom, may be compared to a pleasant meadow planted with heavy laden trees wherein a person may wander at peace, gathering now one, now another fruit for his soul's nourishment. The early history of the doctrine of the Ascension, which has now been outlined, may also be approached in this spirit of careful selection, choosing now one, now another idea in order to direct attention to those features which must be borne in mind when seeking to assess the importance and the significance of the Ascension for Christian believers at the present day.

Certainly the first, if not the most important, observation to be made is that the Lucan record, as we have seen from our examination of the New Testament evidence, is not to be regarded as having exclusive authority.[1] The acceptance of it as such has indeed bedevilled much of the history of the doctrine, since it has led scholars and exegetes to concentrate upon the details of the pericope in Acts to the neglect of the meaning of the event in the light of the New Testament witness as a whole. Moreover, even when the teaching of the other Apostolic writers has not been passed over, the tendency has been to approach it from the Lucan standpoint, without recognizing that this is entirely *sui generis*. We may see this clearly in several contemporary articles and in numerous sermons, whose main burden is to assert, with St. Luke, that the Ascension marks the termination of the Resurrection Appearances. There is, it is true, a certain finality about the Ascension, which will be considered below, but it is a finality that differs from that with which St. Luke invested it; and if we reject his account as historically unreliable we must also conclude that this frequent modern emphasis is misplaced.

[1] cp. A. M. Ramsey, "What was the Ascension?", *Studiorum Novi Testamenti Societas, Bulletin*, II, 1951, p. 50.

This is not to say that St. Luke has nothing to teach us about the Ascension, but it does involve a loosening of the bonds which have for so long narrowly confined our understanding of the doctrine. At the same time it provides an answer to those who would dismiss it as connected with an outmoded cosmology and a corrective to those who persist in an equally outmoded approach to the Biblical record. We need not then believe that the Ascension involved transportation to a localized heaven but transference to a new condition of being which, in the felicitous words of an early eighteenth-century writer on the subject, "far better becometh the Divine Residence than the Top of our Atmosphere".[1]

The acceptance of that tradition which associates the Ascension closely with the Resurrection as one element in a single process, rather than as an event separated from the Resurrection by a period of nearly six weeks, provides further the opportunity to assess its true importance in the economy of redemption. It can no longer be regarded as a mere appendage, as no more than an imprimatur which adds nothing to that which had already been accomplished.[2] It is part of the redemptive act. If it is through the Ascension that Jesus entered upon the office of Son of man, became no longer *Messias designatus* but Messiah indeed, and received the regal dignity and title of "Lord", then the Ascension belongs not to the periphery but to the heart and substance of the Gospel.

The Ascension indeed demonstrates that what has taken place in Jesus Christ is not some casual story: it reveals that "here an ultimate and supreme thing comes into action, behind which there is no other reality".[3] It consummates the reconciliation between man and God which is effected by God putting Himself in man's place at the Incarnation and by man being put in God's place at the Ascension.[4] It was an appreciation of this that led the Fathers to declare so frequently that Ascension Day was the crown of all Christian feasts—a theme that Augustine expressed with unimpeachable

[1] J. Wright, *Some Remarks on Mr. Whiston's Dissertation about Christ's Ascension*, 1709, p. 14.
[2] Contrast Theodore of Mopsuestia: the Resurrection "is the end of all the economy of Christ" (*Lib. ad Bapt.*, *Woodbrook Studies*, VI, 1933, ed. A. Mingana, p. 75).
[3] K. Barth, *Dogmatics in Outline*, E.T., 1949, p. 126.
[4] *Ibid.*, p. 115.

clarity: "This is that festival which confirms the grace of all the festivals together, without which the profitableness of every festival would have perished. For unless the Saviour had ascended into heaven, His Nativity would have come to nothing . . . and His Passion would have borne no fruit for us, and His most holy Resurrection would have been useless."[1]

There are those who claim that the Cross is the heart of the Gospel; others that the Resurrection should occupy this position. It is not my intention to seek to displace either of these two by the Ascension, but to add the Ascension to them, so that this triad in unity is recognized as forming the heart of the Gospel, i.e. that which Bultmann designates "the salvation-occurrence".[2] It is from these three, and not from the first two only, that Christian preaching began, and moreover, Christian worship and Christian belief. The disciples preached the Lord Jesus;[3] they confessed Him as Lord;[4] they met to eat the Lord's Supper,[5] and they did so because they knew that salvation rested upon belief in the Lord Jesus,[6] in Him who had been exalted to the right hand of God. Hence the modern realization that the New Testament record was written in the light of the Resurrection requires modification, in so far as it must be affirmed that these writers lived not only in the days of the Resurrection but also in the days of the Ascension. Nor is this mere tautology: the two are distinct, however intimately they be connected.

The Resurrection accomplished the vanquishing of death, and through it the humanity of Christ was transformed so that it was no longer subject to the conditions of mortality; hence the Resurrection was the necessary precondition of the Ascension when that transformed humanity entered upon new conditions of existence in heaven. The one established the hope of immortality, the other the certainty of reconciliation through the Lord Jesus. Hence we may agree with H. Sasse that "it is of profound significance that the New Testament distinguishes the resurrection from the exaltation of Christ. As the Risen One, Christ would only be the firstfruit from the dead, the firstborn among many brethren. His resurrection

---

[1] *Sermo* 53.4 (*Coll. Selec. SS. Ecclesiae Patrum*, ed. D. A. B. Caillau, 131B, 1842, p. 278).
[2] *Theology of the New Testament*, E.T., 1952, p. 293.
[3] Acts 11: 20. [4] Phil. 2: 11; 1 Cor. 12: 3. [5] 1 Cor. 11: 20. [6] Acts 16: 31.

would thus only be the beginning of the general resurrection of the dead. There would be no fundamental difference between His resurrection and ours. His 'Lordship' would be inconceivable apart from the resurrection, but it would not be accounted for by it alone. For this reason the New Testament draws a logical distinction between the resurrection and the exaltation."[1] It is indeed one thing to say that Christ is risen, meaning that death and corruption no longer hold Him: it is another thing to say that He has ascended, meaning that He is not only alive but sovereign.[2]

We conclude then that the Ascension with the Resurrection form two distinct elements in Christ's redemptive work, and we may therefore express the meaning of the first in a variety of ways depending upon which particular interpretation of the economy we may have in mind. Thus if we accept the Classical theory of the Atonement, we may see in the Ascension the final act which marks the overthrow of the demonic powers and the triumphal procession of the victor; on the other hand, if we prefer the sacrificial theory, then the Ascension is the occasion of the offering to the Father of that perfect humanity which was sacrificed upon the Cross.[3] It marks not only the bringing of humanity to God, but also the conclusion of the days of humiliation and the consummation of the process of glorification whereby man, in whose nature God had become a participant through the Incarnation, was made a participant in the glory of the Godhead.

It is, however, the conception of the offering of the firstfruits, a recurring feature in the patristic teaching, which most vividly interprets the Ascension with the aid of Biblical imagery.

The simplest formulation of the rule governing the offering of the firstfruits is to be found in the Book of the Covenant and in the law of the Two Tables: "The first of the firstfruits (*rē'shīth bikkūrīm*) of thy ground thou shalt bring into the house of the Lord thy God."[4] The first (*bikkūrīm*) is that part of the crop which both ripens first and is reaped first, while the firstfruits (*rē'shīth*) denotes both the first, the beginning,

---

[1] *Mysterium Christi*, ed. G. K. A. Bell and D. A. Deissmann, 1930, p. 105.
[2] cp. A. M. Ramsey, *The Resurrection of Christ*, 1945, p. 122.
[3] We may indeed question the satisfactoriness of certain other theories, e.g. the Abelardian, on the grounds that they assign no adequate place to the Ascension.
[4] Exod. 23: 19; 34: 26.

and the best, the main part. The full meaning of the term is thus not conveyed by the English translation, and moreover it applies not only to crops but also to the beginning of a period of time. The first day of a period embodies the character of the whole period so that the following days unfold from it; and the first Israelite is the archetype in whom the whole Israelite nation is inherent. "Every totality", comments Pedersen, "is concentrated in its first origin."[1] Hence the importance to the Hebrews of the offering of the firstfruits—as the first they represent the whole; the entire blessedness of the harvest is concentrated in them. So "the firstfruits have a special possibility of being holy and acting by their holiness on the growth of the rest of the produce".[2] By their offering and consequent sanctification the whole of the harvest is affected. The treatment of the firstborn[3] is strictly analogous to this, for they are the firstfruits of the herd or, in the case of human beings, of the family or clan; they too must be offered to God so that the way may be prepared for the next generation which is to perpetuate the life of the race to which they belong.[4]

This then is the background to the statement that the Ascension is the offering of the firstfruits of human nature to God; the application is not difficult to make,[5] indeed St. Paul was both familiar with the underlying principle and made use of it. Thus he enunciated the rationale: "If the firstfruit is holy, so is the lump."[6] He applied it: "Now hath Christ been raised from the dead, the firstfruits of them that are asleep."[7] Similarly Christ is the firstborn in a threefold sense: the first-born of all creation[8] according to His divine nature; the firstborn of Mary[9] according to His human nature; the first-born of the dead[10] according to the unity of His Person.

Christ then is the firstfruits because He is the first to attain to the Resurrection and Ascension, and He is the beginning because He is the *fons et origo* of the Ascended life. As the first-fruits He must be brought into the Temple of God in order that mankind might be consecrated through the offering of His human nature. This is accomplished through the Ascension,

---

[1] J. Pedersen, *Israel*, III-IV, 1940, p. 301.
[2] Pedersen, *loc. cit.*
[3] Exod. 22: 29f.; 34: 19f.
[4] Pedersen, *op. cit.*, p. 314.
[5] cp. above, p. 116.

[6] Rom. 11: 16.
[7] I Cor. 15: 20.
[8] Col. 1: 15; Heb. 1: 6.
[9] Luke 2: 7.
[10] Col. 1: 18; Rev. 1: 5.

and it is apposite to recall that ἀναβαίνω in its LXX usage means not only to mount up but also to offer sacrifice.[1] So by means of the Ascension His manhood was offered and finally sanctified, and then received the Holy Spirit, thus becoming the source of blessing to all mankind. "Being therefore by the right hand of God exalted, and having received of the Father the promise of the Holy Ghost, he hath poured forth this, which ye see and hear."[2] The appropriateness of the imagery of the firstfruits may be illustrated further from the fact that the firstfruits of the barley harvest were offered "on the morrow after the sabbath",[3] which is most probably the Sunday of Passover week,[4] i.e. the very day on which, according to our previous argument, Christ's Resurrection and Ascension took place and the Age to come began to dawn.

Christ is also the firstborn in so far as being the Image of God He is the archetype of the first Adam, and in so far as He was Himself the second Adam, whose nature was fashioned afresh in the Virgin's womb, He is the beginning of the new creation. As the firstborn He must be offered to God that the new race of which He is the origin may draw its life from His self-consecration whereby it too is sanctified; this is the function of the Ascension when the Son of God brought His manhood to the Father. Rightly is the Church, His Body, of which He is the risen and ascended Head, termed "the church of the firstborn".[5]

His Body, glorified through Resurrection and Ascension, is now the centre and substance of His mystical Body, the Church —hence the virtual identity between them. But since "it is not yet made manifest what we shall be,"[6] since, that is to say, our present condition is in contrast with His present condition, the two must be distinguished in our understanding. We have received the pledge but not the fulness of our inheritance.

It is at this point that we must recognize that the doctrine of the Church, with its essentially Christological basis, also sheds light upon the subject of the Ascension. It was the realization of this that underlay Augustine's teaching concerning the Head and the Body, to the effect that as members of

---

[1] See above, p. 24.
[2] Acts 2: 33.
[3] Lev. 23: 11.
[4] Pedersen, *op. cit.*, pp. 303, 400.
[5] Heb. 12: 23.
[6] 1 John 3: 2.

Christ we now have access to heaven through our ascended Head. Since the Church is *totus Christus*, there can be no separation of Head and Body, and therefore the ascent of the One necessarily includes the uplifting of the other. In Christ we are highly exalted—no less than the Crucifixion and the Resurrection, the Ascension, too, has its profound consequences for the community of the redeemed.

The first of these consequences that we may note is related to the fact that the Ascension, in the words of Karl Barth, "is the beginning of this time of ours".[1] *Now* is the time of the Church's mission to the world: it is "end-time": the time between the Ascension and the Parousia, and our entrance upon this eschatological dimension is marked by the Ascension. The Church militant is of course inescapably involved in space and time. It is the instrument of God's saving purpose within history, but it nevertheless possesses a life beyond itself in the ascended Christ who is to come. The Ascension therefore means that "the Church is sent to live its life and to exercise its ministry within the limitations of history, but here by the Spirit the limitations of history cease to be mere limitations for their finality is taken away".[2] So the Ascension determines the eschatological reference of the Church's life, for it points us forward to the Second Coming. Already the present age is interpenetrated by the age to come, but the final revelation of glory is held "in eschatological reserve"[3] that the Gospel may be preached and that, in this time of God's patience, the opportunity for repentance and response may be offered.

It follows therefore—and this is the second consequence to be noted—that the Ascension is the foundation of Christian faith, for "faith is the assurance of things hoped for, the proving of things not seen".[4] By His withdrawal of Himself at the Ascension from the realm of the visible, Christ provides the occasion for faith, which is the bond of union with Him in His exalted state. *Now* is the time of faith, not of sight. And this withdrawal has taken Him out of the visible succession of history, thereby making it impossible to relegate Him to the distant past. Christ is indeed our contemporary in whom we may trust. But since His Ascension was the climax of what

---

[1] *op. cit.*, p. 128.
[2] T. F. Torrance, *Royal Priesthood*, 1955, p. 56.
[3] *Ibid.*, p. 60.
[4] Heb. 11: 1.

He had done in history, we are directed to the historical Jesus, "not just as an object for historical investigation by the canons of credibility available for all other events in fading time, but as real historical happening in which the past is fully present reality. Through the Ascension then Christ has withdrawn Himself from sight that we may find Him alive and risen in the historical Jesus as communicated through the Apostolic witness and tradition and through the Spirit be united to Him in His Humanity as the forgiven and redeemed."[1]

Yet faith which thus unites us with the ascended Lord is inseparable from hope by which we stretch out to the final consummation at Christ's Second Coming, for Christians believe, with Augustine, that the Head, who has entered into glory, will draw His members after Him. "Hope", according to Calvin, "is the anchor of the soul which presses on into the innermost sanctuary, but only because Christ has gone before."[2] The aim of the Christian towards the heavenly life is indeed grounded in the Ascension of Christ, and the whole man and the whole of his temporal life must be orientated towards the future goal already realized in Christ; i.e. Christian moral endeavour is itself involved in the Ascension, for, to quote Calvin once more: "If Christ has been raised to heaven, then how far removed from a Christian must be all lust. For what has Christ, after His Ascension into heaven, in common with the filth of this world?"[3] And again: "Since our soul and body are appointed to heavenly life and immortality and to a crown that fadeth not away, we must therefore exert ourselves to see that they are kept pure and blameless unto the day of His appearing."[4]

But the Christian is not left to "exert" himself alone. "Christ has departed from us in order that He may be present to us in a way that is far richer in blessing than was possible during His incarnate life, when He was yet confined to the humble abode of the flesh. . . . He has been received into heaven and has thereby withdrawn from our gaze His bodily presence, but His purpose was not to withdraw His help from the faithful who are still pilgrims on earth but to govern heaven and earth

1 Torrance, *op. cit.*, p. 58.
2 On 1 Peter 1: 21, quoted by T. F. Torrance, *Kingdom and Church*, 1956, p. 20.
3 On 1 Cor. 6: 14, quoted Torrance, *Kingdom and Church*, p. 44.
4 Calvin, *Inst.*, III.6.3.

with more effectual power."[1] Thus, although the Ascension was the final act in the redemptive process, it did not mark any final parting of Christ from His followers. Christ's promise, given *after* the Ascension, if our interpretation of the Matthean account is correct: "Lo, I am with you alway, even unto the consummation of the age"[2]—this promise still stands. But in very few instances does this involve a visual presence, rather the ascended Christ is known in the breaking of the bread whereby the members are offered to the Father by the ascended Head in union with His perfect manhood sacrificed once and for all on Calvary. Hence, as Bede remarked, the Sacraments too are involved in Christ's Ascension and look towards His return.[3] "We teach that if believers would find Christ in heaven, they must begin with the Word and Sacraments. We turn this view to Baptism and the Supper, that in this way they may rise to the full height of celestial glory."[4]

This participation in the ascended humanity through Word and Sacrament[5] is an essential element in the eschatological context of the Church's life, because that humanity is the humanity of Him who is to come. The Sacraments indeed belong to the time between the two Advents and, together with faith, are the medium of Christ's presence until that presence is revealed in all its fulness at His return in glory.

This reference to "fulness" may serve to remind us of the sole New Testament passage which gives an explicit definition of the purpose of the Ascension. According to Eph. 4: 10, Christ ascended "that he might fill all things".[6] To understand this statement we must take account of the threefold relation of πλήρωμα—to Christ, to the Church and to the universe.

In the Old Testament to "fill heaven and earth" is a note of Deity,[7] and in the New Testament it is affirmed that in Christ "dwelleth all the fulness of the Godhead bodily".[8] Christ therefore possesses the sum total of the divine perfections and qualities. He ascended that He might enter into regal relations with the whole world; He was exalted in order that He

---

[1] Calvin, *Inst.*, II.16.14.   [2] Matt. 28: 20.   [3] cp. Augustine, *c. Faust.*, 20.21.
[4] Calvin, *Sec. Def. c. Westphalum*, quoted Torrance, *op. cit.*, p. 129n.
[5] For the relation between the Ascension and the ministry of the Church, see Torrance, *Royal Priesthood*, especially pp. 38ff., 61.
[6] ἵνα πληρώσῃ, a final clause expressing purpose.   [7] Jer. 23: 24.   [8] Col. 2: 9.

might fill the universe with His divine activity as Sovereign and Governor, thereby claiming it as His rightful possession. The Church also is referred to as the fulness of Christ,[1] that is to say, it is a vessel into which the fulness of Christ is poured, and it is the fulness of Christ because that fulness cannot be manifested among men without the human vessel that contains it.[2] But the Church has still to attain to its maturity, "unto the measure of the stature of the fulness of Christ".[3] Πλήρωμα or fulfilment is thus a movement which takes place intensively within the Body of Christ. "Potentially that organism includes the whole human race in its Christ-filled maturity",[4] and it is the Church's task to embody this fulness and so extend it to incorporate all mankind.[5] Thus the σῶμα reaches out through the Spirit to the πλήρωμα or fulfilment,[6] which is consequently also an extensive movement spreading out to the ends of the earth and to the end of the ages. The new humanity which appeared in Christ is then to be universalized, and for this the Ascension is the necessary precondition, issuing in the mission of the Spirit and so of the Church. Christ is therefore the Divine Fulfiller who is to bring the universe to its predestined goal. He ascended to bring the whole of God's creation to its πλήρωμα.[7] Thus the Incarnational process reaches its end and in this process we notice a recurring pattern.

Christ descends in order that He might ascend with our humanity: He ascends in order that the Spirit might descend through that assumed humanity which is the fount and source of this blessing: the Spirit descends in order that we, in due season, might ascend whither our Head has preceded us. On earth the immanent Spirit is the earnest of our inheritance, the firstfruits of our redemption: in heaven the ascended manhood is the pledge of our consummated destiny, the firstfruits of our risen and ascended human nature.

To speak of the Incarnational process is, however, to call attention to the fact that our understanding of the Ascension must rest not only on its integration with the Crucifixion and

[1] Eph. 1: 23.
[2] cp. L. S. Thornton, *The Common Life in the Body of Christ*, 1941, p. 310.
[3] Eph. 4: 13.
[4] Thornton, *op. cit.*, p. 317.
[5] cp. J. A. T. Robinson, *The Body*, 1952, p. 71.
[6] cp. Torrance, *Royal Priesthood*, p. 24.
[7] cp. Calvin, *Inst.*, IV.6.10.

the Resurrection, as part of the salvation-occurrence, nor just on the doctrine of the Church and the Sacraments, but upon our interpretation of the initial act of divine condescension. This is very clearly revealed in the teaching of Hilary of Poitiers,[1] whose belief that the Incarnation involved a partial severance in the divine unity led him logically and inevitably to posit a restoration of that unity at the Ascension: what he thought of the one thus rightly determined what he taught of the other. Although we may hesitate to follow Hilary in his daring speculation, his perception that Incarnation and Ascension are not to be separated is one that should not be neglected.

There are four features of Christology which are especially relevant to this present study. The first of these is the acknowledgment that the Incarnation involved no movement in space —to say that the Son of God descended is to refer to His condescension and not to a physical descent. There is scarcely need to press this point further, and its bearing upon the Ascension equally requires no labouring since it demands no more than a reaffirmation of what has already been stated, viz. that the Ascension involved no physical movement to a localized heaven. The second feature, however, requires more extended treatment, i.e. the fact of *kenosis*.

Kenotic Christology is based upon a passage in the second chapter of St. Paul's Epistle to the Philippians, vv. 5-11—a passage in which the Apostle associates the same two themes that we are considering, i.e. Incarnation and Ascension. St. Paul's thesis is that though Christ was by nature divine ($\dot{\epsilon}\nu$ $\mu o\rho\phi\hat{\eta}$ $\Theta\epsilon o\hat{v}$), He did not treat equality with God as "something to be seized" or "a prize" ($\dot{a}\rho\pi a\gamma\mu\dot{o}\nu$), as did the first Adam who, wishing "to be as God", snatched at the prize and, in his fall, dragged mankind down with him. On the contrary, the second Adam voluntarily denuded or emptied Himself ($\dot{\epsilon}av\tau\dot{o}\nu$ $\dot{\epsilon}\kappa\dot{\epsilon}\nu\omega\sigma\epsilon\nu$) and through His obedience exalted mankind to God, receiving consequently the name of Godhead[2] so that all may worship Him as they worship the Father. The implication of this passage is that the Incarnation involved a voluntary self-limitation of the eternal Son to an historical

---

[1] See above, pp. 100-03.
[2] The "name" of God in the Old Testament stands for the character and power of God revealed in His mighty acts; so the redemptive act of Christ has revealed that He is entitled to the "name" of God.

human consciousness and human faculties of knowledge and action. The original form of this theory, with its too crude discrimination between those attributes of the Godhead which the Son gave up and those He retained, has few if any supporters at the present time, and there are many, too, who would still reject even a modified form of this teaching.[1] But I would endorse the judgment of the late Dr. O. C. Quick that its central principle, viz. the voluntary self-abnegation of the Son, "has proved itself to be the most important contribution to Christology which has been made since the time of Irenaeus"[2]—it being understood that what is involved in this reformulation of the theory is a limitation of consciousness rather than of actual being.

What contribution then does the *kenosis* make to our understanding of the Ascension? Clearly the Ascension was the occasion when the period of self-humiliation and self-renunciation came to an end; when the consciousness of absolute unity and communion with the Father, which in varying manners and degrees, most notably shown in the cry of dereliction on the Cross, had been limited by the flesh, was fully restored. We may even then go as far as Hilary in asserting that the Incarnation involved a partial disruption of the divine unity, which was restored by the Ascension, *if we understand that disruption not in a metaphysical sense but as taking place in the sphere of consciousness.*

At this juncture a further emphasis of modern Christological teaching may prove of value, viz. that Christ, in so far as He was truly human, was subject to conditions of human growth and development.[3] We must therefore go on to affirm that it was through the Ascension that this process reached its consummation, when the manhood, in indissoluble unity with the Godhead, entered upon a new mode of being and was liberated from its previous limitations. But the removal of these limitations did not involve the obscuring of the distinction between Creator and creature. The perfection then revealed was the perfection of the persisting manhood of Christ "who, being the eternal Son of God, became man, and so was, and continueth

---

[1] cp. D. M. Baillie, *God was in Christ*, 1948, pp. 94-98.
[2] *The Doctrines of the Creed*, 1938, pp. 132-33.
[3] L. Hodgson, *And Was Made Man*, 1928, pp. 40f., 50-56, 159, 192f.

to be, God and man in two distinct natures, and one person, for ever".[1] Henceforth the Second Hypostasis of the Godhead is divine humanity and, in the words of Berdyaev, "the eternal face of man abides in the very heart of the Divine Trinity Itself".[2]

The third feature of Christology upon which we are to touch is the *enhypostasia*, i.e. the doctrine that the manhood of Christ was inpersonal. According to this teaching, which is a refinement by Leontius of Byzantium of the views of Cyril of Alexandria, there was no man Jesus existing independently of the divine Son of God: the human element in the Incarnation was human *nature* assumed by the Second Person of the Trinity— the *persone* was the pre-existent Son, the human nature being inpersonal.[3] As applied to the Ascension this means that it was not the occasion of the exaltation of an individual man, but of human nature. It was therefore a unique event; it cannot be compared, for example, with the apotheosis of a Hercules or with the translation of an Elijah; it was the taking up of human nature itself into the Godhead, being the completion of the redemptive act begun in the womb of the Virgin. Thus the Ascension confirms the twofold nature of the Incarnate Lord: it was not man but God in man who ascended. As man He appears before the face of God for us in order to bring us in Himself to God; as Son He now sits at the right hand of the Father to bestow the glory of adoption on all humanity. Equally the Incarnation confirms the reality of the Ascension, for the unity of Person in the Incarnate Lord necessarily entailed the entry of the manhood with the Godhead into the heavenlies as the final act in the drama of redemption.

It is this unity that eternally secures the relation of man to God, and the Ascension reveals that this relation, established by the hypostatic union, was no mere passing phenomenon but an abiding reality. Consequently through the exaltation of the Incarnate Son man may approach God and this may be expressed in terms of mediation, which itself is inseparable from the exercise of the office of high priest. It is the manhood of Christ, which has entered heaven through

[1] *Westminster Shorter Catechism*, Ans. to Q. 21.
[2] *Freedom and the Spirit*, 1935, p. 207.
[3] For a modern statement of this, see E. L. Mascall, *Christ, The Christian and The Church*, 1946, pp. 1-10.

the Ascension, that provides the point of contact between God and us in our creaturely state. Moreover, by the Ascension one of the indispensable preconditions of the high priest's continual intercession was fulfilled—Christ has entered "into heaven itself, now to appear before the face of God for us".[1] The Ascension was indeed a necessary stage in the mission of Christ which culminated in the Session at the right hand of the Father[2] and in the consequent mission of the Holy Spirit.

The fourth and final feature of Christology with which we are concerned is that which turns upon the absoluteness of the Incarnation. The Fathers were unanimous that the Incarnation was dependent upon the Fall.[3] "It was our state", affirms Athanasius, "that was the cause of the great descent; our transgression that evoked the loving kindness of the Word."[4] But many of the mediaeval Divines,[5] of whom Rupert of Deutz († 1131) would seem to have been the first, were of the opinion that the "taking of the manhood into God" was the goal of creation from the beginning. The schools therefore debated the question: whether Christ would have been incarnate if Adam had not sinned. Thus Thomas Aquinas states: "some say that since by the Incarnation of the Son of God there was accomplished not only the liberation from sin, but also the exaltation of human nature, and the consummation of the whole universe, for these reasons even if sin had not existed, the Incarnation would have taken place."[6] If this were not so, it was argued, man would have gained an advantage from his wickedness and the Incarnation would have rested upon a contingency instead of being part of God's purpose for mankind: this, however, has not been frustrated by the Fall, and although the circumstances of the Incarnation—the sufferings, the Cross, etc.—were due to man's sin, the Incarnation itself was included in the mystery of God's eternal plan.

[1] Heb. 9: 24.
[2] A. J. Tait, *The Heavenly Session of Our Lord*, 1912.
[3] The only patristic writer who suggested that the Incarnation belonged to the original plan of Creation, and in this sense was independent of the Fall, was Maximus the Confessor (*Quaest. ad Thal.*, 60; *P.G.* 90.620-25).
[4] *De Inc.*, 4.2; cp. "His becoming man would not have taken place had not the need of man become a cause", *Or. c. Arianos*, 2.56.
[5] Their teaching is surveyed by B. F. Westcott, *The Epistles of St. John*, 1883, pp. 273-314.
[6] *Sent.*, iii. *Dist.*, i. *Quaest.*, 1.

It will be evident that the meaning of the Ascension will be defined with differing emphases depending upon how we answer this question concerning the contingency or absoluteness of the Incarnation.[1] Thus to apply the former first.

Through the Resurrection the power of death has been broken and we may sing with the Apostle: "O death, where is thy sting? . . . Death is swallowed up in victory."[2] But this exultant affirmation does not exhaust the content of Christian hope. Not only has Christ triumphed over death, He has also entered heaven. The two are not identical. To have triumphed over death is to have reversed the adverse verdict passed upon the sons of Adam, but the consequence is not, as might have been expected, a return to the earthly Paradise but an entrance into the heavenlies—an entrance which has been effected through the Ascension which therefore consummates the economy of redemption, while being an integral part of it. Hence, from the standpoint of the contingency of the Incarnation, it is through the Resurrection *and* the Ascension, and not through the former alone, that man can now say: *"Felix culpa!"* To be restored to the condition of unfallen Adam would no doubt be an occasion for rejoicing, but to enter with the second Adam into heaven itself is something which surpasses even that which the Resurrection by itself would have effected. Hence St. Augustine could open a sermon on the Feast of the Ascension with the words: "To-day we have received by grace a greater place of refuge through the Ascension of Christ than we had lost through the envy of the devil."[3]

If, however, we now consider the Incarnation in its absolute character, then we must affirm that the Ascension has not enabled us to say *"Felix culpa!"* of the Fall: instead, it provides us with an insight into God's plan for mankind. It is the revelation of what God has eternally purposed for man. Thus the Ascension manifests the final condition of those who are in Christ. We may indeed see man's ultimate goal revealed and already attained by Jesus, who has trodden the whole path of human destiny.

[1] Either position is of course tenable and it is not my task to decide in favour of one or the other, but the Scriptural interpretation of the Ascension does seem to accord better with the absoluteness of the Incarnation.
[2] I Cor. 15: 55, 54.
[3] *Sermo* 54.1 (Caillau, *op. cit.*, p. 281).

What is man, that thou art mindful of him?
Or the son of man, that thou visitest him?
Thou madest him a little lower than the angels;
Thou crownedst him with glory and honour,
And didst set him over the works of thy hands:
Thou didst put all things in subjection under his feet.[1]

Christ thus embodies in Himself the long course of human history as purposed by God in His original creation. This, we may say, borrowing Scriptural phraseology, is the "mystery" of the divine will,[2] which has now been made known through the Ascension of Christ, that He "chose us in him before the foundation of the world . . . having foreordained us unto adoption as sons . . . to sum up all things in Christ".[3]

This revelation affects the Christian eschatological hope which is seen to be centred not only in the Parousia and in the Resurrection of the dead, but also in the Ascension of the redeemed. In the New Testament this is expressed in a variety of ways. In his First Epistle to the Thessalonians, St. Paul asserts that we are "to be caught up in the clouds, to meet the Lord in the air: and so shall we ever be with the Lord".[4] In the Epistle to the Hebrews, Christ is styled the forerunner,[5] He who at His Ascension has gone before us whither we are to follow. In the fourth Gospel Jesus is represented as saying: "I go to prepare a place for you. And if I go and prepare a place for you, I come again, and will receive you unto myself; that where I am, there ye may be also."[6]

This belief in the Ascension of the redeemed is enshrined in the phrase "life everlasting", which was apparently inserted in the Apostles' Creed to reassure those many Christians who feared that their resurrection might only lead to their dying again.[7] That this was an issue at the beginning of the fifth century is evident from statements by Augustine[8] and John Chrysostom,[9] who, faced with the anxiety that believers might rise and yet die again like Lazarus, affirmed that after the Resurrection they would enter upon life everlasting, i.e. upon

---

[1] Ps. 8: 4-6, cited in Heb. 2: 6-8.　　[4] 1 Thess. 4: 17.
[2] Eph. 1: 9.　　[5] Heb. 6: 20.
[3] Eph. 1: 4, 5, 10.　　[6] John 14: 2, 3.
[7] J. N. D. Kelly, *Early Christian Creeds*, 1950, pp. 387-88.
[8] *Enchir.*, 84 (*P.L.* 40.272); *Ep.*, 102 (*P.L.* 33.371ff.).
[9] *Hom.*, 40.2 (*P.G.* 61.349).

the life of the world to come. This theme is implicit in the argument of Nicetas of Remesiana that life everlasting is life with Christ in heaven, eternal and blessed life.[1] So we see that "the Resurrection and Ascension of Christ are two moments in the anticipation of the ultimate home-gathering of the whole people of God".[2]

At the Ascension the eternal Son of God reassumed that glory which He had with the Father before the world was, and the glorification of His manhood was then perfected. Christians, whose "citizenship is in heaven"[3] and who already reflect that glory by the agency of the Spirit,[4] will themselves, as His members, be changed into glory.[5] "As we have borne the image of the earthy, we shall also bear the image of the heavenly."[6] At the Parousia we shall "see him even as he is"[7] and no longer "in a mirror darkly; but then face to face".[8] We shall behold Him in His ascended glory and will in our turn ascend with Him, to join the chorus of heavenly praise to Him whose glorification enables us to laud Him here below in the words of the doxology:

Glory be to the Father, and to the Son, and to the Holy Ghost: As it was in the beginning, is now, and ever shall be, world without end. Amen.

---

[1] *De Symb.*, 12.
[2] C. F. D. Moule, "The Ascension—Acts i. 9", *Expository Times*, LXVIII, 1957, p. 209.
[3] Phil. 3: 20.
[4] 2 Cor. 3: 18.
[5] 2 Cor. 4: 17; 2 Thess. 2: 14; 2 Tim. 2: 10.
[6] I Cor. 15: 49.
[7] I John 3: 2.
[8] I Cor. 13: 12.

Table A

PARALLELS BETWEEN TOBIT 12 AND LUKE 24

TOBIT 12	LUKE 24
12. Tobit complimented on care for dead	1-3. women go to care for dead
16. καὶ ἐταράχθησαν οἱ δύο καὶ ἔπεσον ἐπὶ πρόσωπον	38. τί τεταραγμένοι ἐστέ 5. καὶ κλινουσῶν τὰ πρόσωπα εἰς τὴν γῆν
ὅτι ἐφοβήθησαν	5. ἐμφόβων δὲ γενομένων 37. ἔμφοβοι γενόμενοι
17. καὶ εἶπεν αὐτοῖς Μὴ φοβεῖσθε εἰρήνη ὑμῖν ἔσται	36. καὶ λέγει αὐτοῖς Εἰρήνη ὑμῖν
18. τὸν δὲ θεὸν εὐλογεῖτε	53. εὐλογοῦντες τὸν Θεόν
19. πάσας τὰς ἡμέρας ὠπτανόμην καὶ οὐκ ἔφαγον οὐδὲ ἔπιον	23. ὀπτασίαν ἀγγέλων 43. ἐνώπιον αὐτῶν ἔφαγεν
20. ἀναβαίνω πρὸς τὸν ἀποστείλαντά με	51. διέστη ἀπ' αὐτῶν καὶ ἀνεφέρετο εἰς τὸν οὐρανόν
21. καὶ ἀνέστησαν καὶ οὐκ εἶδον αὐτόν	46. καὶ ἀναστῆναι ἐκ νεκρῶν 24. αὐτὸν δὲ οὐκ εἶδον

Table B

PARALLELS BETWEEN LUKE 9 AND ACTS 1[1]

LUKE 9	ACTS 1
1. Commissioning of the apostles Reference to δύναμιν and to ἐξουσίαν	2,8. Commissioning of the apostles Reference to δύναμιν and to ἐξουσίᾳ
2, 11, 27. Reference to βασιλείαν τοῦ Θεοῦ	3. Reference to βασιλείας τοῦ Θεοῦ
5. μαρτύριον	8. μάρτυρες
7-9, 18-21. Reference to John the Baptist and to Elijah	5. Reference to John the Baptist and (implicitly) to Elijah
10. Return of the apostles (ὑποστρέψαντες)	12. Return of the apostles to Jerusalem (ὑπέστρεψαν)
10-17. Feeding of the 5,000	4. Feeding together (συναλιζόμενος)
16. Jesus ἀναβλέψας εἰς τὸν οὐρανὸν	11. The apostles βλέποντες εἰς τὸν οὐρανόν
22. Reference to Death and Resurrection	3. Reference to Death and Resurrection
26. Reference to Parousia	11. Reference to Parousia
28. εἰς τὸ ὅρος	12. ἀπὸ ὄρους
29. ἱματισμὸς λευκὸς	10. ἐσθήσεσι λευκαῖς
30. καὶ ἰδοὺ ἄνδρες δύο	10. καὶ ἰδοὺ ἄνδρες δύο
31. ἔξοδος	11. ἀναλημφθεὶς... εἰς τὸν οὐρανὸν
34. νεφέλη	9. νεφέλη

[1] I am grateful to the editors of the *Journal of Theological Studies* for permission to reprint this table.

Table C

PARALLELS BETWEEN LUKE 24 AND ACTS 1

LUKE 24: 46-53	ACTS 1: 4-14
46. εἶπεν αὐτοῖς	7. εἶπεν πρὸς αὐτούς
48. ὑμεῖς μάρτυρες	8. ἔσεσθέ μου μάρτυρες
47. καὶ κηρυχθῆναι ... εἰς πάντα τὰ ἔθνη,— ἀρξάμενοι ἀπὸ Ἰερουσαλήμ	ἔν τε Ἰερουσαλήμ καὶ ἐν πάσῃ τῇ Ἰουδαίᾳ καὶ Σαμαρίᾳ καὶ ἕως ἐσχάτου τῆς γῆς
49. καὶ ἰδοὺ ἐγὼ ἐξαποστέλλω τὴν ἐπαγγελίαν τοῦ Πατρός ὑμεῖς δὲ καθίσατε ἐν τῇ πόλει	4. περιμένειν τὴν ἐπαγγελίαν τοῦ Πατρός παρήγγειλεν αὐτοῖς ἀπὸ Ἱεροσολύμων μὴ χωρίζεσθαι
ἕως οὗ ἐνδύσησθε ἐξ ὕψους δύναμιν	8. λήμψεσθε δύναμιν ἐπελθόντος τοῦ Ἁγίου Πνεύματος ἐφ' ὑμᾶς
50. ἐξήγαγεν δὲ αὐτοὺς ἕως πρὸς Βηθανίαν	12. ἀπὸ ὄρους τοῦ καλουμένου Ἐλαιῶνος, ὅ ἐστιν ἐγγὺς Ἱερουσαλὴμ σαββάτου ἔχον ὁδόν.
51. διέστη ἀπ' αὐτῶν καὶ ἀνεφέρετο εἰς τὸν οὐρανόν	9. βλεπόντων αὐτῶν ἐπήρθη, καὶ νεφέλη ὑπέλαβεν αὐτὸν
	10. ... εἰς τὸν οὐρανόν
52. καὶ αὐτοὶ ... ὑπέστρεψαν εἰς Ἱερουσαλὴμ	12. τότε ὑπέστρεψαν εἰς Ἱερουσαλὴμ
53. καὶ ἦσαν διὰ παντὸς ἐν τῷ ἱερῷ εὐλογοῦντες τὸν Θεόν	14. οὗτοι πάντες ἦσαν προσκαρτεροῦντες ὁμοθυμαδὸν τῇ προσευχῇ

PARALLELS BETWEEN MARK 16: 9-20 AND LUKE 24

MARK 16	LUKE 24
9. Christ appears to Mary Magdalene	10. Mary Magdalene is among those to whom the angels make known the Resurrection
from whom He had cast out seven devils	tion (cp. Luke 8: 2)
11. Her report is disbelieved	11. Their report is disbelieved
12, 13. Jesus appears unto two of them as they go into the country—they return and inform the others	13-35. Jesus appears unto two of them as they go into a village—they return and inform the eleven
14. Jesus appears to the eleven as they eat	36, 41. Jesus appears to the eleven as they eat
He condemns their unbelief	37-43. He condemns their unbelief
15. He charges them to preach the Gospel to the whole creation	47b. He charges them to preach in His name to all the nations
16. He that believes and is baptized shall be saved	47a. Repentance and remission of sins shall be preached
17. Devils shall be cast out	(cp. Acts 5: 16)
Glossolalia	(cp. Acts 2: 4)
18. Serpents shall be held	(cp. Acts 28: 3-5)
Hands shall be laid on the sick	(cp. Acts 28: 8)
19. Jesus	51. He parted from them and
was received up into heaven	was carried up into heaven

(It will be noticed that the parallelism is one of content and not of vocabulary, which is to be expected where a brief summary of a longer passage is involved.)

Table E

PARALLELS BETWEEN 1 KINGS 19
AND ACTS

1 KINGS 19	ACTS
8. καὶ ἀνέστη	2: 24. ὃν ὁ Θεὸς ἀνέστησεν
καὶ ἔφαγεν	10: 41. οἵτινες συνεφάγομεν
καὶ ἔπιεν	καὶ συνεπίομεν
	αὐτῷ μετὰ τὸ ἀναστῆναι αὐτὸν
καὶ ἐπορεύθη . . .	1: 11. πορευόμενον
τεσσεράκοντα ἡμέρας . . .	1: 3. δι' ἡμερῶν τεσσεράκοντα
ἕως ὄρους	1: 12. ἀπὸ ὄρους
11-12. πνεῦμα . . .	2: 4. Πνεῦμα
συνσεισμός . . .	4: 31. ἐσαλεύθη ὁ τόπος
πῦρ . . .	2: 3. γλῶσσαι ὡσεὶ πυρός
φωνὴ . . .	2: 6. φωνῆς

Table F

THE ASCENSION SERMONS OF
ST. AUGUSTINE

In volume 38 of Migne, *Patrologia Latina*, the following Ascension sermons are printed:

1. *Sermo* 261 (1202-7).
2. *Sermo* 262 (1207-9).
3. *Sermo* 263 (*al. de Temp.* 174) (1209-12).
4. *Sermo* 264 (1212-18).
5. *Sermo* 265 (1218-24).

In volume 39, we have:

6. *Sermo* 395 (1716-17).

and in the Appendix of the same volume:

7. *Sermo* 176 (*al. de Temp.* 176) (2081-82).
8. *Sermo* 177 (*al. de Temp.* 175) (2082-83).
9. *Sermo* 178 (*al. de Temp.* 177) (2083-84).
10. *Sermo* 179 (*al. de Temp.* 178) (2084-85).
11. *Sermo* 180 (*al. de Temp.* 179) (2085-86).
12. *Sermo* 181 (*al. de Temp.* 180) (2086-87).

In *Collectio Selecta S.S. Ecclesiae Patrum*, ed. D. A. B. Caillau, 130, 1836, there are the following Ascension sermons:

13. *Sermo* 40 (224-28).
14. *Sermo* 41 (228-31).

and in the Appendix of the same volume:

15. *Sermo* 5 (364-66).
16. *Sermo* 6 (367-70).

In volume 131B (1842) of the same series, there are:

17. *Sermo* 53 (275-80).
18. *Sermo* 54 (280-86).
19. *Sermo* 55 (287-91).
20. *Sermo* 56 (292-305).
21. *Sermo* 57 (305-7).

In *Miscellanea Agostiniana*, ed. G. Morin, I, 1930, there are:

22. Mai XCVIII (347-50).
23. Liverani VIII (391-95).
24. Biblioth. Casin. II. 76 (413-15).
25. Guelferb. XX (504-6).
26. Guelferb. XXI (507-9).
27. Morin IX (619-23); also in *Rev. Bénéd.*, XXIX, 1912, pp. 253-56.
28. Morin XVII (659-64); also in *Rev. Bénéd.*, XLI, 1929, pp. 136-40.

Finally, in the *Revue Bénédictine*, in addition to the last two, there has been published:

29. Lambot (LI, 1939, pp. 25-27).
30. Lambot (LXII, 1952, pp. 97-100).

Of the above: 6, 15, 19 and 21 are of unknown authorship; 7 is by Faustus of Riez; 8 by Caesarius of Arles; 11 and 12 are doubtfully attributed also to Fulgentius of Ruspe; 16 is possibly by Leo, while 20 is a Latin translation of Chrysostom's Ascension sermon (*P.G.* 50.441-52). The remainder, with the possible exception of 10 and 14, are probably all by Augustine. They are not, however, all distinct the one from the other.

$$3.1 = 26.1, 2$$
$$3.2 \text{ (to } intuemur) = 26.3 \text{ (to } intuemur)$$
$$3.2 \text{ (} intuemur \text{ to } super\ caelos) = 22.1 \text{ (to } super\ caelos)$$
$$3.2 \text{ (} Neque\ enim \ldots in\ caelo) = 22.2 \text{ (} neque\ enim \ldots in\ caelo)$$
$$3.2 \text{ (} cum\ ascendit \ldots \text{ to end)} = 22.2 \text{ (} cum\ ascendit \ldots \text{ to end)}$$
$$3.3 = 22.3$$
$$3.4 = 22.4$$
$$9.1 \text{ (} \ldots maior\ est) = 23.1$$
$$9.2 = 23.7, 8$$

Appended Note I

THE OBSERVANCE OF ASCENSION DAY

IT is a very widely held belief among scholars that Ascension Day did not exist as a festival before the latter part of the fourth century.[1] Prior to that period, so it is argued, there was a unitive commemoration on Whit Sunday, when the Ascension and the Descent of the Spirit were observed together. Only with the development of the Church's Calendar were these separated, the former being celebrated on the fortieth and the latter on the fiftieth days after Easter.

The evidence adduced for a unitive festival is as follows:

1. In the *Doctrine of Addai*, a Syriac document which in its present form probably dates from *c.* 400, the statement is made that the Apostles "received powers and authorities at the time that He ascended".[2] This, to say the least, is a little vague, and it is going somewhat beyond the evidence to assert that "in the *Doctrina Addaei* the Ascension and Pentecost (i.e. the outpouring of the Spirit) are expressly placed on the same day, the fiftieth after the Resurrection".[3]

2. In the *Doctrine of the Apostles*, another Syriac document of the same period as the preceding, the Ascension is described and is apparently followed immediately by the gift of the Spirit.[4] It is further prescribed: "At the completion of fifty days after His Resurrection make the commemoration of His Ascension to His glorious Father."[5] This is an unambiguous affirmation that the Ascension is to be observed on what we now call Whit Sunday; surprisingly no reference is made to the commemoration of the descent of the Spirit.

3. In his *Commentary on Matthew*, written towards the end of his life, Jerome states: "*Montanus, Prisca et Maximilla etiam*

[1] So e.g. L. Duchesne, *Christian Worship*, 1904, p. 240; *Liturgy and Worship*, ed. W. K. Lowther Clarke, 1943, p. 208; G. Dix, *The Shape of the Liturgy*, 1945, p. 358; A. A. McArthur, *The Evolution of the Christian Year*, 1953, pp. 152-57.
[2] G. Phillips, *The Doctrine of Addai the Apostle*, 1876, p. 9.
[3] G. Kretschmar, "Himmelfahrt und Pfingsten", *Z. für K.*, LXVI, 1954-55, p. 217.
[4] W. Cureton, *Ancient Syriac Documents*, 1864, pp. 24-25.
[5] *Ibid.*, p. 27.

post Pentecosten faciunt quadragesimam: quod ablato sponso, filii sponsi debeant jejunare."[1] The reliability of this report, written some 250 years after the death of the people to whom it refers, is not beyond question. But in any case the observance of the obscure Montanist sect is scarcely evidence for the practice of the Church as a whole.

4. In his *Life of Constantine, c.* 337, Eusebius records: "Εκαστα δὲ τούτων ἐπὶ τῆς μεγίστης συνετελεῖτο ἑορτῆς, τῆς δὴ πανσέμνου καὶ σεβασμίας πεντηκοστῆς ἑβδομάσι μὲν ἑπτὰ τετιμημένης, μονάδι δ' ἐπισφραγιζομένης, καθ' ἥν τὴν εἰς οὐρανοὺς ἀνάληψιν τοῦ κοινοῦ σωτῆρος τήν τε τοῦ ἁγίου πνεύματος εἰς ἀνθρώπους κάθοδον γεγενῆσθαι λόγοι περιέχουσι θεῖοι. ἐν δὴ ταύτῃ τούτων ἀξιωθεὶς βασιλεύς, ἐπὶ τῆς ὑστάτης ἁπασῶν ἡμέρας, ἥν δὴ ἑορτὴν ἑορτῶν οὐκ ἄν τις διαμάρτοι καλῶν, ἀμφὶ μεσημβρινὰς ἡλίου ὥρας πρὸς τὸν αὐτοῦ Θεὸν ἀνελαμβάνετο.[2]

This may be translated into English as follows: "All these events occurred during a most important festival, I mean the august and holy solemnity of Pentecost, which is distinguished by a period of seven weeks, and sealed with that one day on which (καθ' ἥν) the holy Scriptures attest the Ascension of our common Saviour into heaven, and the descent of the Holy Spirit among men. In the course of this feast the emperor received the privileges I have just described; and on the last day of all, which one might justly call the feast of feasts, he was removed about mid-day to the presence of his God."

According to this rendering the Ascension was commemorated on the day of Pentecost itself,[3] but it is at least open to doubt whether this was the meaning intended by Eusebius, since καθ' ἥν could also be translated "during which" referring to the preceding πεντηκοστή rather than to μονάς.

Three considerations make this interpretation the more likely:

(i) All the statements in this passage, except the last, which concerns the Emperor's death on Whit Sunday itself, refer to the *season* of Pentecost.

(ii) The two participles, viz. τετιμημένης and ἐπισφραγιζομένης are in the nature of parentheses defining πεντηκοστῆς, with

---

[1] *Comm. in Evang. Matt.*, I.9 (*P.L.* 26.58D).   [2] 4.64.
[3] U. Holzmeister, "Der Tag der Himmelfahrt des Herrn", *Zeitschrift für katholische Theologie*, LV, 1931, p. 62; McArthur, *op. cit.*, p. 151.

which they are in apposition. καθ' ἥν is thus most naturally to be linked grammatically with πεντηκοστῆς.

(iii) This is confirmed by the phrase ἐν δὴ ταύτῃ, which certainly means "during the period of Pentecost".

We therefore translate: "the august and holy solemnity of Pentecost (distinguished by seven weeks, sealed by one day) during which the holy Scriptures attest the Ascension. . . .''

5. In the *Pilgrimage of Egeria*, c. 395, the writer records a celebration at Bethlehem on the fortieth day after Easter,[1] and then describes a gathering on Whit Sunday in the Imbomon and "the place from the Gospel is read where it speaks about the Lord's Ascension, and also from the Acts where it speaks of the Lord's Ascension into heaven after His Resurrection".[2] The account of the Bethlehem festival is incomplete and contains no reference to the Ascension, though one might reasonably suppose that no other event was being commemorated on that day.[3] This supposition is supported by the fact that Egeria was not writing a travel diary but a general report of all the services which were held day by day and year by year in the Holy Places. In other words, she was concerned with what was the normal practice, and there is no hint that what took place at Bethlehem was in any way extraordinary. What then of the readings in the Church of the Ascension on the Mount of Olives on Whit Sunday? It is obvious from Egeria's account that the Church authorities at Jerusalem made good use of the buildings at their disposal. On all great festivals services were held successively in each church, the worshippers progressing from one to the other throughout the day. A service in the Imbomon was therefore quite usual, so, e.g. services were also held there on Palm Sunday, Maundy Thursday, Easter

[1] *Itin. Hieros.*, *C.S.E.L.*, 38, ed. P. Geyer, p. 93.
[2] *Ibid.*, p. 94.
[3] In my article ("The *Peregrinatio Egeriae* and the Ascension", *Vig. Christ.*, VIII, 1954, pp. 93-100), I have advanced a hypothesis to explain why the Ascension was observed at Bethlehem and not at Jerusalem. This suggestion turns upon the late date of the construction of the Imbomon, and at the time of writing I had not noted the thesis of A. Grabar (*Martyrium. Recherches sur le culte des reliques et l'art chrétien antique*, I, 1946, pp. 283-89) that the Imbomon was in fact a Constantinian foundation. His argument, however, has been devastatingly criticised by L. H. Vincent ("L'Eléona, sanctuaire primitif de l'Ascension", *Revue Biblique*, LXIV, 1957, pp. 48-71), who demonstrates afresh that the Church of the Ascension was not built until c. 375, whereas the Eleona was a Constantinian building erected close to the traditional site of the Ascension to enshrine the cave where Jesus was believed to have spoken to His disciples of the Last Things.

Day and Easter Monday. We cannot assume then that a gathering in the Imbomon necessarily implies an Ascension festival. The readings for Whit Sunday itself in the Church of the Ascension were undoubtedly Luke 24: 49-53 and Acts 1: 6-12. In each passage there is a direct reference to the imminent descent of the Spirit, and they are therefore eminently suitable for reading on Whit Sunday which saw the fulfilment of this promise. To go further than this would be to read into the account more than it can be said certainly to contain, and to allow one's presuppositions as to the existence of a unitive festival to colour one's interpretation of the evidence upon which it is supposed to rest.

To sum up. Of the evidence adduced for a unitive festival, 1. is vague: 2. may possibly support it: 3. raises serious doubts on historical grounds: 4. is probably to be understood as affirming the opposite: 5. is at least ambiguous.[1] The most that one can say is that in a part of the Syriac speaking Church in the fourth century there *may have been* a unitive festival.[2] To generalize from this slender evidence is a dangerous proceeding,[3] and moreover it fails to take account of other evidence which indicates that the fortieth day after Easter was observed from the earliest days of the fourth century. This other evidence may now be summarized.

1. According to Canon 43 of the Council of Elvira (*c.* A.D. 310): *Pravam institutionem emendari placuit iuxta auctoritatem Scripturarum, ut cuncti diem Pentecostes celebremus, ne si quis non fecerit, novam haeresem induxisse notetur.*[4]

Several MSS. read *non quadragesimam* after *celebremus*, and an ancient abridgement also adds *post Pascha quinquagesima teneatur, non quadragesima.* Thus apparently the custom had arisen in certain parts of Spain of celebrating the fortieth day after Easter, not the fiftieth, i.e. Ascension not Pentecost. It has

---

[1] If Egeria is speaking of a unitive festival this would represent an anachronism (as the evidence detailed below will indicate) which is unlikely in view of the important role played by Jerusalem in the development of the Calendar.

[2] I stress the words "may have been" because one just does not know how far the prescription in the *Doctrina Apostolorum* was ever observed in practice.

[3] Kretschmar (*op. cit.*) argues that the Ascension was observed on the fiftieth day under the influence of a Moses' typology, Moses having ascended the mount to receive the Law on the fiftieth day. His ingenious argument might explain the reference in the *Doctrina Apostolorum*; it cannot be said to do more, if my argument as to the dearth of evidence is correct.

[4] Mansi, *Concilia*, II, p. 13.

been suggested that this abbreviation of the festal season was due to a Montanist party, wishing to suppress Pentecost because they believed that the Holy Spirit had not descended until He came in the person of Montanus,[1] but this seems unnecessarily ingenious, since in Cassian's time there were still those among the orthodox who thought that the season of rejoicing would be most fittingly brought to an end by the fortieth day because after that Jesus' presence was withdrawn from His disciples.[2] The council ordained that the period must be prolonged to Pentecost according to the universal tradition of the Church, based upon the Scriptures, but its canon testifies clearly to the observance of the fortieth day after Easter, at least in certain areas of Spain, by the beginning of the fourth century.

2. According to Canon 5 of the Council of Nicea: Αἱ δὲ σύνοδοι γενέσθωσαν, μία μὲν πρὸ τῆς τεσσαρακοστῆς, ἵνα πάσης μικροψυχίας ἀναιρουμένης τὸ δῶρον καθαρὸν προσφέρηται τῷ Θεῷ, δευτέρα δὲ περὶ τὸν τοῦ μετοπώρου καιρόν.[3]

This is usually translated: "and let these synods be held, the one before Lent (τεσσαρακοστῆς), in order that, having put away all low-mindedness, we may present a pure offering to God, and the second in the autumn." There are, however, two considerations which, to say the least, should make one hesitant to accept this rendering without further question. In the first place, it would involve the holding of the first synod in January or February, i.e. in winter when travel would be anything but easy. In the second place, it is extremely doubtful if a forty-day Lent was so widespread a practice at this period that the term τεσσαρακοστή as applied to it could be assumed to bear a precise connotation in both East and West.[4] Even as late as Sozomen[5] and Socrates[6] there was still a wide divergence of practice as regards the pre-Easter fast, so much

---

[1] Herbst, "Synode von Elvira", *Tübinger Quartalschrift*, III, 1821, pp. 39ff.; A. W. W. Dale, *The Synod of Elvira*, 1882, pp. 306f.

[2] *Coll.*, 21.18-20.

[3] Mansi, II, p. 669.

[4] It is sometimes suggested that Athanasius' *Festal Letters* reveal an initial ignorance on his part of the existence of Lent; if this were so, it would provide additional support for the thesis outlined above, but in view of McArthur's arguments (*op. cit.*, p. 121), I am inclined to doubt its validity.

[5] *H.E.*, 7.19.

[6] *H.E.*, 5.22.

so that the latter can express surprise that the term τεσσαρακοστή should be applied to it.[1]

We need, however, be left in no doubt as to the exact meaning of the term in this canon, since Canon 20, ascribed to the Dedication Council but now regarded as emanating from one held at Antioch shortly after Nicea, is no more than a rephrasing of Canon 5 of Nicea.[2] Canon 20 reads: Διὰ τὰς ἐκκλησιαστικὰς χρείας καὶ τὰς τῶν ἀμφισβητουμένων διαλύσεις, καλῶς ἔχειν ἔδοξε συνόδους καθ᾿ ἑκάστην ἐπαρχίαν τῶν ἐπισκόπων γίνεσθαι δεύτερον τοῦ ἔτους. ἅπαξ μὲν μετὰ τὴν τρίτην ἑβδομάδα τῆς ἑορτῆς τοῦ πάσχα, ὥστε τῇ τετάρτῃ ἑβδομάδι τῆς πεντηκοστῆς ἐπιτελεῖσθαι τὴν σύνοδον . . . τὴν δὲ δευτέραν σύνοδον γίνεσθαι ἰδοῖς ὀκτωβρίαις, ἥτις ἐστὶ δεκάτη ὑπερβερεταίου.[3]

It is thus ordained that of the two synods "one is to be held after the third week of the feast of the Pascha, so that it is finished in the fourth week of Pentecost . . . the second is to be held on the Ides of October, that is the tenth of Hyperberetaios". Hence the two annual assemblies are here determined more precisely than in the previous canon. Where the Fathers of Nicea said "autumn", those of Antioch provided a twofold indication, by means of the Roman calendar and the Asiatic—the autumnal council is to be held on the Ides, i.e. October 15, which corresponds to the 10th of the Macedonian month Hyperberetaios. Where the Nicene canon said "before the τεσσαρακοστή", the Antiochene gave another twofold indication—the spring council is to be held after the third week of the festival of Easter in such fashion as to be finished by the fourth week of Pentecost, i.e. the fourth week of the fifty days succeeding Easter.[4] This interpretation of the Nicene canon, which is repeated by the Canones Apostolici 38,[5] is to be preferred to those that derive from a later period when τεσσαρακοστή had become a technical term for Lent. Consequently we have here a distinct reference to the fortieth day after Easter.

3. Evidence that a feast of the Ascension was observed during the first decades of the fourth century, at least in certain parts

[1] The evidence has been very carefully investigated by S. Salaville, "La Τεσσαρακοστή du Vᵉ Canon de Nicée", Echos d'Orient, XIII, 1910, pp. 65ff.

[2] P.L. 56.35-41.

[3] Mansi, II, p. 1316.

[4] cf. Salaville, op. cit., p. 69.

[5] C. J. Hefele, A History of the Christian Councils, I, 1894, p. 473.

of Christendom, is provided by the writings of Eusebius of Caesarea.[1] In his *De solemnitate paschali*, V, published *c.* 332, he refers to the seven weeks which followed Easter and continues: Οὐ μὴν ἐπὶ ταύτας ὁ τῆς πεντηκοστῆς ἀριθμὸς ἵσταται· ὑπερακοντίσας δὲ τὰς ἑπτὰ ἑβδομάδας, μονάδι τῇ μετὰ ταύτας ὑστάτῃ τὴν πανέορτον ἡμέραν τῆς Χριστοῦ ἀναλήψεως ἐπισφραγίζεται.

His thesis is that since seven weeks is only forty-nine days, a further day is needed to make up the number fifty, i.e. Pentecost. It is this extra and final day that ratifies or confirms (ἐπισφραγίζεται, Middle) the great feast day of the Ascension of Christ. So the last day of the season of Pentecost confirms and seals the Ascension which has preceded it, i.e. the descent of the Spirit at Pentecost ratifies the truth of the Ascension and Christ's accompanying promise that the disciples were to be baptized with the Holy Ghost.[2]

It is unnecessary to go on to consider the undisputed evidence for the observance of Ascension Day later in the fourth century;[3] enough has been said to indicate that in all probability it was in existence at least from the first decades. It is this that both justifies and explains St. Augustine's declaration to Januarius (A.D. 400)—a statement that itself would preclude a recent origin—that the feast of the Ascension was of apostolic foundation or at least was instituted by an oecumenical council, as those of the Passion, the Resurrection and Pentecost.[4]

[1] Since the name of Eusebius of Caesarea heads the list of signatures to the canons of the Council held at Antioch shortly after Nicea, of which *c.* 20 has been cited above, his knowledge of the fortieth day is quite apparent.

[2] V. Larrañaga (*L'Ascension de Notre-Seigneur dans le Nouveau Testament*, 1938, p. 519) cites an apt parallel from Polybius (32.6.3), who records how Charops, after his murderous career in Greece, went to Rome to obtain from the Senate the ratification of his illegal actions, βουλόμενος ἐπισφραγίσασθαι διὰ τῆς συγκλήτου τὴν αὐτοῦ παρανομίαν.

[3] Larrañaga, *op. cit.*, pp. 581-99.

[4] *Ep.*, 54.1.

Appended Note II

EARLY ENGLISH HOMILIES[1]

TOWARDS the end of the period to which this history of the doctrine of the Ascension is limited, the vernacular homily began to make its appearance in Western Europe. Whereas Latin continued to be the language of the scholar and indeed that in which most sermons were delivered, from the seventh century in England verse and prose exegetical paraphrases were composed in the native tongue. They add little or nothing to our understanding of the Ascension, but for the sake of completeness they are listed here.

Bede records how Caedmon (*c.* 680) received the "heavenly gift" and spent his days converting the Scriptural narratives into "most harmonious verse". Of this nothing now remains, but it appears that "he sang . . . the Incarnation, Passion, Resurrection of our Lord, and His Ascension into heaven".[2]

Cynewulf (*c.* 750-825), of Northumbrian or possibly Mercian origin, is usually considered to be the author of a long poem in Anglo-Saxon entitled *Christ*. This work is in three parts, the second of which is in the main a versification of Gregory the Great's Ascensiontide homily,[3] known to the poet either directly or possibly from extracts in the Breviary. So Cynewulf borrows the interpretation of the white robes of the angels, the five "leaps"—increased to six by the addition of a "leap" into Hell—and the appeal for the faithful to ascend in heart and mind whither Christ has gone before.[4]

A more slavish reproduction of Gregory's thought is to be noted in the eleventh of the *Blickling Homilies*.[5] The white of the angels' clothes emphasizes the joy of the occasion:

because the ruin and the grievous doom of mankind was abolished, and the sorrowful sentence reversed which our Lord in His wrath

[1] I am most grateful to my colleague, G. T. Shepherd, Lecturer in English in the University of Birmingham, for not only drawing my attention to these homilies but also both transcribing and translating those contained in unpublished manuscripts.
[2] *E.H.*, 4.24.   [3] See above, p. 156.
[4] A. S. Cook, *The Christ of Cynewulf*, 1909, pp. 18-33.
[5] R. Morris, *The Blickling Homilies*, 1880, No. XI, pp. 114-30.

had previously pronounced on the first man: "Dust thou art and to dust thou shalt return." The same human nature that He previously in His wrath had so denounced—the same our Lord raised, in Himself, above heaven, and above the company of angels, at this holy season.[1]

Aelfric, Abbot of Eynsham (*fl.* 1000), translates, with—an unusual feature—due acknowledgment, long passages from Gregory, including the latter's specious recommendation of chastity.[2] Less derivative, though no more illuminating, is a homily preserved in the library of Corpus Christi College, Cambridge.[3] The preacher begins with the Resurrection of Christ, affirming that at His first appearance He gave "precious kisses" to His disciples—apparently a reference to the breathing on them for the bestowal of the Spirit. Then, after referring to the world-wide mission of the Church, he gives a paraphrase of the Acts' account of the Ascension, declaring that it marks the victory of Christ in which all mankind will eventually share, i.e. he predicates a General Ascension of the faithful after the General Resurrection. Two novel features are, first, the linking of Jacob's dream[4] and possibly of Christ's saying to Nathanael[5] with the Ascension to the effect that the disciples saw a ladder from earth to heaven with angels in white ascending and descending to give the message of the Parousia, and, second, the description of the disciples seeing Christ enter heaven and stand before the altar to praise His Father, there being beneath it those who had been delivered from the devil.[6]

Also preserved at Cambridge is an eleventh-century homily for the Vigil of the Ascension which makes much use of the Elijah typology.[7]

[1] There is also a description of the Church of the Ascension on the Mount of Olives, derived from Bede (*E.H.*, 5.17). Bede, in his turn, had taken this from one named Adamnai who was indebted to Arculf. It is possible that Cynewulf had the same description in mind when, describing the Ascension, he said: "Our King passed through the roof of the temple, where they were beholders" (*l.* 495).
[2] *Hom.* 21. B. Thorpe, *The Homilies of the Anglo-Saxon Church*, I, 1844, pp. 294-311.
[3] CCCC 162, pp. 431-41.   [4] Gen. 28: 12.   [5] John 1: 51.   [6] Rev. 6: 9, 10.
[7] CCCC 303, pp. 223-25. On pp. 72-76 of this MS. there is another homily which M. R. James (*A Descriptive Catalogue of the Manuscripts of the Library of Corpus Christi College, Cambridge*, II, 1912, p. 96) describes as concerned with the Resurrection. In his first volume, however (p. 84), referring to CCCC 41, pp. 295-301 which is a copy of Bede's *Ecclesiastical History*, containing a homily written in the margins, he states that this is an Ascension homily and is the same as CCCC 303, pp. 72-76. In fact the homily, in both MSS., is primarily concerned with the Harrowing of Hell.

From the twelfth century and from the East-Midland area of England comes another sermon[1] which has increased the five leaps of Gregory and the six of Cynewulf to seven, by the addition of a leap from Hell to earth at the Resurrection.[2]

All these homilies[3] have the same characteristics as their contemporary Latin counterparts, i.e. they are essentially moralistic in tone and they are plagiaristic—St. Gregory being the primary source, which is not surprising in view of his relationship to St. Augustine's mission in 597. The obsession with the Second Advent and more particularly with the Last Judgment, exemplified in the *Dies Irae*, also begins to find its place, these two eschatological elements being presented, together with the Ascension, as the grounds for moral endeavour.

[1] *Hom.* 19. R. Morris, *Old English Homilies*, 1873, pp. 108-16.
[2] cp. Peter Abelard, *Carmina*, 46 (*P.L.* 178.1795).
[3] For the most recent description of Anglo-Saxon manuscripts containing Ascension sermons see N. R. Kerr, *Catalogue of Manuscripts Containing Anglo-Saxon*, 1957, p. 529.

BIBLIOGRAPHY

A. *Ascension Homilies*

(Except where otherwise indicated, the sermons are without number and have only a title, usually in the form *In Ascensione* or *De Ascensione Christi*.)

Absalom: *Sermo* 31 (*P.L.* 211.182-87).
—— *Sermo* 32 (*P.L.* 211.187-93).
—— *Sermo* 33 (*P.L.* 211.193-99).
Alefric: *Sermo* 21 (D. Thorpe, *The Homilies of the Anglo-Saxon Church*, I, 1844, 294-311).
Aelred: *Sermo* 13 (*P.L.* 195.283-90).
—— *In Ascensione* (C. H. Talbot, *Sermones Inediti B. Aelredi Abbatis Rievallensis*, 1952, 100-4).
Anonymous: 1. (J. Leclercq, *Rev. Bénédictine*, LVIII, 1948, 53-72.)
—— 2. (C. P. Caspari, *Briefe, Abhandlungen und Predigten*, 1890, 185-90.)
Atto: *Sermo* 10 (*P.L.* 134.845-46).
Augustine: *Sermo* 261 (*P.L.* 38.1202-7).
—— *Sermo* 262 (*P.L.* 38.1207-9).
—— *Sermo* 263 (*P.L.* 38.1209-12).
—— *Sermo* 264 (*P.L.* 38.1212-18).
—— *Sermo* 265 (*P.L.* 38.1218-24).
—— *Sermo* 178 (*al. de Temp.* 177) (*P.L.* 39.2083-84).
—— *Sermo* 40 (*Coll. Selec. SS. Patrum*, 130.224-28).
—— *Sermo* 53 (*Coll. Selec. SS. Patrum*, 131B. 275-80).
—— *Sermo* 54 (*Coll. Selec. SS. Patrum*, 131B. 280-86).
—— Mai XCVIII (*Misc. Agost.*, I, 347-50).
—— Liverani VIII (*Misc. Agost.*, I, 391-95).
—— Biblioth. Casin II.76 (*Misc. Agost.*, I, 413-15).
—— Guelferb. XX (*Misc. Agost.*, I, 504-6).
—— Guelferb. XXI (*Misc. Agost.*, I, 507-9).
—— Morin IX (*Misc. Agost.*, I, 619-23).
—— Morin XVII (*Misc. Agost.*, I, 659-64).
—— Lambot (*Rev. Bénédictine*, LI, 1939, 25-27).
—— Lambot (*Rev. Bénédictine*, LXII, 1952, 97-100).

Pseudo-Augustine: *Sermo* 395 (*P.L.* 39.1716-17).

—— *Sermo* 179 (*al. de Temp.* 178) (*P.L.* 39.2084-85).

—— *Sermo* 180 (*al. de Temp.* 179) (*P.L.* 39.2085-86).

—— *Sermo* 181 (*al. de Temp.* 180) (*P.L.* 39.2086-87).

—— *Sermo* 5 (*Coll. Selec. SS. Patrum*, 130.364-66).

—— *Sermo* 41 (*Coll. Selec. SS. Patrum*, 130.228-31).

—— *Sermo* 55 (*Coll. Selec. SS. Patrum*, 131B.287-91).

—— *Sermo* 57 (*Coll. Selec. SS. Patrum*, 131B.305-7).

Basil of Seleucia: *P.G.* 28.1091-1100.

Bede: *Hom. Genuin. II. Hom.* 9 (*P.L.* 94.174-81)=*Hom.* II.15 (*Corpus Christ.*, 122.280-89).

Bernard: *P.L.* 183.299-301.

—— *P.L.* 183.301-4.

—— *P.L.* 183.304-9.

—— *P.L.* 183.309-16.

—— *P.L.* 183.316-24.

Blickling Homilies: 11 (R. Morris, *The Blickling Homilies*, 1880, 114-30).

Caesarius of Arles: Augustine, *Sermo* 177 (*P.L.* 39.2082-83)= *Sermo* 21 (*Corpus Christ.*, 104.837-40).

John Chrysostom: *P.G.* 50.441-52.

Pseudo-Chrysostom: *P.G.* 52.773-92.

—— *P.G.* 52.791-94.

—— *P.G.* 52.793-96.

—— *P.G.* 52.797-800.

—— *P.G.* 52.799-802.

—— *P.G.* 52.801-2.

—— *P.G.* 61.711-12.

—— *P.G.* 62.727-30.

—— *P.G.* 64.45-48 (also assigned to Eusebius of Alexandria, *P.G.* 86.422).

—— *Traditio*, IX, 1953, 116-19 (? by Nestorius).

—— *Traditio*, IX, 1953, 122-24.

Diadochus: *P.G.* 65.1141-48.

Pseudo-Epiphanius: *P.G.* 43.477-86.

Faustus of Riez: Augustine, *Sermo* 176 *de Temp.* (*P.L.* 39.2081-82). G. Morin, *Rev. Charlemagne*, I, 1911, 161-4.

Garnier: *Sermo* 20 (*P.L.* 205.700-4).

Goffridus: *Sermo* 6 (*P.L.* 157.258-62).

Gregory the Great: *Hom.* 29 *in Evang. Lib.* II (*P.L.* 76.1213-19).

Gregory of Nyssa: *P.G.* 46.689-93.
Gregory Palmas: *Hom.* 21 (*P.G.* 151.276-85).
—— *Hom.* 22 (*P.G.* 151.285-96).
Haymo of Auxerre: *Hom.* 96 *de Temp.* (*P.L.* 118.542-49).
Helinand: *Sermo* 14 (*P.L.* 212.591-95).
—— *Sermo* 15 (*P.L.* 212.595-611).
Hugh of St. Victor: *Sermones Centum*, 69 (*P.L.* 177.1114-19).
Leo the Great: *Sermo* 73 (*al.* 71) (*P.L.* 54.394-96).
—— *Sermo* 74 (*al.* 72) (*P.L.* 54.397-400).
—— *Sermo* 6 (*Coll. Selec. SS. Patrum*, 130.367-70).
Pseudo-Leo: M. Schanz, *Geschichte der römischen Literatur*, IV.2, 1920.60.
Leo Imperator: *Oratio* 11 (*P.G.* 107.113-20).
Martin of Legio: *Sermo* 30 (*P.L.* 208.1085-1198).
—— *Sermo* 31 (*P.L.* 208.1197-1204).
Maximus of Turin: *Hom.* 60 *de Temp.* (*P.L.* 57.367-70).
—— *Sermo* 44 *de Temp.* (*P.L.* 57.623-26).
—— *Sermo* 45 *de Temp.* (*P.L.* 57.625-26).
—— *Sermo* 46 *de Temp.* (*P.L.* 57.625-28).
Pseudo-Maximus: *Sermo* 47 *de Temp.* (*P.L.* 57.627-30).
Old English Homilies: 19 (R. Morris, *Old English Homilies*, 1873, 108-15).
Odilo of Cluny: *Sermo* 8 (*P.L.* 142.1011-14).
Peter of Blois: *Sermo* 23 (*P.L.* 207.627-30).
Peter of Celles: *Sermo* 50 (*P.L.* 202.785-88).
—— *Sermo* 51 (*P.L.* 202.788-91).
—— *Sermo* 52 (*P.L.* 202.791-94).
Proclus: *P.G.* 65.833-37.
—— *P.G.* 79.1500-1.
Rabanus Maurus: *Hom.* 21 *de Fest.* (*P.L.* 110.42-43).
—— *Hom.* 44 *in Evang.* (*P.L.* 110.226-28).
—— *Hom.* 45 *in Evang.* (*P.L.* 110.228-31).
—— *Hom.* 46 *in Evang.* (*P.L.* 110.231-33).
—— *Hom.* 47 *in Evang.* (*P.L.* 110.233-36).
Radulphus Ardens: *Hom.* 68 (*P.L.* 155.1917-22).
—— *Hom.* 69 (*P.L.* 155.1922-27).
Rather: *Sermo* 8 (*P.L.* 136.734-40).
—— *Sermo* 9 (*P.L.* 136.740-45).
Theophanis Ceramei: *Hom.* 39 (*P.G.* 132.744-64).

Werner: *Libri Deflorationum ex Melliflua diversorum Patrum*, I.35 (*P.L.* 157.970-76).

B. *Critical Studies*

B. W. Bacon: "The Ascension in Luke and Acts", *Expositor*, VII, 1909.

D. M. Baillie: *God was in Christ*, 1948.

O. Bardenhewer: *Patrology*, 1908.

P. C. Baur: "Drei Unedierte Festpredigten", *Traditio*, IX, 1951.

G. K. A. Bell, ed.: *The Meaning of the Creed*, 1918.

—— and A. Deissmann: *Mysterium Christi*, 1930.

P. Benoit: "L'Ascension", *Rev. Biblique*, LVI, 1949.

N. Berdyaev: *Freedom and the Spirit*, 1935.

G. Bertram: "Die Himmelfahrt Jesu vom Kreuz aus und der Glaube an seine Auferstehung", *Festgabe für A. Deissmann*, 1927, pp. 187ff.

G. H. Boobyer: *St. Mark and the Transfiguration Story*, 1942.

L. Brun: *Die Auferstehung Christi in der urchristlichen Überlieferung*, 1925.

R. Bultmann: *Theology of the New Testament*, I, 1952.

—— *Primitive Christianity in its Contemporary Setting*, 1956.

C. F. Burney: *Israel's Hope of Immortality*, 1909.

—— *Outlines of Old Testament Theology*, 1930.

Archimandrîte Cassien: *La Pentecôte Johannique*, 1939.

R. H. Charles: *A Critical History of the Doctrine of a Future Life*, 1899.

W. K. Lowther Clarke: "The Clouds of Heaven. An Eschatological Study", *Theology*, XXXI, 1935.

D. Daube: *The New Testament and Rabbinic Judaism*, 1956.

J. G. Davies: "Pentecost and Glossolalia", *J.T.S.*, III, 1952.

—— "The *Peregrinatio Egeriae* and the Ascension", *Vig. Christ.*, VIII, 1954.

—— *The Spirit, The Church and The Sacraments*, 1954.

—— "The Prefigurement of the Ascension in the Third Gospel", *J.T.S.*, VI, 1955.

—— "An Addition to the Reconstituted Creed of Jerusalem", *Vig. Christ.*, IX, 1955.

—— "Proclus and Pseudo-Nilus", *H.T.R.*, XLIX, 1956.

W. D. Davies and D. Daube, edd.: *The Background of the New Testament and Its Eschatology*, 1956.

G. Dix: *The Shape of the Liturgy*, 1945.

C. H. Dodd: *According to the Scriptures*, 1952.

M. Dorenkemper: *The Trinitarian Doctrine of St. Caesarius of Arles*, 1953.

J. A. Dorner: *The Person of Christ*, I, 1870.

J. Endres: *Honorius Augustodunensis*, 1906.

I. Engnell: *Studies in Divine Kingship in the Ancient Near East*, 1943.

M. S. Enslin: "The Ascension Story", *Journ. Bib. Lit.*, XLVII, 1928.

A. Farrer: *A Study in St. Mark*, 1951.

A. Fridricksen: "Die Himmelfahrt bei Lukas", *Theol. Blätter*, VI, 1927.

R. H. Fuller: *The Mission and Achievement of Jesus*, 1954.

J. de Ghellinck: *Littérature Latine au Moyen Age*, 1939.

—— *Le Mouvement Théologique du XIIᵉ Siècle*, 1948.

T. F. Glasson: *The Second Advent*, 1945.

H. M. Grant: "Athenagoras or Pseudo-Athenagoras", *H.T.R.*, XLVII, 1954.

—— "The Chronology of the Greek Apologists", *Vig. Christ.*, IX, 1955.

S. L. Greenslade: *Schism in the Early Church*, 1953.

H. Gunkel: *Ausgewählte Psalmen*, 1904.

—— *Die Psalmen*, 1926.

E. Haenchen: *Die Apostelgeschichte*, 1956.

A. Harnack: *Das apostolische Glaubensbekenntniss*, 1892.

A. Heidel: *The Gilgamesh Epic and Old Testament Parallels*, 1949.

L. Hodgson: *And was Made Man*, 1928.

U. Holzmeister: "Der Tag der Himmelfahrt des Herrn", *Zeitsch. für kath. Theol.*, LV, 1931.

S. H. Hooke: *The Origins of Early Semitic Ritual*, 1938.

—— ed. *Myth and Ritual*, 1933.

—— ed. *The Labyrinth*, 1935.

J. Jeremias: *The Parables of Jesus*, 1954.

—— *The Eucharistic Words of Jesus*, 1955.

A. R. Johnson: *Sacral Kingship in Ancient Israel*, 1955.

M. de Jonge: *The Testaments of the Twelve Patriarchs*, 1953.

J. N. D. Kelly: *Early Christian Creeds*, 1950.

H. Koch: *"Quod idola non sint:* ein Werk Cyprians", *Cyprianische Untersuchungen,* 1926.

G. Kretschmar: "Himmelfahrt und Pfingsten", *Zeitsch. für Kirchengeschichte,* LXVI, 1954-55.

K. Lake: *The Resurrection of Jesus Christ,* 1907.

G. W. H. Lampe: *The Seal of the Spirit,* 1951.

—— and K. J. Woollcombe, *Essays on Typology,* 1957.

V. Larrañaga: *L'Ascension de Notre-Seigneur dans le Nouveau Testament,* 1938.

J. Lebon: "La Position de saint Cyrille de Jérusalem dans les Luttes provoquées par l'Arianisme", *Rev. d'Hist. Eccl.,* XX, 1924.

A. A. McArthur: *The Evolution of the Christian Year,* 1953.

J. Mánek, "The New Exodus in the Books of Luke", *Novum Testamentum,* II, 1957.

C. S. Mann, "The New Testament and the Lord's Ascension", *C.Q.R.,* CLVIII, 1957.

A. D. Martin: "The Ascension of Christ", *Expositor,* XVI, 1918.

E. L. Mascall: *Christ, The Christian and The Church,* 1946.

P. Menoud: "Remarques sur les textes de l'ascension dans Luc-Actes", *Neutestamentliche Studien für R. Bultmann,* 1954.

W. Milligan: *The Ascension and Heavenly Priesthood of Our Lord,* 1901.

C. F. D. Moule: "The Ascension—Acts i. 9", *Expository Times,* LXVIII, 1957.

S. Mowinckel: *Psalmenstudien,* II, III, 1922-23.

—— *He That Cometh,* 1956.

D. Nineham, ed.: *Studies in the Gospels,* 1955.

J. Pedersen: *Israel,* III-IV, 1940.

D. Plooij: *The Ascension in the "Western" Textual Tradition,* 1929.

J. R. Porter: "The Interpretation of 2 Samuel vi and Psalm cxxxii", *J.T.S.,* V, 1954.

O. C. Quick: *Doctrines of the Creed,* 1938.

A. M. Ramsey: *The Resurrection of Christ,* 1945.

—— *The Glory of God and the Transfiguration of Christ,* 1949.

—— "What was the Ascension?" *Studiorum Novi Testamenti Societas, Bulletin* II, 1951.

A. E. J. Rawlinson: *The New Testament Doctrine of the Christ,* 1949.

J. A. T. Robinson: "The Second Coming—Mark xiv. 62", *Expository Times*, LXVII, 1956.

S. Salaville: "La Τεσσαρακοστή du Vᵉ Canon de Nicée", *Echos d'Orient*, XIII, 1910.

H. Schrade: "Zur Ikonographie der Himmelfahrt Christi", *Vorträge der Bibliothek Warburg, Vörtrage* 1928-1929. *Über die Vorstellungen von der Himmelsreise der Seele*, 1930.

W. J. Sparrow Simpson: *Our Lord's Resurrection*, 1905.

N. H. Snaith: *The Jewish New Year Festival*, 1947.

H. F. D. Sparks: *The Old Testament in the Christian Church*, 1944.

C. Spicq: *Esquisse d'une Histoire de l'Exégèse Latine au Moyen Age*, 1944.

E. Stauffer: *New Testament Theology*, 1955.

B. H. Streeter: *The Four Gospels*, 1930.

W. J. Swaans: "A propos des 'Catéchèses Mystagogiques' attribuées à S. Cyrille de Jérusalem", *Muséon*, LV, 1942.

H. B. Swete: *The Apostles' Creed*, 1905.

—— *The Ascended Christ*, 1910.

A. J. Tait: *The Heavenly Session of Our Lord*, 1912.

T. F. Torrance: *Royal Priesthood*, 1955.

—— *Kingdom and Church*, 1956.

L. H. Vincent: "L'Eléona, sanctuaire primitif de l'Ascension", *Rev. Biblique*, LXIV, 1957.

G. Widengren: *Psalm 110 och det sakrala kungsdömet i Israel*, 1941.

A. N. Wilder: "Variant Traditions of the Resurrection in Acts", *Journ. Bib. Lit.*, LXII, 1943.

C. S. C. Williams: *Alterations to the Text of the Synoptic Gospels and Acts*, 1951.

J. Wright: *Some Remarks on Mr. Whiston's Dissertation about Christ's Ascension*, 1709.

INDEX

INDEX

(c) *Apocrypha and Apocryphal Writings*